SOCIAL ENTERPRISE

Social enterprise has become a much discussed term in recent years, often in conjunction with the public sector – the idea that entrepreneurship might somehow step in and save the public purse has taken hold in a number of areas.

This book introduces and explains the terminology surrounding social enterprise and brings much-needed rigour to proceedings by demonstrating how this can be measured, evaluated and held accountable. A range of validated evaluation measures, tools and techniques, such as social return on investment (SROI), the 'Outcomes Star' and randomized control trials, are presented in individual research projects, conducted by an exciting and eclectic mix of international authors who are recognized experts in the field of social enterprise.

Wrapping up with the ground-breaking use of a General Self-Efficacy scale, a reflective critique of social finance and a challenge to the actual concept of social enterprise, the book discusses the potential disadvantages that can arise from the commodification of social enterprise activities, resulting in a fascinating summary of current thinking surrounding this topic.

Simon Denny is Professor of Entrepreneurship and Social Enterprise Development Director at the University of Northampton. His research interests are in the areas of social enterprise, entrepreneurship and social inclusion, and effective support for new enterprises. He is joint head of the Centre for Entrepreneurship, Enterprise and Governance (CEEG).

Fred Seddon is Social Enterprise Researcher in the School of Social Sciences at the University of Northampton. Prior to taking up his current post he held research posts at the Open University, UK, and Padua University, Italy. He has published extensively in the fields of social enterprise and music psychology and education.

'A brilliant book to provide insights into what makes a social enterprise successful and how to evaluate its efficiency and efficacy. A unique book for students, social entrepreneurs, investors, and policy makers.'

Mariarosa Scarlata, Newcastle University Business School

'This new book provides a refreshing and informed international perspective on social enterprise. Based on contributions from 17 leading scholars from several countries, it is essential reading for those with an interest in the study and practice of social enterprise.'

Jonathan Bland, Managing Director, Social Business International, founder of E3M and member of GECES

'For many within the social enterprise movement, evaluation, which this book interrogates conceptually and empirically, represents the most promising strategy for encouraging social redress.'

Boris Urban, University of Witwatersrand, South Africa

'This book will be welcomed by practitioners and researchers alike, offering as it does a disciplined and knowledgeable account of the key issues.'

Peter Lawrence, Loughborough University

SOCIAL ENTERPRISE

Accountability and evaluation around the world

Edited by Simon Denny and Fred Seddon

Routledge
Taylor & Francis Group

LONDON AND NEW YORK

First published 2014
by Routledge
2 Park Square, Milton Park, Abingdon, Oxon OX14 4RN

Simultaneously published in the USA and Canada
by Routledge
711 Third Avenue, New York, NY 10017

Routledge is an imprint of the Taylor & Francis Group, an informa business

British Library Cataloguing in Publication Data
A catalogue record for this book is available from the British Library

Library of Congress Cataloging in Publication Data
Social enterprise : accountability and evaluation around the world /
edited by Simon Denny and Fred Seddon.
pages cm.
Includes bibliographical references and index.
1. Social entrepreneurship. 2. Social responsibility of business. I. Denny, Simon, Professor of Entrepreneurship. II. Seddon, Frederick A.
HD60.S5854 2013
361.2'5–dc23   2013002724

ISBN: 978-0-415-62609-5 (hbk)
ISBN: 978-0-415-62610-1 (pbk)
ISBN: 978-0-203-10291-6 (ebk)

Typeset in Bembo
by Deer Park Productions

CONTENTS

PART V
The future for evaluation of social enterprise

ILLUSTRATIONS

Figures

Tables

CONTRIBUTORS

Malin Arvidson is a research fellow at the Third Sector Research Centre, University of Southampton, UK and a lecturer at the Department of Social Work, University of Lund, Sweden. She works with research on third-sector organizations, including the use, role and effect of evaluations, and organizational change in the context of a mixed economy of welfare. Malin has a background in international development, with research focusing on NGOs and poverty alleviation strategies.

Jo Barraket is Associate Professor of Social Enterprise at the Australian Centre for Philanthropy and Nonprofit Studies, Queensland University of Technology. Her research interests include social enterprise, social innovation and the role of the social economy in new public governance.

Belinda Bell is a social entrepreneur who has established and grown a number of social enterprises. She has worked in a range of fields including financial exclusion, community asset ownership, young people and ageing. As well as her academic interests, Belinda is currently working with social enterprises to secure social invest-ment, and continues to develop new social enterprise ideas that seek to address intractable social problems. Belinda holds a Masters degree in Community Enterprise from the University of Cambridge, a Bachelors degree in Social Anthropology from Goldsmiths College, University of London, and is a fellow of the RSA.

Ingo Bode holds the Chair of Social Policy, Organization and Society at the Department of Social Work and Social Welfare, University of Kassel (Germany). His areas of work embrace the comparative analysis of public and non-profit sectors as well as organization studies in social and health care. He is chairing the research network 'The sociology of social policy and social welfare' of the European

Sociological Association and is a member of various academic boards, including the 'Organizational Sociology' section of the German Association of Sociology. Prior to moving into his current position, he has been a lecturer or guest professor in the UK, France and Canada.

Carlo Borzaga is a full Professor of Economic Politics at the University of Trento where he lectures in labour economics and economics of cooperatives and non-profit enterprises. His specific interests are economic analysis of the employment market and economic analysis of non-profit organizations, focusing on cooperatives in general as well as social cooperatives and the evolution of this sector in Europe. Since 2008 he has been the chairman of the Euricse (European Research Institute on Cooperative and Social Enterprises). He has written and co-edited numerous papers dedicated to the theory of social and non-profit enterprises.

Simon Denny is Social Enterprise Development Director at Northampton University. In this role he leads on the development and implementation of the University's social enterprise strategy. In 2006, Professor Denny received the University of Northampton Court Award in recognition of his achievements in the area of knowledge exchange and enterprise. He was elected a Fellow of the RSA in 2008. In April 2010 he received the Queen's Award for Enterprise Promotion. He has published several articles in international, peer-reviewed academic journals.

Sara Depedri is Senior Researcher at the Euricse (European Research Institute on Cooperative and Social Enterprises) in Trento. She also teaches economics of welfare systems and social enterprises at the University of Trento, Italy. Her research activity mainly concerns the economic analysis of cooperatives and social enterprises. She has carried out several investigations, especially at national and local level, in order to support theory with empirical analyses and formulate policy advice. She has published on the topics of governance structures and participation, members' involvement, human resource management and labour policies in cooperatives, and work integration social cooperatives.

Bob Doherty is Chair of Marketing at the York Management School, University of York. Bob specializes in the marketing aspects of fairtrade social enterprises. He is an Honorary Research Fellow at the Third Sector Research Centre at the University of Birmingham. Bob is also a member of the organizing committees for both the International Social Innovation Research Conference and the International Fair Trade Symposium. For the past five years he has been editor of the *Social Enterprise Journal*. Prior to moving into academia Bob spent five years as Head of Marketing at the social enterprise, Divine Chocolate.

Suzanne Grant completed her PhD at the Waikato Management School, University of Waikato, Hamilton, New Zealand, where she now teaches in the areas of social enterprise and organizational behaviour. Part of her teaching and research contributes to New Zealand's only post-graduate qualification in Social Enterprise. Taught entirely online, this qualification attracts students from throughout New Zealand and around the world. Her research interests include organizational behaviour, social enterprise and community/not-for-profit organizations. Suzanne has a particular interest in transformative methodologies encompassing action research, critical appreciative processes and critical theory perspectives.

Kelly Hall is a Senior Lecturer in Sociology at the University of Northampton, having previously worked as a Research Fellow at the University of Birmingham. Her current research interests focus on social enterprise and health, especially on NHS spin-outs. She has previously published on social enterprise evaluation tools, focusing primarily on Social Return on Investment (SROI). She also recently completed an evaluation of the Social Enterprise Investment Fund (SEIF).

Helen Haugh is Senior Lecturer at Judge Business School and Deputy Director of the MBA. Her research interests focus on social and community entrepreneurship, community economic regeneration, business ethics and corporate social responsibility. Her research in the social economy has examined community-led regeneration in peripheral rural communities, cross-sector collaboration between organizations in the social economy and the private and public sectors, and innovations in governance. This work has been published in the *Academy of Management Education and Learning, Organization Studies, Entrepreneurship Theory and Practice, Journal of Business Ethics, Cambridge Journal of Economics,* and *Entrepreneurship and Regional Development.*

Richard Hazenberg is a Social Enterprise Researcher at the University of Northampton. His research focuses upon the performance evaluation of work integration social enterprises that deliver employment enhancement programmes to young unemployed individuals. He also has research interests in the area of social finance, social enterprise governance, as well as cross-cultural research in the social enterprise field in relation to Anglo-Swedish social enterprise comparisons. He has published research in international, peer-reviewed academic journals and has also presented several research articles at conferences in Europe and America.

Chris Mason is a Senior Lecturer at the Faculty of Business and Enterprise, Swinburne University of Technology in Melbourne, Australia. His research covers a number of areas, although he is principally concerned with social enterprise and entrepreneurship, and how competing notions of these concepts and practices are formulated and contested. Recent work has examined the impact of social enterprise policies on discourse and identity, and he maintains a strong interest in the governance of social enterprises. The latter research strand brings together a number of ideas, including legitimacy, institutional theory, corporate social responsibility and critical studies of social enterprise.

Alex Nicholls is the first tenured Lecturer in Social Entrepreneurship appointed at the University of Oxford and was the first staff member of the Skoll Centre for Social Entrepreneurship in 2004. His research interests range across several key areas within social entrepreneurship and social innovation, including: the nexus of relationships between accounting, accountability and governance; public and social policy contexts; social investment; and fairtrade. To date Nicholls has published more than 40 papers, chapters and articles and five books. Most appear in a wide range of peer-reviewed journals and books, including four sole-authored papers in Financial Times Top 30 journals.

Jonathan M. Scott is a Reader in Entrepreneurship at Teesside University Business School, having completed a PhD (University of Ulster, 2003) on the trading relationships between Northern Ireland and Hungarian manufacturers. He is a Director of Enterprise Educators UK (2011–14) and a member of the Higher Education Funding Council for England (HEFCE)/UnLtd (the Foundation for Social Entrepreneurs) Higher Education Support Initiative for Social Entrepreneurs (2012–13). His collaborative research focuses on access to finance for SMEs and social enterprises. He was a Visiting Research Fellow at the University of Turku, Finland in 2009, 2010 and 2012.

Fred Seddon is a Social Enterprise Researcher at the University of Northampton. His research interests include 'social enterprise governance' and 'social impact measurement'. He has published several journal articles in international peer-reviewed academic journals. He was awarded his PhD in Music Psychology from the University of Keele in 2001. He was a professional researcher in the field of Music Psychology at the Open University (UK) and the University of Padua (Italy) until his appointment as Social Enterprise Researcher at Northampton University in 2009.

John Thompson is Emeritus Professor of Entrepreneurship at the University of Huddersfield; he has had visiting links with universities in Australia, Finland and New Zealand. He is a Board Member of the European Case Clearing House and he has served on the boards for the Institute for Small Business and Entrepreneurship, Enterprise Educators UK and UK Business Incubation. He has written over a dozen texts on entrepreneurship and strategy and is an active researcher and case writer. His main interests are identifying people with the potential to be entrepreneurs and social entrepreneurs. In 2009 John received the Queen's Award for Enterprise Promotion.

FOREWORD

This is a book that is absolutely of its time and should be read by all those interested in the future of business. In that sense, it is a book of its age.

I write this because I run a business, and that business is one that is driven by the need to contribute to society through the provision of health and social care, do no harm to the environment while doing so, and return a surplus not to shareholders and/or to the ever-demanding open maw of the market in shares but to the very people who add value to society – the public.

The business I run, Turning Point, is a social enterprise and while much has been said about what social enterprises are or are not, I can tell you that we are a business. It is simply that our model of doing business acknowledges the existence of society and the need to do no harm to society in pursuing our business aims. Indeed, the value of our business is in improving the value of society itself.

In this book, Professor Simon Denny and Dr Fred Seddon have attempted to encapsulate curved thinking on the subject of social enterprise in a way that is open, engaging and relevant to anyone who is interested in the future of business and not just the nomenclature.

The University of Northampton has taken a brave and necessary decision to assume the academic crown of leading the understanding of social enterprise, its impact, its worth and its leadership. In this way, the University is furthering the cause of social enterprise; more importantly, it is recreating the purpose of business in a modern society.

I do not believe that it is an accident that social enterprise has become the model of the moment across both the commercial and non-commercial sectors. I believe it is simply the result of many years of individuals searching for a better way to deliver goods and services.

This book is a contributory factor in changing the way we understand and do business.

Lord Victor Adebowale CBE
Chief Executive, Turning Point

PART I

Overview

1

EVALUATING SOCIAL ENTERPRISE

An international perspective

Simon Denny and Fred Seddon

Social enterprise is not new. In the UK Thomas Firmin (1632–97) provided employment for London's tradesmen thrown out of work as a result of the plague of 1665. Later, and more ambitiously, from 1676 until the 1690s he ran a purpose-built factory employing up to 1,700 of London's poor in linen manufacturing. Sadly the scheme never paid its way, but we can see Firmin as one of the earlier British social entrepreneurs, running a business with overtly social values. Some 350 years after Firmin social enterprise has become a subject of global interest. Politicians from all parts of the Western political spectrum are looking to social enterprise to deliver existing, and new, services that have been provided by the state for the past several decades. The global financial crisis and the increasing unaffordability of the services we in the West have given ourselves, has led to social enterprises (including cooperatives) being seen as a 'way out' as well as an attractive model for politicians to support. Public sector managers are increasingly looking to contract with social enterprises and to work with them. More directly, many public sector managers are, willingly or unwillingly, becoming social entrepreneurs themselves, spinning out their unit or function into a new, more commercial form. Private sector managers are starting to seek to gain competitive advantage by partnering with social enterprises (either as part of the supply chain, or as partners in the delivery of services). Others are perhaps seeking to 'steal the clothes' of social enterprises by using the same language. High profile business leaders, including Sir Richard Branson, have warned in 2012 that large corporations have to change their business models and contribute more to society. It would seem that the business of business is no longer simply about maximizing profit.

Business school academics with an interest in social enterprise, previously marginalized by their more traditional and mainstream colleagues, have suddenly found themselves in demand for media appearances, conferences and new accredited course development. Academia faithfully follows the curve, and we invite people to count the number of undergraduate and postgraduate courses for existing and would-be social entrepreneurs that have sprung up since 2010. Our employer, the University of Northampton, has gone so far as to position itself as the UK's number one HEI for social enterprise, and has put huge resources into achieving its mission.

Given the attention increasingly being paid to social enterprise, the time is ripe and right for a new book with a broad and critical scope. We have set out to challenge the all too often implicit assumption that social enterprise must be good because it sets out to do good. We have been determined to review the evidence and to examine what works, and what does not. Here we present and add to the work of eminent authors from six countries to make a contribution to the policy, practice and study of social enterprise.

Following the global financial crisis in 2008, governments are increasingly moving towards alternative methods of financing their social services (Pearce 2003; Doherty et al. 2009; SEC 2009, 2011). The global growth in social enterprise (SE) is accompanied by a 'wind of change', which is developing a demand for more ethical ways of financing, producing and making available goods and services, especially to the more disadvantaged members of society. Increases in the amount of finance directed towards SE demands rigorous forms of evaluation to ensure finances are being directed effectively. In order to be able to perform essential micro and macro evaluative functions, it is first necessary to establish a clear concept of exactly what SE is. Part II of this book (Chapters 2–4) explores definitions of SE from a theoretical perspective with authors drawing distinctions between the concepts of SE, SE organizations, actors, management and SE identity. Moving on from issues of definition, Part III (Chapters 5–9) examines the variety of ways SEs can be evaluated. This section focuses on evaluation and involves contributing authors drawing from prior and emerging research, while reporting the findings of their own research conducted in the UK, Italy and Australia. In Part IV of the book (Chapters 10–12), authors from the UK, Germany and New Zealand examine SE through a critical reflection in relation to issues of finance, management and social construction.

On the surface, the term 'social enterprise' would seem to be the juxtaposition of two opposing phenomena (Cooper 1989). The term 'social' can be perceived as, and related to, notions of caring, collaboration and support whereas the term 'enterprise' can have connotations of competition and profit-making. How do these two potentially diametrically opposite concepts comfortably coalesce to form what is currently perceived as social enterprise? Defining SE is an activity that has occupied academics for some time now without resolution (Stayaert and Dey 2010; Curtis 2008; Haugh 2012) and in the first section of the book, three well-established and authoritative authors from the UK and Australia offer their perspectives on SE. In Chapter 2, John Thompson and Jonathan Scott explore the intricacies of defining social enterprise, social enterprises, social entrepreneurs and social entrepreneurship. The authors provide a detailed and well-referenced account of these concepts and their complex interactions, drawing from examples of well-known international businesses. The purpose of social enterprises, what they are, their desired outcomes and values are discussed in relation to SE actors and organizations. In Chapter 3, Bob Doherty examines SE from a management perspective and considers how SEs can manage the balance between social and commercial objectives when competing against larger, resource-rich rivals. Doherty applies Resource Advantage (R–A) theory, a recently revised competition theory, to explain how SEs can maintain a balance between social and commercial objectives within their limited resources. In the chapter, R–A theory is applied to three case studies of leading farmer-owned fair trade SEs: Liberation CIC (Community Interest Company), Divine Chocolate Company and Cafedirect plc. Doherty's research identifies 'social resources' consisting of three interrelated components: ethical and social commitments, connections with partners and consistency of behaviour. Doherty argues that in SEs, strategic choices are influenced by social and ethical values more so than in private or public sector organizations. In Chapter 4, Chris Mason seeks to define SE by focusing on SE 'identity' and the importance of discourse in shaping that identity. Mason critically reviews research by Parkinson and Howorth (2008) and Jones *et al.* (2008), which connects SE discourse and identity. Within this framework, Mason argues that spoken articulations of SE identity are inherently incomplete. Based upon prior research (Jones *et al.*, 2008), Mason proposes that SE identity is dynamic, fragmentary and unstable and argues that social entrepreneur self-identity has a distinctive political dimension. Mason employs notions of 'self' and 'the suppressed self' (Jones *et al.* 2008; Parkinson and Howorth 2008) and Derrida's concepts of *différance* and *supplementarity* (Derrida 1967) to emphasize meaning-making *processes*, which he argues are political, discursive, asymmetrical and open-ended. Mason embraces the openness of SE debate but is mindful of the inherent challenges of the discursive process.

SE evaluation can be conducted on different levels, depending upon whether the focus of the evaluation is on *output*, *outcome* or *impact* as defined in the SIMPLE methodology (McLoughlin *et al.* 2009). For example, when evaluating a work integration social enterprise (WISE), *output* can be defined as the relationship between the number of unemployed individuals accessing the programme and the number who subsequently gain employment. Considering *output* as a method of evaluation is useful for tracking the success of a programme from this particular perspective. However, if *output* is employed as a singular measure, the evaluation will not include important longer-term participant and societal benefits, i.e. *outcome* and *impact*. In the context of our WISE example, an *outcome* represents positive psychological changes (e.g. increased self-efficacy) that can enhance participants' future employability. *Impact* is an even longer-term benefit and is the *impact* on society resulting from the reduction of unemployment. For example, reduced unemployment benefits payments, lower costs to the criminal justice system and the health service, and higher income tax receipts. As will be demonstrated in Part III of this book (Chapters 5–9), there are numerous methods and focuses of evaluation, and the section begins with a chapter reporting a research project that examines the role of altruism in the motivation of employees working in UK community

development finance institutions. The section continues with a research study that proposes new indexes of evaluation for evaluating Italian work integration social cooperatives (WISC) and continues with a further three chapters that consider *outcome* and *impact* measures based upon research studies conducted in Australia and the UK. Two of the studies report on *outcomes* for the individuals and the *impact* on society and the other draws comparisons between social return on investment (SROI) and two further *impact* measurement tools. The research studies reported in Part III of the book employ a mixture of quantitative and qualitative measures, which are fully described and evaluated.

Chapter 5, by Belinda Bell and Helen Haugh, reports an interesting UK study that examined employee motivation influencing employees who worked in community development finance institutions (CDFI) having previously worked in private sector financial services. Bell and Haugh found that the majority of their research participants earned less working in CDFI than they did when previously working in the private sector. According to Bell and Haugh, a combination of personal factors and the characteristics of the organization the participants worked for, indicated some employees were motivated by altruism. The study adopted a qualitative methodology collecting interview data from 17 employees currently working in CDFI. Interview data was analyzed following the principles of grounded theory, and concepts of altruism, job satisfaction, employee engagement and psychological empowerment are presented to support the proposition that some of the research participants were motivated by altruism. Chapter 6, by Carlo Borzaga and Sara Depedri, brings an Italian perspective to SE evaluation with an evaluation of Italian work integration social cooperatives (WISCs). This highly informative chapter reports a research study conducted by the authors, which examined the efficiency and efficacy of Italian WISCs. The study focuses on evaluating how WISCs support the integration of disadvantaged workers (e.g. individuals suffering from addiction problems, ex-prisoners, people with mental health problems and young people with low levels of education) into the labour market, particularly during the current economic crisis. A comprehensive description of Italian WISCs, their beneficiaries and the supportive legal structure is provided along with proposed indexes of evaluation based on commercial, personal and social dimensions. Borzaga and Depedri present the results of an investigation conducted in 2011 by Euricse (European Research Institute on Cooperative and Social Enterprises) in the Trento province of Italy. The results of this quantitative study, undertaken with ten social cooperatives and 194 disadvantaged workers, present a comprehensive cost-benefit analysis including guaranteed cost savings for the public sector gained as a result of disadvantaged workers being employed by WISCs and therefore placing lower demands on public services. Chapter 7, by Jo Barraket, examines the *outcomes* and *impact* of work integration social enterprise (WISE) this time in Australia. Barraket draws from an evaluation conducted by Adult Multicultural Education Services (AMES) on seven WISEs in the Australian state of Victoria. The WISE programmes, which provided an alternative training and employment model, were designed to facilitate employment for highly disadvantaged individuals (referred to in Barraket's chapter as enterprise operators) through skill development and employment creation. Participants in the WISE programme were immigrants and refugees experiencing multiple barriers to economic and social participation. The evaluation focused on *outcome* and *impact* measures and data was gathered through semi-structured interviews with 33 people (thirteen enterprise operators; eleven staff; two programme volunteers; one contractor; four representatives from partner organizations; and two representatives from the main funding body). Results of the evaluation reported positive *outcomes* in terms of improvement in self-esteem and self-efficacy for all the enterprise operators with improved *impact* in terms of positive intergenerational and intercultural effects in their local communities. Richard Hazenberg, in Chapter 8, provides us with a comparative intervention study, comparing *outcome* benefits of employment enhancement programmes (EEP) delivered by a 'for-profit' private company and a WISE. The EEP programmes were designed to help and support young people not in employment, education or training (NEET). Hazenberg employs a general self-efficacy (GSE) scale and semi-structured interviews in an intervention-style study to measure the changes in GSE before and after NEET engagement in the EEPs. Results from the analysis of quantitative and qualitative data are triangulated to provide a rigorous evaluation of the *outcome* benefits provided by the EEPs for the NEET clients in both the 'for-profit' and WISE organizations. Hazenberg furthers the comparison between the 'for-profit' company and the WISE by investigating the organizational factors (e.g. aims, values and structures) of the two entities via further interviews and focus groups discussions with their owners and staff. Results of the study suggest that although no significant difference between the *outcome* benefits perceived for the NEETs at either organization were revealed, the WISE had *outcome* improvement with more socially excluded individuals when compared with the 'for-profit' organization's clientele. In Chapter 9 the authors Kelly Hall and Malin Arvidson discuss the importance of the evaluation of *impact* and focus on the choices of *impact* evaluation tools available to different organizations. Hall and Arvidson discuss how these tools are perceived by the SE community, commissioners, grant-making bodies and social investors. Three specific impact evaluation tools are considered, Social Return on Investment (SROI), Outcomes Star (OS) and Randomized Control Trials (RCT). Analysis of the use of these impact evaluation tools informs the authors' proposal that the tools do not merely assess achievement but influence value systems in current debate surrounding assessing SE performance. Detailed description and critique of the three impact evaluation tools are provided by the authors prior to the presentation of insightful comparisons between the measures and how they can influence definition of *impact*, the role evaluation plays and what counts as evidence.

The three chapters (Chapters 10–12) in Part IV provide an overarching critique of the evaluation of SE from social, political and financial perspectives. Together, these three chapters engage in a broad philosophical debate that informs the reader about past and current developments in SE. The contributing authors also indicate potential future developments for SE and raise issues of ethics and morality in the development of social finance, management, organizational challenges and support for disadvantaged individuals in society. In Chapter 10, Alex Nicholls performs a forensic examination of 'social finance' in a wide-ranging critical review of past, current and future developments in the landscape of social finance. Nicholls argues that ethical financial investment can support SEs in achieving a triple-bottom line of financial surplus, fulfilment of social mission and environmental sustainability. Nicholls examines social finance from the perspectives of supply, demand and intermediation. Supply includes individuals, institutions and governments; demand is from the recipients of social finance (e.g., social enterprises, charities, cooperatives, social businesses and hybrid organizations) and intermediaries are organizations that link the supply and demand elements (e.g., Bridges Ventures, Acumen Fund and Big Society Capital). Nicholls distinguishes between capital allocation logics (the outcome of placing capital) and investor rationalities (the objectives of placing capital) proposing that social finance is institutionalized in a complex market, which constitutes the institutionalization of hybridity. Nicholls argues three possible future scenarios of institutionalization: 'absorption' – social finance is absorbed into mainstream finance; 'parallel' – social finance continues to operate on the margins of the mainstream; and 'institutional' – social finance institutionalizes value-driven rationalities and imports them into mainstream capital markets. In Chapter 11, Ingo Bode presents a critical evaluation of the increasing dominance of 'social enterprise' over 'public sector culture'. Bode discusses the mounting pressure on traditional 'non-profit' service providers to adopt the 'social enterprise model'. He also considers whether or not existing 'non-profit' managers have the entrepreneurial skills necessary to achieve the required 'double bottom line'. Bode includes evidence from WISE and 'social care' organizations across three European countries (UK, Germany and France) to illustrate his argument that volatile financial conditions, affecting interfaces between contemporary 'non-profits' and welfare bureaucracies, make 'chance' an important factor in their wider development and result in a 'muddling-through' style of management. In Chapter 12, Suzanne Grant extends the critical review of SE by challenging 'positive' and 'glowing' accounts of SE, often projected by policymakers, practitioners and academics through examining the social construction of SE. Grant examines the potential paradox between 'social' and 'enterprise' through the lens of 'critical appreciative processes' (CAP) (Grant 2006). The chapter begins with an overview of 'appreciative inquiry', to familiarize the reader with this action research approach, and introduces CAP, which is then applied to SE considering key themes such as policy capture, heroic and deliverance claims and increased marketization identified within social enterprise/entrepreneurship. Grant concludes with a discourse examining the cultural dimension. Grant argues that SE must take culture into account or risk endangering targeted communities by failing to appreciate traditional values and not accepting the limitations of Western ideologies.

This well-respected group of authors has contributed individual specific perspectives on evaluating SE from a truly international perspective. Within the book's chapters, the debate surrounding the definition of SE is not resolved but stimulated.

Authors present their own rigorous research in support of their assertions and propositions that definition and evaluation of SE should remain flexible and developmental as the phenomenon of SE is still a relatively new and dynamic concept. The contributing authors provide many examples of how SEs and SE itself may be evaluated but draw to the readers' attention the importance of selecting the appropriate measure for the target of evaluation. One of the more exciting aspects of the compilation of these excellent chapters is how they interrelate with each other, often citing fellow authors' work, to provide stimulating and thought-provoking critical debate around SE at a political, financial, social and philosophical level.

This book has an international approach, but it is not intended to be a global review. Our authors are based in the so-called developed world and their subject matter is largely SE in mature market economies. SE in much of Africa, Asia and South America is different in scale and scope. A review of the purposes and effectiveness of SE in the industrializing world, and the lessons that can be learnt from different practices, will be the subject of a different book.

References

Cooper, R. (1989) 'Modernism, post modernism and organizational analysis 3: The contribution of Jacques Derrida', *Organisational Studies*, 10: 479–502.

Curtis, T. (2008) 'Finding that grit makes a pearl – a critical re-reading of research into the development of social enterprises by the public sector', *International Journal of Entrepreneurial Behaviour and Research*, 14(5): 276–90.

Derrida, J. (1967) [1974] *Of Grammatology*. Baltimore, MD: John Hopkins University Press.

Doherty, B., Foster, G., Mason, C., Meehan, J., Rotheroe, N. and Royce, M. (2009) *Management for Social Enterprise*. London: Sage Publications.

Grant, S. L. (2006) 'A paradox in action? A critical analysis of appreciative inquiry', PhD Thesis, University of Waikato.

Haugh, H. (2012) 'The importance of theory in social enterprise research', *Social Enterprise Journal*, 8(1): 7–15.

Jones, R., Latham, J. and Betta, M. (2008) 'Narrative construction of the social entrepreneurial identity', *International Journal of Entrepreneurial Behaviour and Research*, 14(5): 330–45.

McLoughlin, J., Kaminski, J., Sodagar, B., Khan, S., Harris, R., Arnaudo, G. and McBrearty, S. (2009) 'A strategic approach to social impact measurement of social enterprises: The SIMPLE methodology', *Social Enterprise Journal*, 2(1): 154–78.

Parkinson, C. and Howorth, C. (2008) 'The language of social entrepreneurs', *Entrepreneurship and Regional Development*, 20(3): 285–309.

Pearce, J. (2003) *Social Enterprise in Anytown*. Lisbon: Calouste Gulbenkian Foundation.

SEC (2009) *State of Social Enterprise Survey 2009*. London: Social Enterprise Coalition.

SEC (2011) *Enjoy What You Do, Work in Social Enterprise*. London: Social Enterprise Coalition.

Stayaert, C. and Dey, P. (2010) 'Nine verbs to keep the social entrepreneurship research agenda "dangerous"', *Journal of Social Entrepreneurship*, 1: 231–54.

PART II

Defining social enterprise: a theoretical perspective

2

SOCIAL ENTERPRISE OR SOCIAL ENTREPRENEURSHIP

Which matters and why?

John Thompson and Jonathan M. Scott

Introduction and context

While there are many definitions of social enterprise (discussed later in this chapter), social enterprises, social entrepreneurs and social entrepreneurship, these are replete with abstractness, bias, contradiction and debate (Department for Trade and Industry 2002; Jones and Keogh 2006; Birch and Whittam 2008; Dacin *et al.* 2011) and 'confusion' (Jones and Keogh 2006). Without clear agreement on meaning and purpose, it is difficult to evaluate performance, value and success. Moreover, the value attributed to the contribution of those engaged in social enterprises will be influenced by the assessment and evaluation used. Social entrepreneurship, social enterprise and social enterprises have all grown in significance over the last twenty years – both as noticeable activities and as research topics, as evidenced by a growing body of literature (for example, Chell 2007; Curtis 2008; Haugh 2005; Leadbeater 1998; Nicholls 2006; Peattie and Morley 2008; Shaw and Carter 2007). Their prominence and popularity is one of the reasons why there is a need and a demand for this book.

The thesis of this chapter is that social enterprise and social entrepreneurship are needed for the value they generate. This argument assigns these terms as verbs and activities, rather than as nouns or 'entities'. Hence, this argument and perspective does not necessarily mean that social enterprises are needed or, indeed, that the majority of the people who populate the social enterprises in question should be called social entrepreneurs. This chapter, therefore, endeavours to (i) explore sense and meaning in this field, which is confused by the loose use of terminology (**theory**), and (ii) provide practical guidance for readers into how innovation and creativity can be stimulated, given its key role in the sustainability of social enterprises (**practice**).

Whilst we may not have a 'universal' definition of a social enterprise, we do have a number that are frequently cited, capture the ethos of social enterprises and which are broadly similar (Birch and Whittam 1998; Department of Trade and Industry (DTI) 2002; Dees 2001; Thompson and Doherty 2006; Nicholls 2006). But if we then look at the key elements of entrepreneurship, whether it is practised in social enterprises or elsewhere (Bolton and Thompson 2004), it becomes apparent that an organization can be a social enterprise without being entrepreneurial. Correspondingly, social entrepreneurship is manifest in organizations that are not social enterprises when benchmarked against the popular and prevalent definitions. Therefore, and in turn, social enterprises may not be led by people we might describe as social entrepreneurs. And people we call social entrepreneurs may be active in activities and organizations that are not social enterprises. To 'complete the circle', a person who might be described as a social entrepreneur might well be involved in an activity or organization that is not socially entrepreneurial in the way that it behaves.

This chapter is structured as follows. First, we consider the influence of social enterprises' purpose. Second, we explore definitions and terminology to clarify what social enterprises actually (we think) are and, third, how the desired outcomes, values and actors are linked. The fourth section attempts to make sense of the preceding findings and discussion whilst the final section concludes the chapter.

A sense of purpose

At the most basic level, the test of the value of any social enterprise or community-based initiative would be the extent to which it would be missed if it was no longer there. The outcome, then, is arguably more important than the reason why it was established in the first place, the declared purpose it might have and the way it is run – tested against measures of efficiency (how well it does what it does). Its effectiveness, what it achieves in the eyes of key stakeholders, becomes the critical issue (for insight into stakeholder theory, see Freeman 1984; Friedman and Miles 2002; Freeman 2011; Freeman et al. 2010; Freeman and Phillips 2002; Phillips et al. 2003). But a debate on values and perspectives is still a relevant one to have.

When we look at social enterprises, at the actors and organizations involved, we can begin to debate the extent to which it is about being:

Value driven: A new (and different) type of organization that has distinctive governance and a more social and less commercial perspective – to conform with the values that are often attributed to social enterprises generally and also because (i) some hold a belief that the commercial model will not deal with the relevant needs; (ii) the public sector arguably does not possess the resources required, as it involves some very difficult choices and rationing (demand for services exceeds resource-driven supply potential), as well as a desire for a better way of providing the services in question. The new model ought to be all-round more effective and reinvest any relevant surpluses into the organizations. This perspective will be attractive to people who would shun the traditional commercial, capitalist or neo-liberal model.

Financially driven: Delivering public services more efficiently by moving them out of the so-called public sector and into social enterprises. Successive governments have encouraged this innovative approach, but for some people it became a contentious issue in the context of 'private sector competition' in the debates on the 2012 Bill that introduced fresh reforms to the National Health Service. On the one hand, there is an argument that already stretched resources can achieve more with different ways of working; on the other hand, there is a fear that some jobs might be lost.

This view can be taken in a different direction and extended into a displacement argument. If there are grants, subsidies or cheap loans available to declared non-profit or social enterprises contracting for work, then this can give them an unfair advantage when set alongside private sector providers with a declared profit orientation, although there might be no attempt on the part of such organizations to make anything more than a modest profit.

It is very important in this debate not to lose sight of the need for both efficiency in the utilization of resources and expectations of high levels of service. Those in favour of competition, whatever form this might take and from whichever provider, would emphasize this point.

Values and social responsibility most closely align with strategic purpose in social enterprises and not-for-profit firms in terms of both vision (Ruvio *et al.* 2010) and mission (Brinckerhoff 2009; Kirk and Nolan 2010; McDonald 2007). Furthermore, other novel business models include social ventures, for example, which have social objectives, including poverty reduction, and a distinct business model (Seelos and Mair 2005, 2007). One particularly pertinent example is the Grameen Bank, whose business model exposes some key lessons, namely 'challenging conventional wisdom', 'finding complementary partners', 'undertaking continuous experimentation', 'favouring social profit-oriented shareholders' and 'specifying social profit objectives clearly' (Yunus *et al.* 2010). Consequently, Yunus *et al.* (2010) have developed a social business model framework which has four elements: (i) social and environmental profit equation; (ii) value proposition (stakeholders and product/service); (iii) internal and external value constellation; and (iv) economic profit equation.

Definitions and terminology

The Department of Trade and Industry (2002) in the UK has defined a social enterprise as 'a business with primarily social objectives whose surpluses are principally reinvested for that (social) purpose in the business and the community' (DTI 2002: 7). We might then think of a social enterprise as one that provides 'business solutions to social problems' and one that is 'good at doing good'. It has a clear orientation and purpose and it is run efficiently. Many other organizations and community-based, often volunteer, initiatives look to provide solutions to social problems, but they may not be 'business solutions' and the way they operate may not be very business-like or particularly innovative. But their contribution might still be of great significance and value. The following characteristics (taken from Thompson and Doherty 2006) seem to be criteria for identifying a social enterprise:

- It has a social purpose.
- Its assets and wealth are used to create community benefit.

- It pursues this with (at least in part) trading activities. If it delivers services to clients, which are paid for by a third party as distinct from direct sales to a customer, this is still regarded as trading.
- Profits and surpluses are reinvested in the business and community rather than distributed to shareholders.
- Employees (or members) have some role in decision-making and governance.
- The enterprise is held accountable to both its members and a wider community.
- There is either a double or triple bottom-line paradigm with an acceptable balance of economic, social and possibly environmental returns – which are audited.

Entrepreneurship, whatever the context, is a way of thinking and behaving that has both opportunity and the individual entrepreneur at its heart (Shane and Venkataraman 2000; Shane 2003). Creativity and innovation are typically in evidence (Schumpeter 1934; Drucker 1985a, 1985b; Hébert and Link 2006). Entrepreneurs – and entrepreneurial people – recognize, create, engage and exploit opportunities (Kirzner 1997) – and they do this habitually and instinctively, with entrepreneurial orientation, comprising: 'autonomy, innovativeness, risk taking, proactiveness and competitive aggressiveness' (Lumpkin and Dess 1996: 136), and with effectual reasoning, 'the logic of control' rather than the 'logic of prediction' or causation (Sarasvathy 2001). They find ways to secure the resources they are going to need, although these may not be available when they set out on their journey. They often accomplish this through having entrepreneurial talent, such as with accessing finance (Evans and Jovanovic 1989), and through networking, which is one key aspect of their social capital (Davidsson and Honig 2003). Risks have to be understood, taken and managed (Knight 1921; Stewart and Roth 2001). Setbacks, which are inevitable, have to be overcome. The outcome is something of perceived value for the target client or audience; they have to value whatever it is, whether they have to pay for it or not. Where this is a social benefit, it should be sustainable. In simple terms, we would think of something as entrepreneurial, as distinct from business-like or even enterprising, if it is genuinely different in some distinctive way, if it is finding innovative solutions or resolutions for problems, and if it is hungry to achieve, find a fresh challenge (related or unrelated to the existing activity or cause) and move on.

Bolton and Thompson (2004) define the entrepreneur as 'a person who habitually creates and innovates to build something of recognized value around perceived opportunities' (Bolton and Thompson 2004: 16). For a true social entrepreneur we might rework this and say 'builds something that has a sustained and meaningful impact on the lives of others'. Similarly, Nicholls (2006: back cover) summarizes it as 'activities which address a range of social and environmental issues in innovative and creative ways'. It can take place within or outside a social enterprise as defined by the criteria above. And, to reinforce the point and the dilemma, it may not always be evident in a social enterprise.

Whether the enterprise is entrepreneurial or not we might look for evidence of:

- a clear idea, opportunity – or at the extreme, a cause – at the heart
- the necessary resources, however they are acquired – *sometimes this can be very entrepreneurial*
- clear outcomes – maybe communicated as a vision
- 'actioning' – *again, entrepreneurial behaviour might or might not be evident*
- measured outcomes
- demonstrated benefits – including social outcomes
- management and business discipline
- a leader – or a team – who will take and manage the risk.

Sykes (1999) argues that the responsibility for these can be shared amongst a group of people and that one or more people can be responsible for three essential contributions: envisioning, enabling and enacting. The envisioner sees the opportunity; the enabler gathers together the necessary people and resources; the enactor manages the subsequent delivery (ibid.) and, further, there is another element that needs separate identification and that is *engaging* (see Thompson *et al.* 2000; Thompson 2008). Things happen when someone makes them happen. It is the link between seeing an opportunity and responding to it (Singh 2001; Corbett 2005). Many of us see possibilities and choose to do nothing about them. There are people 'out there' willing to commit their time (paid or otherwise) or other resources if their contribution can be harnessed. Similarly, there are people who are good at finding money if they can be introduced to a worthy cause. When there is a team involved, sharing the responsibilities, it is always interesting to consider who the most entrepreneurial driver is.

In summary, entrepreneurship, regardless of its context, involves three key elements:

- a vision
- someone with leadership skills who can operationalize the vision – which often involves finding a suitable partner, engaging the support of a range of, sometimes voluntary, helpers and dealing with the inevitable setbacks (*the vision may be that of the social entrepreneur who starts the venture or one which is 'bought in', as we shall see later*)
- a will to build something that will grow and endure.

Bolton and Thompson (2004) introduced the FACETS mnemonic to capture the core characteristics of entrepreneurs. In summary, the details of this framework are:

- **F** represents **focus**, the key ability to deliver and achieve.
- **A** is **advantage**, the ability to spot real opportunities which are more than ideas.
- **C** is the **creativity** that underpins advantage and starts the process off.

- **E** or **ego** is the temperament that drives everything. It has an inner core based around motivation and an outer core linked to the ability to deal with one's motivation.
- **T** is the **team** element that is central to growth and development.
- **S** is the **social** characteristic that helps determine the direction the person will take; it is the only characteristic that directly affects the ego.

They argue that temperament is the key driver and that strengths in different 'roles' are reliant on the presence of particular talents. Focus is required by a manager just as much as it is by an entrepreneur, for example. Team characteristics are relevant for leaders and managers as well as entrepreneurs, although perhaps with an emphasis on different sub-characteristics. Social can affect everyone. Their social characteristic has four sub-characteristics, which can be likened to the rungs of a ladder. The two lower rungs are beliefs and values. Individually entrepreneurs may have beliefs that have a direct impact on the values manifested by their business. But they may not and, of course, need not. Brian Souter (of the transport company Stagecoach) has strong personal beliefs, based upon his Christian upbringing and beliefs, but these are not automatically Stagecoach values. His sister, and partner in the business when it started, Ann Gloag, an ex-nurse, has invested money and spent time doing charity work for Mercy Ships, where medics provide free surgical care for people in developing countries who would otherwise not receive treatment. This was always kept separate from Stagecoach. When evident in the business, values will relate to the ways a business treats its various stakeholders – customers, suppliers and employees. Social responsibility and ethical issues can be critical.

The third rung is related to finding a cause that affects the direction of the business or enterprise. The social 'direction' can vary markedly. The late social entrepreneur Anita Roddick discovered a cause related to the Third World and the environment. The more she focused on this the greater was the impact on The Body Shop as a business, both positively (image and reputation) and negatively (falling profits and a weaker competitive position, which had a real bearing on her losing control). J. Arthur Rank found a cause when he realized the impact film (movies) could have on people's lives and this proved to be the foundation of the modern British cinema industry.

The examples in the last two paragraphs feature entrepreneurs who have run businesses with which they are very closely associated. Anita Roddick has been described by some as a social entrepreneur, but The Body Shop is not a social enterprise. It has shareholders. Brian Souter could not logically be described as a social entrepreneur. To Bolton and Thompson (2004), the real social entrepreneurs – as distinct from people running social enterprises or being socially enterprising – dedicate their lives to the service of others. They find and embrace a cause and it becomes everything to them. There are strong spiritual and social elements in their work. They care – and do something about it. Generally we have here moved away from entrepreneurs running businesses, however conventional or unconventional, to something else. Historically William and Catherine Booth (founders of the

Salvation Army) and more recently Mother Teresa and Lord Michael Young (systematically the founder of The Open University, the Consumers' Association and *Which*? magazine and The School for Social Entrepreneurs) would be good examples.

It might be pedantic, but it is important to distinguish people who are socially entrepreneurial from those we celebrate as true social entrepreneurs. This view is reinforced by comments on the Ashoka Foundation website (www.ashoka.org): 'social entrepreneurs are individuals with innovative solutions to society's most pressing social problems ... ambitious and persistent ... offering new ideas for wide-scale change ... [they] find what is not working and solve the problem by changing the system, spreading the solution, and persuading entire societies to take new leaps ... often possessed by their ideas they commit their lives to changing the direction of their field'. Using their team characteristic to effect they often galvanize support from socially entrepreneurial people in communities everywhere. Bill Drayton, founder of Ashoka, is himself a social entrepreneur.

The expression social entrepreneur, then, should arguably be used more cautiously and more discriminately than it often is. Related to this are four other interesting issues. The first concerns how we classify the successful and wealthy entrepreneurs and business people who 'give back' some of their wealth to causes they believe in. Bill Gates – through the Bill and Melinda Gates Foundation – is a generous benefactor and philanthropist. Indeed, billionaire Warren Buffett has donated substantial sums to the Gates Foundation rather than start his own. By matching dollar for dollar the money that Rotary International donates to polio vaccination across the developing world Gates has helped to eradicate this terrible disease in many countries, thus affecting lives in a serious and positive way. Such generosity is an expression of belief; in itself it does not automatically make an entrepreneur a social entrepreneur.

Bolton (2006) has gone a step further and identified those entrepreneurs he would describe as 'Kingdom Entrepreneurs'. Here he is taking a religious perspective – and, of course, William and Catherine Booth had this. Similarly, Florence Nightingale believed she had been called by God to do the work she did. Kingdom entrepreneurs are concerned with building something of value that all of us can be proud of, and through which they leave a legacy and 'footprints'.

It is also fair to argue that Mohamed Yunus, Nobel Prize winner, founder of the Grameen Bank and provider of microfinance to women in the developing world, is a social entrepreneur. A similar contribution has been made by David Bussau, retired wealthy business entrepreneur and founder of Opportunity International, which has again provided microfinance to help small enterprises start up in various developing countries. Although we would call David Bussau a social entrepreneur, he is also an enterprise enabler. If we use terminology loosely we would probably call him an entrepreneur enabler! But really he enables entrepreneurship to flourish; he has no direct link to the individuals who start the micro-businesses. His contribution is to help others who want to start something modest to be able to do so.

When social enterprises and many community-based initiatives are successful they are often publicized widely and the people behind them receive attention.

They become visible figures. Paradoxically, this then makes them a target for others who are in need of advice and support. Because they are socially committed people they are frequently drawn to help others, which at one level is defensible and good. The danger is they lose focus and their own enterprise suffers as they get involved in other things. Here their serial nature can work against them rather than for them.

Desired outcomes, linked values and actors

Whilst the triple bottom line has been exhaustively explored since the seminal Elkington (1997, 1998), social enterprise performance and its social impact remains under-researched (Barratt 2007; Paton 2003; Peattie and Morley 2008; Thompson *et al.* 2012), despite some efforts (Bull 2007; Haugh 2007), as do the reasons for failure, such as the example of Aspire and its ill-fated franchising business model (Tracey and Jarvis 2006, 2007).

When we discuss double and triple bottom line achievements we are looking at economic, social and environmental impacts. It is an easy trap to think of organizations creating different capitals as outcomes – after all, profit-seeking organizations do generate economic or financial capital. The recipients of this capital then have the opportunity to become wealthy, and, again, because it is an easy measure, we often evaluate the success of business people and entrepreneurs through their financial wealth. Social capital is, though, an *input* that helps in the creation of social wealth. Fukuyama (1995) captures this by defining social capital as 'a set of informal values or norms shared among members of a group that permits co-operation among them' (Fukuyama 1995: 16). The way people use their networks to make other things happen is an important determinant of what they achieve – whether it is financial, social or environmental.

We should also account in some way for important buildings, works of art, great music and so on because they can also have a major impact on people's lives. Design – and the ensuing artefacts – creates aesthetic wealth. To what extent, though, do we create environmental wealth as distinct from arguably potentially destroying something that is there as a natural resource? Thompson and Scott (2010) have pointed out that a positive impact on the environment can be achieved through organizations and the people behind them truly caring about the environment – and it can be achieved through carefully crafted legislation that restricts particular business practices that would have a potentially harmful impact.

Whilst some organizations strive to, and succeed in, achieving multiple outcomes, others fail in this. The American energy business, Enron, was a case in point. Enron traders were happy to see Californian residents short of electricity as Enron shut down its power stations unnecessarily, and exported power out of California to drive up energy prices through the natural laws of supply, demand and scarcity. By doing this they made huge trading profits for Enron. This challenge will never be easy. The 'paradigm of greatest good' might not be financially viable, and the most financially sustainable option might deliver only modest social outcomes.

Relevant for social enterprises, where faith communities frequently have a major involvement, Bolton (2006) flags the importance of spiritual capital. He defines this as 'the blessings of the Father's love' (Bolton 2006: 19) and sees it reflected in the ways that people deal with and support each other. Caring would then be a key manifestation. It will become apparent just how important spiritual capital can be for true social entrepreneurs.

From earlier arguments, it will be apparent just how diverse social enterprises are. There are, though, some obvious clusters and 'actors', including charities. But, of course, charities and the charity sector range from large international charities to national ones, to organized and formal local ones linked to specific causes (such as a local hospice) and to *ad hoc* and more informal charities set up by individuals with a specific concern. Some seek to help people directly (Oxfam, those linked to famine relief); some carry out research that they hope will ultimately 'do good' (Cancer Research UK); some look to spread important messages, and so on. Where they come together is in competition for scarce funding. They all look for donations through collections and events; some have trading operations such as charity shops. Many employ professional fundraisers; others rely on volunteers. Funding is a big challenge for without financial resources their ability to carry out good work is severely constrained.

National and local government are actors because they sometimes opt to commission the provision of specific services from private providers rather than retain them as public sector activities – and they often favour social enterprises, sometimes ones that have been set up deliberately by ex-public sector employees. Instances can be found in healthcare, education and social services, both adult and children's services. We have already discussed the people we would describe as true social entrepreneurs. Entrepreneurs (in business) who have a strong social (and/or environmental) orientation are still very important and relevant actors even if we might choose not to see them as true social entrepreneurs. Similarly, there are many different types of social enterprise, including those spun out from the public sector to provide services under commissioning agreements. Organizations that declare themselves to be 'fairtrade' may or may not be included. Cooperatives and credit unions might also fit the social enterprise framework outlined earlier in this chapter.

Although often included, one might separate out those that operate in 'civil society'. Museums and art galleries, which are sometimes established as charities and are typically non-profit making (but perhaps heavily grant subsidized), would be examples. The term 'civil entrepreneur' can be found being used to describe those who champion such organizations (Leadbeater and Goss 1998).

In addition, the different types of community initiative are too many to mention. These can vary from those that are entirely reliant on volunteers, to those that require grant funding to survive, to those that raise their own funding. It is no exaggeration to say that many of these fit the base evaluation criteria very closely – if they no longer existed they would be sorely missed. Many people benefit enormously from these initiatives and local organizations; they are the Big Society, in many instances. They may not grow, they may not be particularly well managed, they may operate 'on the breadline' but they are arguably very important contributors to society and the economy.

The 'third sector' as a whole survives because there is support for it. Government supports the third sector with both grants and commissioning; benefactors often see such organizations as an ideal vehicle for 'giving back' – which they may do as individuals or through such vehicles as Community Foundations; individuals give modest amounts every time they pass a street collector – and they also often give their time.

Charity shops are arguably social enterprises, although they are largely dependent upon volunteer staff and so are seen by many as part of the voluntary sector – where many local organizations would also be placed. Within the voluntary sector there can be evidence of significant entrepreneurship; without innovation and a real desire to secure resources and make a difference many community initiatives would soon disappear. Many organizations that we do think of as social enterprises are those which sub-contract service delivery work that might otherwise be provided by the public sector, as we have pointed out above. They are again often well managed and do what they do efficiently and effectively, but they are responding to a government-defined need; they are not innovatory and different in the way that entrepreneurs are.

Fairtrade organizations present an interesting challenge for us. They need to be innovative and entrepreneurial if they are to help suppliers, such as African cocoa growers, to gain access to markets in the developed world, and if they are to persuade consumers to pay a premium price for the products. Divine Chocolate, for example, is priced some 15 to 20 per cent higher than the 'mainstream' chocolate bars (Doherty and Meehan 2006). Ideally, their consumers will be persuaded that they are buying a superior quality product, as well as being willing to pay more for the fairtrade promise. In this way the business will be more sustainable in the long run, for the fact that something is fairtrade is not in itself a guarantee of success. Aspire was set up in the late 1990s to enable homeless people to sell fairtrade products through a direct mail catalogue. Initially successful, the business was franchised. But its product range was limited and consequentially its target market was limited. It grew too quickly and was wound up in 2004 (Tracey and Jarvis 2006, 2007).

The popularity of social enterprises has increased, in part because the government believes they can be an efficient way of delivering services that meet important social needs – it therefore commissions work from them. When this happens it would be quite normal for the purchaser/funder to specify the target outputs and so, in that way, the service remains supply-driven. But others have been set up because an individual 'entrepreneur' has seen a need and set out to do something about it. Thus some activities are reactive to funding opportunities whilst others are more proactively demand-driven. With the latter, it is often the case that if the opportunity is viable and consumers will pay for a product that provides value for them, it could be provided by a profit-seeking competitor in just the same way that it can by a social enterprise. Equally, some customers will pay a premium price for a product that can demonstrate fairtrade origins. Here success lies in the ability to add and deliver the value that matters to the customer.

These activities operate alongside the voluntary (or third stream) sector where a huge range of organizations also meet important social needs. In fact, volunteers will often be required to meet needs that the public sector cannot and will not pay for, and for which those with a need (or in some cases a desire rather than a need) cannot or will not pay a market price. But volunteering, even when it is enterprising, does not amount to an 'enterprise' and yet many active volunteers might well be loosely described as social entrepreneurs meeting a social need in an entrepreneurial way. They are certainly achieving the latter, but it is debatable whether we really should call them entrepreneurs. Given important differences between an entrepreneur recently involved in a start-up and someone who has been running a small business for some time, recently started-up entrepreneurs have a real emphasis on difference, habitual activity and growth. People involved in social and economic regeneration behave entrepreneurially, because that is the way they make things happen and bring results. Recent entrepreneurs and established small business owners/managers, then, may be very different in how they behave and in what they do. Being an entrepreneur and behaving entrepreneurially are not synonymous, and this also holds if we prefix both with the word 'social'.

Beginning to make sense

From our discussions we might summarize that social entrepreneurship in action requires:

- doers – people who get things done – including volunteers
- leaders – champions – organizers
- enablers – who in various ways smooth the road and make things possible
- opportunity spotters
- people who care enough about the need to do something.

Although these criteria fit, many of those who are engaged in community-based activities would not see themselves as entrepreneurs or want to be called an entrepreneur (although they might tolerate social entrepreneur!) and, tested against the definition adopted earlier, they are not genuine entrepreneurs, but some (not all) of them are entrepreneurial. They can do what they do in a wide raft of organizations and initiatives – they are not restricted to what we would define as a social enterprise.

If we also look at the link between activity and outcome (returning here to our economic and social value debate), then many of the initiatives and organizations will deliver value without being enterprising (innovative) or entrepreneurial in any way.

We should also consider issues of sustainability and how many organizations start and disappear because of funding issues (Ramsden 2005; Darby and Jenkins 2006). There is then a danger that much of their attention is given over to external funding because simply the market itself cannot pay for all the relevant services. This can be another distraction from the core purpose.

There is clearly both scope and need for more social innovation and social entrepreneurship if, on the one hand, the identifiable requirements of the community are to be met more effectively, and, on the other hand, new opportunities to create additional benefits are to be found and exploited proactively. To accomplish this, more social champions need to be found and many of the people involved in existing ventures need to be encouraged to become more ambitious and more professional – in the context of increased efficiency. This increased incidence implies increased visibility and new forms of support. The former can be achieved by widening awareness, and the latter by introducing new training and development opportunities for people willing to support the ventures – and perhaps ultimately start a new initiative. Here, the issue of the 'right people' is important. Some people who are willing to volunteer their services and time may be inadequately skilled and qualified, and without appropriate training will inhibit rather than enhance the initiative.

In terms of efficiencies, because many ventures of this nature can avoid the rigorous monitoring found in the profit-generating sector, it is important to ensure that the appropriate performance measures are adopted. By and large, the real effectiveness of anything deemed socially entrepreneurial implies 'soft' or qualitative evaluation, but quantitative measures such as the number of clients benefiting, external monies raised, the number of jobs created and the numbers of volunteers (or honorary professionals) attracted are all ideal for benchmarking purposes.

One important element is that professionals attracted to the third sector often have many of the skills and much confidence already, but what they lack is innovative ideas. But people from more deprived backgrounds, who are very close to the need and who are often very willing to get involved, are perhaps more likely to lack some of the skills and confidence. They are less likely to have been in positions where they have had to take a lead and make decisions for others.

Conclusions

In the end, perhaps it is outcomes that matter more than anything else and where we should be focusing our concerns. How these are achieved does, indeed, matter but sustainability depends only in part on organizational efficiencies. Surely we really should be particularly concerned about the people who need to come forward and what they do rather than what we call them. Actions, we might argue, speak louder than theories and rhetoric. It is actions that were required to meet Tony Blair's desire for an 'explosion of acts of community' and that are required if the 'Big Society' is going to amount to something more than words. We need to study and understand the personal motivation of the relevant actors for what they do and what it takes to keep them engaged. We also need to reflect on how 'we academics' might best support these people and the third sector.

For the 'Big Society' to thrive, people must be willing to get off their metaphorical backsides and do something. As we have argued, it may not be really significant if they are rather inefficient but they should be effective. They need to demonstrate they add value and matter to people. In this regard, innovation and improvement should never be neglected. It is important to try to help people to improve and to persuade them that improvement matters. It is innovation, difference and entrepreneurship that hold the key to continuity and sustainability. Books like this, and the serious academic research that continues in this topic, do matter, but they need to foster action as well as debate – the eternal challenge for academics!

NOTE: *This chapter has been developed (in part) from Thompson et al. (2000) and Thompson (2008).*

References

Barratt, P. (2007) 'Some international evidence', Appendix in Hart, T. and Houghton, G. (2007) *Assessing the Economic and Social Impact of Social Enterprise: Feasibility Report*. Hull: Centre for City and Regional Studies: University of Hull.

Birch, K. and Whittam, G. (2008) 'The third sector and the regional development of social capital', *Regional Studies*, 42(3): 437–50.

Bolton, B. and Thompson, J. L. (2004) *Entrepreneurs: Talent, Temperament, Technique*. Oxford: Elsevier.

Bolton, W. K. (2006) *The Entrepreneur and the Church*. Cambridge: Grove Books.

Brinckerhoff, P. C. (2009) *Mission-based Management: Leading Your Not-for-profit in the 21st Century*. London: John Wiley & Sons.

Bull, M. (2007) '"Balance": The development of a social enterprise business performance analysis tool', *Social Enterprise Journal*, 3(1): 49–66.

Chell, E. (2007) 'Social enterprise and entrepreneurship: towards a convergent theory of the entrepreneurial process', *International Small Business Journal*, 25(1): 5–26.

Corbett, A. C. (2005) 'Experiential learning within the process of opportunity identification and exploitation', *Entrepreneurship Theory and Practice*, 29: 473–91.

Curtis, T. (2008) 'Finding that grit makes a pearl: a critical re-reading of research into social enterprise', *International Journal of Entrepreneurial Behaviour and Research*, 14(5): 276–90.

Dacin, M. T., Dacin, P. A. and Tracey, P. (forthcoming) 'Social entrepreneurship: a critique and future directions', *Organization Science*, 22(5): 1203–13.

Darby, L. and Jenkins, H. (2006) 'Applying sustainability indicators to the social enterprise business model: the development and application of an indicator set for Newport Wastesavers, Wales', *International Journal of Social Economics*, 33(5/6): 411–31.

Davidsson, P. and Honig, B. (2003) 'The role of social and human capital among nascent entrepreneurs', *Journal of Business Venturing*, 18(3): 301–31.

Dees, J. G. (2001) *The Meaning of Social Entrepreneurship*. Stanford, CA: Stanford University.

Department of Trade and Industry (2002) *Social Enterprise: A Strategy for Success*. London: DTI.

Doherty, B. and Meehan, J. (2006) 'Market entry based on social resources: the case of Day Chocolate Company in the UK confectionary sector', *Journal of Strategic Marketing*, 14(4): 299–313.

Drucker, P. F. (1985a) *Innovation and Entrepreneurship: Practice and Principles*. New York: HarperCollins.

Drucker, P. F. (1985b) 'The discipline of innovation', *Harvard Business Review*, 63(3): 67–72.

Elkington, J. (1997) *Cannibals with Forks: The Triple Bottom Line of 21st-Century Business*. Oxford: Capstone.

Elkington, J. (1998) 'Partnerships from cannibals with forks: The triple bottom line of 21st-century business', *Environmental Quality Management*, 8: 37–51.

Evans, D. and Jovanovic, B. (1989) 'An estimated model of entrepreneurial choice under liquidity constraint', *Journal of Political Economy*, 97(4): 808–27.

Freeman, R. E. (1984) *Strategic Management: A Stakeholder Approach*. London: Pitman.

Freeman, R. E. (2011) 'Some thoughts on the development of stakeholder theory', in R. Phillips (ed.), *Stakeholder Theory: Impact and Prospects*. Cheltenham: Edward Elgar, pp. 212–34.

Freeman, R. E. and Phillips, A. A. (2002) 'Stakeholder theory: a libertarian defense', *Business Ethics Quarterly*, 12(3): 331–49.

Freeman R. E., Harrison, J. S., Wicks, A. C., Parmar, B. L. and de Colle, S. (2010) *Stakeholder Theory: The State of the Art*. Cambridge: Cambridge University Press.

Friedman, A. L. and Miles, S. (2002) 'Developing stakeholder theory', *Journal of Management Studies*, 39, 1–21.

Fukuyama, F. (1995) *Trust: The Social Virtues and the Creation of Prosperity*. New York: Free Press.

Haugh, H. (2005) 'A research agenda for social entrepreneurship', *Social Enterprise Journal*, 1(1): 1–12.

Haugh, H. (2007) 'Community-led social venture creation', *Entrepreneurship Theory and Practice*, March, 161–82.

Hébert, R. F. and Link, A. H. (2006) 'The entrepreneur as innovator', *Journal of Technology Transfer*, 31: 589–97.

Jones, D. and Keogh, W. (2006) 'Social enterprise: a case of terminological ambiguity and complexity', *Social Enterprise Journal*, 1(1): 11–26.

Kirk, G. and Nolan, S. B. (2010) 'Nonprofit mission statement focus and financial performance', *Nonprofit Management and Leadership*, 20(4): 473–90.

Kirzner, I. M. (1997) 'Entrepreneurial discovery and the competitive market process: an Austrian approach', *Journal of Economic Literature*, 35(1): 60–85.

Knight, F. H. (1921) *Risk, Uncertainty and Profit*. Boston, MA: Hart.

Leadbeater, C. (1998) *The Rise of the Social Entrepreneur*. London: Demos.

Leadbeater, C. and Goss, S. (1998) *Civic Entrepreneurship*. London: Demos.

Lumpkin, G. T. and Dess, G. G. (1996) 'Clarifying the entrepreneurial orientation construct and linking it to performance', *Academy of Management Review*, 21(1): 135–72.

McDonald, R. E. (2007) 'An investigation of innovation in nonprofit organizations: the role of organizational mission', *Nonprofit and Voluntary Sector Quarterly*, 36(2): 256–81.

Nicholls, A. (2006) *Social Entrepreneurship: New Models of Sustainable Social Change*. Oxford: Oxford University Press.

Paton, R. (2003) *Managing and Measuring Social Enterprises*. London: Sage.

Peattie, K. and Morley, A. (2008) *Social Enterprises: Diversity and Dynamics, Contexts and Contributions*. London: Social Enterprise Coalition and ESRC.

Phillips, R., Freeman, R. E. and Wicks, A. C. (2003) 'What stakeholder theory is not', *Business Ethics Quarterly*, 13(4): 479–502.

Ramsden, P. (2005) *EVALUATION: The Phoenix Development Fund*. London: Final Report, Small Business Service.

Ruvio, A., Rosenblat, Z. and Hertz-Lazarowitz, R. (2010) 'Entrepreneurial leadership vision in nonprofit vs. for-profit organizations', *The Leadership Quarterly*, 21: 144–58.

Sarasvathy, S. D. (2001) 'Causation and effectuation: towards a theoretical shift from economic inevitability to entrepreneurial contingency', *Academy of Management Review*, 26(2): 243–63.

Schumpeter J. A. (1934) *The Theory of Economic Development: An Inquiry into Profits, Capital, Credit, Interest, and the Business Cycle*. Oxford: Oxford University Press.

Seelos, C. and Mair, J. (2005) 'Social entrepreneurship: creating new business models to serve the poor', *Business Horizons*, 48: 241–6.

Seelos, C. and Mair, J. (2007) 'Profitable business models and market creation in the context of deep poverty: a strategic view', *Academy of Management*, 21(4): 49–63.

Shane, S. (2003) *A General Theory of Entrepreneurship: The Individual-Opportunity Nexus*. Cheltenham: Edward Elgar.

Shane, S. and Venkataraman, S. (2000) 'The promise of entrepreneurship as a field of research', *Academy of Management Review*, 25(1): 217–26.

Shaw, E. and Carter, S. (2007) 'Social entrepreneurship: theoretical antecedents and empirical analysis of entrepreneurial processes and outcomes', *Journal of Small Business and Enterprise Development*, 14(3): 418–34.

Singh, R. P. (2001) 'A comment on developing the field of entrepreneurship through the study of opportunity recognition and exploitation', *The Academy of Management Review*, 26(1): 10–12.

Stewart, W. H. and Roth, P. L. (2001) 'Risk propensity differences between entrepreneurs and managers: a meta-analytic review', *Journal of Applied Psychology*, 86: 145–53.

Sykes, N. (1999) 'Is the organisation encoded with a DNA which determines its development?', Paper presented at The Visioneers conference, Putteridge Bury Management Centre, April 1999.

Thompson, J. L. (2008) 'Social enterprise and social entrepreneurship: where have we reached? A summary of issues and discussion points', *Social Enterprise Journal*, 4(2): 149–61.

Thompson, J. L. and Doherty, B. (2006) 'The diverse world of social enterprise – a collection of social enterprise stories', *International Journal of Social Economics*, 33(5/6): 361–75.

Thompson, J. L. and Scott, J. M. (2010) 'Environmental entrepreneurship: the sustainability challenge', Institute for Small Business and Entrepreneurship (ISBE) conference, London, November 2010.

Thompson, J. L., Alvy, G. and Lees, A. (2000) 'Social entrepreneurship – a new look at the people and the potential', *Management Decision*, 38(6): 328–38.

Thompson, J. L., Scott, J. M. and Downing, R. (2012) 'Enterprise policy, delivery, practice and research: largely rhetoric or under-valued achievement?', *International Journal of Public Sector Management*, 25(5): 332–45.

Tracey, P. and Jarvis, O. (2006) 'An enterprising failure: why a promising social franchise collapsed', *Stanford Social Innovation Review*, Spring: 66–70.

Tracey, P. and Jarvis, O. (2007) 'Toward a theory of social venture franchising', *Entrepreneurship Theory and Practice*, September, 31(5): 667–85.

Yunus, M., Moingeon, B. and Lehmann-Ortega, L. (2010) 'Building social business models: lessons from the Grameen experience', *Long Range Planning*, 43: 308–25.

3

SOCIAL ENTERPRISE MANAGEMENT

How do social enterprises compete?

Bob Doherty

Introduction

Social enterprise (hereafter SE) has received much attention from various competing perspectives, particularly its emergence and definition as an organizational type (Dart 2004; Defourny and Nyssens 2006; Kerlin 2006). However, the management of SE has received limited scholarly attention, particularly as regards crafting the balance between the social and commercial objectives, i.e. the double bottom line (Ridley-Duff and Bull 2011; Dees 1998; Meehan 2009; Moizer and Tracey 2010). Even less attention has been given to how SEs compete against much larger, resource-rich rivals. This chapter utilizes a recent revision of competition theory namely Resource Advantage theory (R-A theory) to try to identify the tangible/ intangible resources that social enterprises use to compete and manage the balance between social and commercial objectives.

R-A theory is a general theory of competition that draws on the research traditions of Austrian economics, the historical tradition, industrial organization economics, the resource-based tradition, institutional economics, transaction cost economics and economic sociology (Hunt and Derozier 2004). Identifying the specific resources that enable SEs to compete could help social entrepreneurs ground their business and marketing strategies in a theory of competition. This is important in building a competitive advantage for SE.

This chapter will explore in more depth the resources utilized by SE and the implications of these in managing its hybrid nature. Using Resource Advantage theory (R-A theory) the author will explain how crafting the balance is possible if the unique set of resources which enable SEs to compete are identified and utilized in the management of SE. R-A theory is used as opposed to Porter's 'industrial organization' theory of competition because it is a more recent revision of competition theory that combines a range of interdisciplinary approaches including

Resource-Based Value (RBV), Competence-based theory (CBT) and the industrial organizational approach of Porter. R-A theory argues that the unique set of resources displayed by a firm could constitute a comparative advantage leading to a position of competitive advantage for some market segments, resulting in superior financial performance (Hunt 2001). Through a synthesis of the literature on SE and R-A theory this chapter will aim to identify the resources that need to be considered when crafting the SE strategy. This is of critical importance as a number of authors argue that SEs have limited resources (Di Domenico *et al.* 2010; Foster and Bradach 2005; Smith-Hunter 2008).

Introduction to social enterprise

A wide-ranging review of the SE literature by Peattie and Morley (2008) found that SEs are distinguished from other organizations by the simultaneous possession of two attributes. First, they trade in goods and/or services in a market (so they are an 'enterprise' and not simply a voluntary or community organization) and second there is a primacy of social aims. SEs' primary purpose lies outside the commercial outcomes related to their trading of goods and/or services in a market (beyond the generation of profit or the growth of the enterprise itself).

Mair and Martì (2006) argue that SEs combine resources in new ways to create social value by stimulating social change. These are enterprises putting social welfare first and still maintaining profitability. Moizer and Tracey (2010) argue that the pursuit of a double bottom line creates high levels of complexity in the management of SEs as not only do the organizations have to create sufficient revenue to invest in business operations but they also have to maintain an investment in social projects; for example, Cafédirect (a fairtrade social enterprise) has a target of investing 60 per cent of its operating profit in social/community projects with producer communities in developing economies (Davies *et al.* 2010).

So what are these resources and what is the nature of this social value? Surely it is the answer to these questions that will inform our management of SE and clarify how it is different. Moizer and Tracey (2010) propose that managing the double bottom line requires crafting a careful balance between resource utilization in order to build and maintain competitive advantage whilst engaging with the key stakeholders.

Despite recent interest in SE, the focus in the business and management discipline has tended to be on the similarities and differences between social and commercial enterprises (Mair and Martì 2006; Austin *et al.* 2006); surprisingly limited work has examined the management issues facing SE. So how do SEs compete in these various sectors? Before we explore this, the chapter will outline Resource Advantage theory, a *general theory of competition*.

The Resource Advantage theory of competition (R-A theory)

R-A theory is grounded in a range of interdisciplinary approaches including the Resource-Based Value (RBV), Competence-Based theory (CBT) and the industrial organizational approach. R-A theory is a general theory of competition that integrates the different schools of thought in competition theory.

Hunt and Derozier (2004) propose that when firms have a comparative advantage in resources they will occupy market place positions of competitive advantage for some market segments. R-A theory has been developed in the literatures of marketing, management, economics, ethics and general business (Hunt and Arnett 2005; Hunt and Derozier 2004). The theory also draws on and has affinity with research traditions such as Austrian economics, the historical tradition, industrial organization economics, the resource-based tradition, institutional economics, transaction cost economics and economic sociology, and is therefore interdisciplinary. Schlegelmilch (2002) argues that R-A theory is a treasure chest for promising research avenues and rejects the silo approach of some theories. Morgan and Hunt (1994) propose that utilizing theories of business and marketing strategy requires that managers understand the nature of competition. Therefore Hunt and Derozier (2004) propose that theories of business and marketing must be grounded in a theory of competition.

RBV defines resources as both intangible and tangible, which is consistent with the institutional economic view that intangible resources, not just physical resources, are important to the success of a firm (Hunt 2002). Therefore a key construct of R-A theory (the resource construct) stipulates that firms' resources are not just land, labour and capital, as in neoclassical theory, but include intangibles, as in the RBV of the firm, shown as follows (Barney 1991):

Financial	(cash resources, access to financial markets)
Physical	(e.g. plant, raw materials and equipment)
Legal	(e.g. trademarks, licenses)
Human	(e.g. skills and knowledge of individual employees including their entrepreneurial skills)
Organizational	(e.g. competences, controls, policies, culture)
Informational	(e.g. knowledge from consumer and competitive intelligence)
Relational	(e.g. relationships with competitors, suppliers, employees and customers).

It is the unique set of resources displayed by a firm that could constitute a comparative advantage in resources leading to a position of competitive advantage for some market segments, resulting in superior financial performance (Hunt 2001). R-A theory expands the concept of resources to include such entities as organizational culture, knowledge and competencies. Therefore, according to Hunt and Morgan (1997) a comparative advantage in an intangible resource such as a new organizational form or competency can result in a market place position of competitive advantage. Hence, rewards flow to firms that successfully create new resources (e.g. competencies), which provide them with a powerful motivation to innovate. In fact, R-A theory permits competence-based strategy to be successful. Morgan and Hunt (1999) also propose the concept of Relationship-Competitive

Advantage (RBCA) resulting in trust and cooperation between stakeholders. However, they do not recognize ethical or social dimensions as a relational resource involved in creating trust. Also, it is the relationships with downstream stakeholders that are regarded as key and not those with upstream stakeholders such as suppliers and communities. Related to this, Curtis *et al.* (2010) unveiled the importance of trust as a resource in building social capital between SEs and public sector customers in different national contexts.

The dynamic nature of R-A theory is illustrated by those competitors who try to neutralize and/or leapfrog the advantaged firm through acquisition, imitation, substitution or major innovation. In the terminology of Hodgson's (1993) taxonomy of evolutionary economic theories, R-A theory is non-consummatory: it has no end stage, only a never-ending process of change. Because R-A theory draws heavily on Austrian economics and the Schumpeterian tradition in evolutionary economics, innovation and organizational learning are endogenous to R-A theory.

However, pertinent to this chapter, Hunt and Morgan (1995) argue that social objectives can only be entertained when superior financial performance has been achieved and that financial performance can be constrained by the morality considerations of managers, i.e. the deontological component. Nicholls (2006) later proposes that the ethical element is one of the core products for SEs, and also suggests that fairtrade SEs are in a Kantian analysis, deontological. This appears to suggest that SEs are duty bound to moral behaviour, however a number of authors also discuss those SEs that are not only duty bound but are consequentialist, i.e. the value of their organization is based in the consequences of their moral action (Dees 1998; Low 2006). However, Morgan and Hunt (1994) do stress that a firm's reputation for trustworthiness can become economically advantageous. Hunt's work on R-A theory (1997) also highlights relational resources as a source of comparative advantage (i.e. relationships with suppliers and customers) but not on ethical grounds. However, according to Hunt and Arnett (2003) strategic alliances between firms can through time promote trust-based governance by both signalling non-opportunistic intent and developing the type of concrete social relationships that constitute what Coleman (1988) describes as '*social capital*'.

In conclusion, despite R-A theory being a recent revision of competition theory it fails to explain how SEs establish themselves in competitive market sectors based on their social mission. Our aim in this chapter is to unveil the unique resources that enable SEs to compete in specific market segments and distribution channels.

Management challenges for social enterprise

A number of management challenges have been identified in the SE literature. First are the tensions and conflicts for SEs in meeting both financial and social bottom lines (Zahra *et al.*, 2009). This is a contested area with different schools of thought. Paton (2003) suggests that sometimes the pursuit of social goals can be in conflict with managerial rationality. Speckbacher (2003) argues that profit as a single measure of success does not work as it fails to capture other important SE performance outputs.

Evers *et al.* (2004) describe SEs as 'three-dimensional' hybrids, which combine elements of the goal sets and mixed resource structures from three different spheres, including the market, the state and civil society (reflected in terms of resources as income, grant support and voluntary contributions).

Hockerts (2006) views SEs' ability to create public benefit through running a profitable business that incurs private costs as counterintuitive to the point of virtual paradox, and argues that management research has no theoretical explanation for these phenomena. Second, the difficulties in measuring social performance are also identified by a number of authors (Darby and Jenkins 2006; Aeron-Thomas *et al.* 2004). Arthur *et al.* (2006) argue that the debate around effectiveness is mainly focused on the enterprise narrative and not on the social. A third area of challenge is that of working with multiple stakeholders, and the need to establish adequate governance structures (Hudson 2002). Fourth, Westall and Chalkley (2007) identify the difficulties of accessing appropriate forms of finance at both set-up and scale-up. Finally, Paton (2003) identifies the need for planning and strategic management in the SE sector to realize its potential.

Di Domenico *et al.* (2010) remind us that most entrepreneurs operate under conditions of resource scarcity. However the challenge often for SEs is they are working in resource-scarce environments often delivering to unmet needs in areas of market failure. However, there are authors who question the extent of the distinctiveness of SEs and propose that they do combine resources in new ways at the tacit and explicit levels, but require similar operational processes as commercial entrepreneurs (organizational structures, financial capital, partnerships etc.) to manage resources (Meyskens *et al.* 2010). Moss *et al.* (2011) identify the dual identity of social ventures as comprising a utilitarian identity (i.e. entrepreneurial and product orientated) and a normative organizational identity (social, people orientated). Zahra *et al.* (2009) propose that social entrepreneurs have initiated innovative business models to address social problems previously overlooked by business, governments and NGOs.

Resources in social enterprise

Due to the hybrid nature of SEs a common challenge identified in the literature is the need to manage the complexity and tension arising from having to balance both the social and financial objectives to the benefit of collective rather than individual interests (Chell 2007; Moizer and Tracey 2010; Zahra *et al.* 2009). There have been a growing number of research papers on how SEs craft this balance and manage both the double/triple bottom line and their unique intangible resources. The author has analyzed this literature in Table 3.1, which summarizes and identifies both the central arguments and the key resources identified in these articles.

A number of authors also argue that the creation of social value is closely linked to the successful achievement of economic outcomes that, in turn, produce financial resources SEs can use to achieve their social mission (Dacin *et al.* 2010; Dacin *et al.* 2011). Hockerts (2006) proposes that a market orientation for fair trade SEs

TABLE 3.1 Review of key works on resources utilized by social enterprises

Authors	Key arguments	Resources identified
Thompson et al. (2000)	Social value	Relational resources = better quality relationships
Laville and Nyssens (2001)	> amounts of social capital than public or private organizations	Trust and cooperation = stronger relationships and networks
Westall (2001)	Compete on social values	Stronger relationships with customers, suppliers etc.
Mort et al. (2003), Drayton (2005) and Davies and Ryals (2010)	Competitive edge from ethical capital, individual virtues and team commitment	Stronger networks and partnerships
Peredo and Chrisman (2006), Hockerts (2006)	SEs create opportunities from activism, self-help and philanthropy	Provide distribution of products and services, cheaper labour, targeted marketing communications and cheaper financial capital
Gupta et al. (2003), Wagner-Tsukamoto (2007), Ridley-Duff and Bull (2011)	Ethical capital creates social capital then economic capital	Blended value creation via ethical trading and management practice
Seelos and Mair (2005), Moizer and Tracey (2010)	Social mission creates novel resources and alliances	Resources = new partnerships with corporations doing CSR
Smith-Hunter (2008)	Social value creation = trust and financial capital	Committed teams of paid and unpaid staff, strong networks and financial capital gained at lower cost
Shaw and Carter (2007)	Strong ethical values = trust and credibility	Networks and access to finance
Mair and Martì (2006)	Social capital	Improved access to finance
Haugh (2006)	Innovation in organizational culture and governance	Quality of relationships and engagement with social movements
Chell (2007)	Social mission = unique selling points	Relational assets = partnerships, volunteers and reduced start-up and operating costs
Di Domenico et al. (2010)	Social bricolage = social value	Stakeholder participation co-opting trust and improvisation

helps this type of SE deliver more social value for the money they spend. To achieve this balance, SEs need to discover and exploit opportunities to create social and economic value, i.e. blended value creation (Chell 2007; Emerson 2003).

Hockerts (2006) proposes a conceptual framework to explain three sources of social entrepreneurship opportunity, namely activism, self-help and philanthropy. In addition, a number of authors identify networks as critical in providing key resources for SE (Austin *et al.* 2006; Blundel *et al.* 2011; Davies 2009; Haugh 2007; Shaw and Carter 2007). Davies and Ryals (2010) identify that the type of network partner changes from a category of family member in the pre-venture and early stages of SE creation, which demonstrate homogeneity of shared purpose. As the SEs scale-up, new network partners are required (called associates) that display resource heterogeneity and share other useful resources with SEs.

Bloom and Chatterji (2009) and Bloom and Smith (2010) also identify seven factors (called scalers) that SEs require to ensure growth: staffing, communicating, alliance building, lobbying, earnings generation, replicating and stimulating market forces. Bloom and Smith (2010) argue that in addition to company strategy and industrial contexts access to the necessary financial, human and social capital is key to growth. They suggest that SEs face some distinctive challenges compared to commercial ventures, namely they are less likely to be able to provide financial incentives for investors and employees, plus supply and distribution infrastructures need to be developed for the first time. To overcome these resource constraints Di Domenico *et al.* (2010) propose their theory of social bricolage, which suggests that SEs refuse to be constrained by their limited resources by encouraging stakeholder participation in achieving social and economic goals. They also propose another important construct of social bricolage, which is improvisation. A number of authors have also identified the potential for effectuation in explaining how social entrepreneurship opportunities are shaped and created from messy situations based on the resources available (Corner and Ho 2010; Dees 2007). Sarasvathy *et al.* (2003) propose that effectuation can involve intensive dialogue with various stakeholders.

Short *et al.* (2009) suggest that theory building in social entrepreneurship could benefit from exploring the strategic and managerial consequences of trying to craft the balance between economic and social objectives. Dacin *et al.* (2010) suggest in researching SEs the largest opportunities reside in identifying the distinctive nature of the social mission, the process of building SEs and the resources utilized. Despite the range of works on social enterprise resources discussed above none have grounded their work in a theory of competition. This chapter will aim to bridge this gap.

To investigate the resources utilized this chapter will now investigate the cases of three fairtrade SEs through the lens of R-A theory. The author proposes that to manage the challenges for SE discussed above, identifying the unique set of resources utilized by SEs will enable social entrepreneurs to ground their business and marketing strategies in a theory of competition.

Fair trade social enterprise case studies

Background to social enterprise cases

The cases selected are the three leading farmer-owned fair trade SEs: Liberation CIC (Community Interest Company), Divine Chocolate Ltd. (Divine) and Cafédirect plc (see Table 3.2 below for ownership structure and other company details). Liberation competes in the nut market, Cafédirect in hot beverages and Divine in the chocolate confectionery market. In addition to their social mission and farmer ownership they have a number of other features in common, including their aim to compete in mainstream markets. Hence they all operate in highly competitive sectors dominated by large multinational corporations. All of their

TABLE 3.2 Company information and ownership structure

Company and turnover	Shareholding	Seats on board
Divine Chocolate Set up 1998 2010/2011 turnover was £10.5m	Kuapa Kokoo Farmers Union: 45% Twin Trading: 42% Oikocredit:12%[1]	Divine's board consists of 13 seats: Kuapa Kokoo Farmers Union, 2 seats; Twin, 2 seats; Oikocredit, 1 seat; Comic Relief, 1 seat; Christian Aid, 1 seat. Plus 6 independent board members with a range of expertise and both managing director and finance director.
Liberation CIC Set up 2007 2010/2011 turnover was £3.2m	*ORDINARY SHARES International Nut Producers' Cooperative (INPC) 45% Twin 22% Cordaid 17%[2] Equal Exchange 7% Mustard Seed Finance Trust 6% Equal Exchange US 1.5% The Clarkes 1.5%	Liberation's board consists of 12 seats: INPC, 3 directors; Twin, Equal Exchange and Mustard Seed, 1 director each, 1 chair nominated by EE and Twin plus up to 5 non-execs.
Cafédirect Set up 1991 2010/2011 turnover was £15.7m	Oxfam 11.9% (guardian shareholder from original pioneers) Oikocredit 20% (recently jumped from 11%) Cafédirect Producers Ltd. 6% Rathbone Nominees 4.2% Consumers (public) 66.9%	Cafédirect's board consists of 8 seats: Non-executive chair, chief executive, financial director, 2 independent non-exec. Directors, 2 producer directors (1 from Africa and 1 from Latin America), 1 guardian nominee director.

products carry the Fairtrade mark and they have all been set up with the support of Twin Trading.[3] Ensuring they are from within the same social movement enables high levels of reliability through the conventions of literal replication and multiple case study design (Yin 1994). Cross-case comparison is also conducted to detect any differences.

Yin (1994) recommends in case study research the use of different sources of highly complementary evidence. Building these cases has involved a number of multiple methods of data collection including sourcing of documentary evidence from published and internal company sources (i.e. sales reports, minutes of board meetings), direct observation of key events (i.e. shareholder meetings) and participant observation in key events such as board meetings, strategic planning workshops etc. Finally, a major thrust has been a series of 60 semi-structured interviews. Purposive sampling is employed and key informants are selected based on their idiosyncratic specialized knowledge. In summary, the sample covers the key stakeholders including investors, producers, legal experts, senior management in the case companies, original founders, customers from the key channels of distribution (supermarkets, wholesalers etc.), market analysts, competitors and other key influences in the respective market sectors.

Performance of case social enterprises

Performance is measured in these fair trade SEs by both financial and social returns. All three companies have established viable businesses in high-risk situations by developing mainstream, quality Fairtrade brands. Cafédirect, launched in 1991, is the fourth largest hot beverage company in the UK. Divine, launched in 1999, shows a turnover of £10.4m. Liberation, set up in May 2007, has reached a break-even point of £3.5m, showing a 46 per cent increase in 2010 sales. Also from market estimations, Liberation has a 75 to 80 per cent market share in the UK own-label Fairtrade nut market. All three companies have distribution in all the main UK supermarkets. With regard to social performance a key area is the financial benefits of ownership to farmers. All the case companies go beyond the minimum standards of Fairtrade. The farmers are paid a Fairtrade premium price, a social premium as part of the minimum standards requirement of the Fairtrade system; however these companies also invest significant levels of profit into producer partnership programme funds and shareholder dividends. Divine in 2007 was the first of the case study companies to pay a dividend to farmers; the first dividend received per farmer was US $1, which totalled $47,000. The additional sums paid in 2010 by Divine and Cafédirect in addition to the Fairtrade minimum floor price are shown in Table 3.3.

In addition, Liberation paid a Fairtrade premium of $251,000 to producer organizations up to 2009 and the resulting funded community projects have brought improvements in the quality of life and well being for 440,000 people in producer communities across three continents. As a result of this transformative work Liberation have also secured additional funds of £1.75m from other donors for

TABLE 3.3 Social return to producers in 2010

Company	Social premium	Producer Partnership Programmes (PPP)
Divine	£149k	£236k
Cafédirect	£407k	£706k

producer partnership programmes. In addition, Liberation has influenced the work of Twin in partnering with other organizations such as Sainsbury's in securing $1m of new funding for a new processing company called Afri-Nut based in Malawi. This is adding value in the country of origin and this new facility will enable expansion into value-added processed nut products and nutritional supplements, and aims to return strong developmental benefits to farmers in Malawi. Cafédirect Producers Ltd. was also able to attract further investment of £250k in 2010 to look at research into ways of adapting to climate change for smallholder tea and coffee farmers. These companies demonstrate a positive impact in reducing poverty and transforming markets, and have been a catalyst for change by influencing other companies and facilitating other donors to take part. The producer groups such as Kuapa Kokoo and NASFAM who are owners in these SEs also now have their own political voice and growing international reputation.

Resource analysis of case social enterprises

This following analysis shows that all three social enterprises have established mainstream competitive positions in specific product segments and distribution channels based on combining what the author terms 'social resources' with excellent product quality. The research has identified that 'social resources' are made up of three inter-related components, namely *ethical and social commitments, connections with partners* and *consistency of behaviour*. Evidence to support this novel extension to the resource construct of R-A theory (see above) is now explained.

Ethical and social commitments

This component of the 'social resources' construct has delivered trust and integrity in these SE brands, which has been utilized to both deliver more effective marketing and to attract important financial investment.

Firstly, farmer-ownership by smallholder producer groups appears to have strengthened the position of all three companies by providing authenticity and trust in the brands. Producers are central to the marketing communications of all the companies. Divine paid their first share dividend to Kuapa Kokoo (KK) in 2007 at the KK Annual General Meeting and this resulted in significant press coverage for both Divine and KK. A number of authors (Golding 2009; McDonagh 2002; Strong 1996, 1997) highlight the importance of being able to communicate the human element of sustainability via what they term sustainable marketing communications.

Considering their size, both Divine and Liberation have been excellent in achieving media coverage based on their unique story of farmer-ownership. Both have employed their own in-house PR manager and Divine in particular has, according to Golding (2009), excelled at the dual aspect of fair trade marketing, which involves targeting both chocolate consumers interested in quality and fair trade activists, particularly in campaign organizations such as Christian Aid and fair trade town activist groups.

Another key component of ethical and social commitments is the Fairtrade Mark itself. According to the informants, the Fairtrade Mark provides consumer appeal via the confidence and trust provided via the mark, resulting in consumer loyalty. In relation to this aspect, Zadek *et al.* (1998) explain that social labels such as the Fairtrade Mark can provide consumers with the benefits of self-expression and a positive self- and group social identity. In economic terms social labels also can change consumption patterns by moving the consumers' balance of costs and benefits of finding goods.

Secondly, investment finance has been difficult to secure for all three SEs due to their high risk. This is partly down to the competitive nature of their respective market sectors; however some key investors and supporters have been attracted by the ethical and social commitments. All three SEs have brought together a creative range of investors and finance. Key to the initial set-up and launch of Divine was a loan guarantee facility provided by DfID (UK Department for International Development) to a commercial bank. This was the first time a UK government department had provided such a finance mechanism for a new start-up company. DfID was convinced by the *ethical and social commitments* provided by both the Fairtrade Mark and the organizational model of farmer-ownership.

In the case of Liberation, Comic Relief working with the Hunter Foundation (Thomas Hunter is a venture philanthropist) agreed to fund a total grant of £742,800 over three years; of this £550,000 was allocated to equity finance for part of the International Nut Producer's £650,000 stake in Liberation (Twin donated the other £100,000). Of the £550,000 used to buy shares in Liberation for the INPC, £150,000 is preference shares and £400,000 is ordinary share capital. This shareholding is significant for producers as smallholder farmer cooperatives generally lack the financial means to buy shares. Both Comic Relief and Thomas Hunter were attracted to Liberation due to its social mission.

In addition to initial investment finance these *ethical and social commitments* have also enabled both Cafédirect and Divine to secure further scale-up investment. To bolster its marketing effort Cafédirect in 2004 raised £5m in an Initial Public Share Offering (IPO) on the Triodos Bank's[4] ethical ethex exchange so consumers could join and buy a share in a Fairtrade brand. A further Cafédirect share issue in 2011 led to fresh investment of £1.6m, with Oikocredit investing £1.2m and a further £400k from over 300 shareholders who decided to buy more shares. Oikocredit is motivated by both financial return and creating a social impact in areas of market failure, hence its interest in social enterprise. Oikocredit has also been important in the recent scale-up of Divine, buying a stake of 12 per cent to provide new working capital, which made it possible for Divine to set up and launch Divine US in 2007.

Connections with partners

This component of the 'social resources' construct has clearly played an important role in delivering vital resources at both pre-venture, set-up and growth phases. Firstly, NGOs working in partnership with producer organizations at the pre-venture stage has clearly been important in helping producer groups to get market-ready. This has involved both building organizational capacity and also ensuring the quality of the produce for export. At the pre-venture stage NGOs, particularly Twin Trading, have played a crucial role in the creation of all three enterprises.

In the case of Liberation, despite the tough EU food regulations for aflatoxin,[5] NASFAM (National Association of Smallholder Farmers) from Malawi, working in partnership with Twin, began in 2003 to work with ICRISAT (the International Crops Research Institute for the Semi-Arid Tropics) on a project aimed at both improving the quality and yields of groundnuts in Malawi. As a result of this stakeholder partnership new approaches such as the drying of groundnuts in storage in special small haystacks known as '*Mandela corks*' have emerged, which reduce the risk of mould formation. All this has led to a revival in the Malawi groundnut industry with, for example, NASFAM exporting 48 per cent of its groundnut crop in 2008/09. This work culminated in 2010 with new export sales of 576 tonnes of groundnuts, generating an income of $527k and a Fairtrade premium of $58k for NASFAM resulting in improved livelihoods for 10,709 farmers in Malawi. NASFAM is a member of the International Producers Cooperative (INPC), which has a 45 per cent stake in Liberation. These findings appear to disagree with Zahra *et al.* (2009), who comment that NGOs may have overlooked the opportunity for innovative social ventures to solve social problems.

Bringing together investors, producers and activists with a shared social mission who believe in using trade as a means of reducing poverty has been a key factor in helping these SEs to establish a market position. The original founders of Cafédirect – Traidcraft, Equal Exchange and Oxfam – all provided important distribution routes for Cafédirect in the UK market. Two of Divine's original shareholders, The Body Shop and Christian Aid, were instrumental in helping to establish the Divine brand in the UK chocolate market: The Body Shop by providing an initial retail outlet and merchandizing opportunity for Divine via its 260 UK high-street outlets, and Christian Aid by mobilizing its activists to encourage supermarket chain Sainsbury's to increase the distribution of Divine from 70 to 342 stores.

The direct relationship with producers has led to joint representation with supermarket retailers. Producer representatives on the Liberation board have been directly involved in commercial meetings with supermarket buyers. A commercial executive at Liberation comments:

> You are always starting off on the back foot with buyers due to Liberation's higher prices. However, doing meetings with supermarket buyers as a team with producer representatives just works incredibly well. I remember one meeting with one supermarket chain when Tomy (producer) came along

to talk to the buyer about the difference that Liberation makes to his farming community, the buyers eyes did really light-up!

(Interview, informant P)

These connections between partners have delivered valuable resources for these SEs in a situation of resource scarcity and appear to be a good example of the social bricolage proposed by Di Domenico *et al.* (2010).

Consistency of behaviour

This component of 'social resources', namely *consistency of behaviour*, has strengthened the competitive position of these SE brands by delivering both credibility and integrity for these companies. In addition, they have been a catalyst for change in their respective market sectors by raising industry standards, i.e. *raising the ethical bar*. The research in all three cases shows the importance of being 100 per cent fair trade (23 informants identified this). Also both the producer partnership programmes of Divine and Liberation plus the *Gold Standard* programme of Cafédirect are viewed as key in demonstrating their consistency of behaviour. The importance of producer support is identified by 27 informants in this study. There is also a theme emerging from the interviews (seventeen informants) that view both Cafédirect and Divine as being influential in raising the ethical bar in their respective market sectors.

Another important element is the recognition of the product quality of these SE brands. In addition to winning awards for social performance (Cafédirect 2011, Guardian Newspaper Sustainable Company Award), Divine and Cafédirect continue to win food awards for product quality. In 2010 Cafédirect won five gold great taste awards from the Guild of Food; in 2011 Divine won a gold award at *The Grocer* magazine's food and drinks awards. In addition, the importance of product development and innovation has been important in gaining further awards and distribution for these brands. Divine now has a range of 45 products and Cafédirect lists over 50. The combination of using both 'social resources' and product quality to establish a position of competitive advantage illustrates how SEs can craft the balance in achieving both their social and commercial objectives.

It is also important to note that despite their undoubted success in competing against much larger, resource-rich rivals using 'social resources', these SEs have recently come under increasing competitive pressure. Cafédirect suffered a 19 per cent decrease in turnover in 2010 compared to 2009. However, since the new investment by Oikocredit, sales have stabilized. According to a number of market experts the drop in 2010 is due to a combination of competitive pressure from supermarket own-label Fairtrade products and some poorly executed marketing changes by Cafédirect itself. In the summer of 2010 Cafédirect, all in the same three-month period, changed distributor, increased its prices and changed the brand livery. Despite these commercial difficulties Cafédirect has continued to deepen its social impact with producers via its social programme, Gold Standard.

Divine has also come under increasing competitive pressure with mainstream manufacturers such as Cadburys and Nestlé switching to Fairtrade chocolate in 2009. Sales in 2010 reduced by 12 per cent mainly due to the loss of own-label business with the Cooperative Food group. However, Divine has continued to deepen its social impact with producers by starting to work with cocoa producer groups in Sierra Leone. Liberation is currently planning the development of its own brand. Also Divine's international sales, particularly in the US, have continued to grow beyond plan. In addition its work with NASFAM in Malawi, Liberation has helped to secure $1m of new investment to set up a new processing facility in Malawi called Afri-Nut. This new processing facility will enable expansion into value-added processed nut products and nutritional supplements for both local markets in South Africa and export territories.

Social enterprise and Resource Advantage theory

From analysing both the literature and the case studies a number of key resources for SE have been identified. Clearly 'social resources' combined with good product quality provide the case SEs with the ability to compete in certain market segments and distribution channels. The research underpinning this chapter has highlighted the importance of *ethical and social commitments, connections with partners* and *consistency of behaviour*. These three inter-related elements are not currently acknowledged in R-A theory and therefore this theory does not explain the performance of fair trade social enterprises such as Cafédirect, Liberation and Divine. From this research, the author proposes a model of 'social resources' (see Figure 3.1 below), which shows the important components of 'social resources' and their inter-related nature. The *ethical and social commitments* represent the values element of 'social resources', *connections with partners* represent the structural element and *consistency of behaviour* the behavioural element.

This also means the R-A theory resource construct (see literature review on R-A theory above) could be extended to include the addition of 'social resources'. This resource construct lists seven elements highlighted above. This research provides a novel extension to R-A theory, which previously has not acknowledged ethical and social commitments as a competitive resource. It is therefore proposed that the 'social resources' dimension is added as the eighth element of the resource construct in R-A theory (see below). 'Social resources' appear to be subtly different to other resources such as money, skills, intellectual property, information and key strategic relationships as they depend on the perception of key stakeholders. It is the external perception that appears to give 'social resources' their value and validity. Also the relationship between 'social resources' and reputation is strongly implied in the findings, and this will be the subject of further research.

Financial (cash resources, access to financial markets with lower rates of capital such as ethical banks/investors, social philanthropists, e.g. Hunter Foundation)

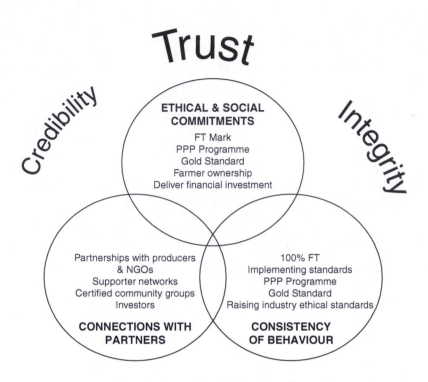

FIGURE 3.1 Diagram of 'social resources' model for fairtrade social enterprises

Physical (e.g. plant, raw materials and equipment)

Legal (e.g. trademarks, licenses)

Human (e.g. skills, knowledge and commitment of individual employees, unpaid volunteers, activist groups including their entrepreneurial skills)

Organizational (e.g. competences such as quality SE brands, controls, policies, culture based on social mission, new forms of stakeholder governance)

Informational (e.g. knowledge from consumer and activist groups and competitive intelligence)

Relational (e.g. relationships with a range of stakeholders including suppliers, employees both paid and unpaid, activist campaign groups and customers)

Social resources (e.g. ethical and social commitments, connections with partners and consistency of behaviour).

In addition, the author has added other key resources elements identified in this study under the existing elements of the resource construct in R–A theory (see above). Firstly, the distinctiveness of a clear social mission, i.e. the social impact on smallholder farmers has delivered financial resources from a blend of investors and supporters. These include NGOs, commercial companies, social investment banks and, of course, activist/campaign groups. The ethical and social commitments provide trust and authenticity and deliver strong connections with a range of stakeholders. If leveraged for commercial opportunity, this can result in cheaper forms of capital, unpaid labour, and economic voting by active consumers providing breakthroughs in mainstream distribution. The investors are attracted by both the social impact and the financial return, whereas the activists are motivated by the social impact. In addition, the choice of investors is also important in providing complementary skills and knowledge to help the SEs build supply chains in competitive markets. Hence this chapter has adapted R-A theory for SE and will provide those managing SEs the opportunity to ground their business and marketing strategies in a theory of competition.

This adaptation of R-A theory for SE also appears to provide some support to the work of Di Domenico *et al.* (2010), who propose their theory of social bricolage. The cases suggest that various stakeholders in these fair trade networks provide important resources at different stages.

Another key theme from the case studies appears to be the importance of developing quality brands. This lends some support to those authors who argue that SEs need to manage resources as commercial entrepreneurs do at the operational level (Meyskens *et al.* 2010). However, as already demonstrated, it is the competitive advantage delivered by 'social resources' which is distinctive for SE.

In fact, it also appears that the financial performance of SE is enhanced by moral considerations rather than constrained as proposed by Hunt and Morgan (1995). In addition, the analysis also shows that relational resources are created based on ethical grounds. However, it is the opportunity-seeking culture of SEs that differentiates them from other third-sector organizations. As discussed above, Divine, Cafédirect and Liberation have developed brands and own-label business in the mainstream by leveraging the resources identified. This is in contrast to earlier attempts by large third-sector organizations such as Oxfam, whose own brands of Fairtrade chocolate and coffee were withdrawn from the market. Oxfam failed to take advantage of the commercial opportunities in the mainstream and limited its distribution to its own high-street shops. Hence, I propose that the resource construct of R-A theory explained above can be adapted for SE.

The author therefore argues that SE offers the potential to extend R-A theory. So how does this analysis of resources impact upon the management of SE? The final conclusions will look at some key implications from the above analysis.

Conclusions and implications

Firstly, this chapter has identified a unique set of resources that will enable social entrepreneurs to ground their business and marketing strategies in a theory of competition. It appears that strategic choices are driven more by underlying social and ethical values compared with private or public sector organizations. Most SEs are coalitions of interest groups (connection of partners) each with their own often divergent priorities. In practice, this means that the strategy development process will involve greater time and resources devoted to networking, communicating, lobbying and negotiating with stakeholders to achieve a consensus on key issues.

To galvanize stakeholder groups it is important to have a strong vision and mission that demonstrates the ethical and social commitment of the SE. According to Whetton (2006) having a clear mission is a factor in building a strong organizational identity. SE visions and missions are often based on fairness, justice and social change. They are also often based on a utopian vision for an idealized state of affairs that the SE is striving to achieve (Courtney 2002; Hudson 2002). With the utopian approach, the vision emphasizes what the organization stands for (for example 'a fairer world', 'justice for all', 'education for all' etc.) and the mission clarifies what the organization will actually do to further the vision. For example, the mission of SE Divine Chocolate is to 'improve the livelihoods of smallholder cocoa producers in West Africa by establishing their own dynamic branded proposition in the UK chocolate market, thus putting them higher up the value chain' (Tiffen 2002: 388). In contrast, the mainstream strategy literature often treats vision and mission in a more pragmatic way (Grant 2004; Porter 1996). For SE it is argued that this sense of mission is part of providing legitimacy to the enterprise (Nicholls 2006).

The importance of 'social resources' appears to point towards the potential for exploring the social and ethical dimensions of marketing for SE. A number of authors have identified the important role that relationships play in building trust and cooperation within economic action but have not identified ethical and social dimensions as a basis for this (Gronroos 2006; Morgan and Hunt 1994, 1999; Vargo and Lusch 2004). However, there are a number of perspectives including the work on both the ethical basis to relationship marketing and ethical consumerism based on virtuous behaviour and trustworthiness, which show that markets reward with consumer loyalty (Murphy *et al.* 2007). Mann (2008) proposes that consumers not only purchase the physical dimensions of a product/service but also a certain quality of relations that do not involve themselves.

However, marketers in SE still need to craft the balance between social and commercial objectives. This is illustrated by earlier work on products supplied by initial fair trade pioneers known as Alternative Trade Organizations (ATOs), which were associated with both poor product quality and limited availability in distribution networks (Strong 1996, 1997; Bird and Hughes 1997; Nicholls and Opal 2005). These products did not succeed; subsequently the fair trade movement gave rise to the development of a range of SEs that delivered good quality, appealing products and via their relations with activist campaign groups leveraged new mainstream distribution for their brands due to the campaigning of activist groups. This evidence appears to support the work of Hockerts (2006), who proposes that links with activists create a commercial opportunity for SE.

Also, as identified in this chapter, these case SEs have recently come under competitive pressure from mainstream counterparts, who have switched their own brands to Fairtrade certification. This shows that competitors are also starting to acknowledge the importance of 'social resources'. R-A theory is non-consummatory; it has no end stage, only a never-ending process of change, and competitors will try to mimic and leap frog their competitors. Because R-A theory draws heavily on Austrian economics and the Schumpeterian tradition in evolutionary economics, innovation and organizational learning are endogenous to R-A theory. Hence these SEs will need to continue to innovate via building and leveraging their 'social resources' to maintain a competitive position.

Notes

1 Oikocredit is based in the Netherlands and is a cooperative financial institution that offers loans or investment capital to microfinance institutions, cooperatives, fairtrade organizations and small to medium-sized enterprises in the developing world. Oikocredit promotes socially responsible investment targeted at business models focused on fighting poverty, promoting fairtrade and respecting the planet's environment. Oikocredit has 480 million euros invested in over 800 project partners in more than 70 countries (see www.oikocredit.org).
2 Cordaid is a Catholic organization for development cooperation based in the Netherlands. It is one of the biggest international development organizations with a network of around a thousand partner organizations in 36 countries in Africa, Asia and Latin America and has a disposable annual budget of around 170 million euros.
3 Twin (Third World Information Network) established in 1985 is a leading alternative trading company whose approach is based on establishing long-term trading relationships with small producers to bring producer organizations and the market closer together. Twin set up Cafédirect, Liberation CIC and Divine Chocolate Ltd. Twin is a farmer-driven members' organization.
4 Triodos is a leading sustainable bank with a mission to make money work for positive social, environmental and cultural change. It offers integrated lending and investment opportunities (see www.triodos.co.uk/en/about-triodos/).
5 Aflatoxin is a mould fungal disease, which in agricultural crops reduces the quality and consequently the value of the groundnut crop (peanuts). The long-term consumption of aflatoxin has been linked to a cancer called hepatocellular carcinoma.

References

Aeron-Thomas, D., Nicholls, J., Forster, S. and Westall, A. (2004) *Social Return on Investment: Valuing What Matters*. London: New Economics Foundation.
Arthur, L., Keenoy, T. and Scott-Cato, M. (2006) 'Where is the 'social' in social enterprise?', Paper presented at the Third Annual Social Enterprise Conference, London South Bank University, 22–23 June 2006.
Austin, J. E., Stevenson, H. and Wei-Skillern, J. (2006) 'Social entrepreneurship and commercial entrepreneurship: same, different, or both?', *Entrepreneurship Theory and Practice*, 30(1): 1–22.
Barney, J. B. (1991) 'Firm resources and sustained competitive advantage', *Journal of Management*, 17(1): 99–120.
Bird, K. and Hughes, D. (1997) 'Ethical consumerism: the case of fair trade coffee', *Business Ethics, A European Review*, 6(3): 159–67.
Bloom, P. N. and Chatterji, A. K. (2009) 'Scaling social entrepreneurial impact', *California Management Review*, 51(3): 114–33.

Bloom, P. N. and Smith, B. R. (2010) 'Identifying the drivers of social entrepreneurial impact: theoretical development and an exploratory empirical test of SCALERS', *Journal of Social Entrepreneurship*, 1(1): 126–45.

Blundel, R., Lyon, F. and Spence, L. J. (2011) 'Analysing the growth process in social enterprises: an historical perspective', in *Third EMES International Research Conference on Social Enterprise: Social Innovation through Social Entrepreneurship in Civil Society: EMES Selected Paper Series*, 4–7 July 2011, Roskilde, Denmark.

Chell, E. (2007) 'Social enterprise and entrepreneurship: towards a convergent theory of the entrepreneurial process', *International Small Business Journal*, 25: 5–26.

Coleman, J. S. (1988) 'Social capital in the creation of human capital', *American Journal of Sociology*, 94 (supplement): 95–120.

Corner, P. D. and Ho, M. (2010) 'How opportunities develop in social entrepreneurship', *Entrepreneurship Theory and Practice*, 34(4): 635–59.

Courtney, R. (2002) *Strategic Management for Voluntary Nonprofit Organisations*. New York: Routledge.

Curtis, T., Herbst, J. and Gumkovska, M. (2010) 'The social economy of trust: social entrepreneurship experiences in Poland', *Social Enterprise Journal*, 6(3): 194–209.

Dacin P., Dacin, M. and Matear, M. (2010) 'Social entreprenuership: why we don't need a new theory and how we move forward from here', *The Academy of Management Perspectives*, 24(3): 37–57.

Dacin, M., Dacin, P. and Tracey, P. (2011) 'Social entrepreneurship: a critique and future directions', *Organization Science*, 22(5): 1203–13.

Darby, L. and Jenkins, H. (2006) 'Applying sustainability indicators to the social enterprise business model', *International Journal of Social Economics*, 33: 411–31.

Dart, R. (2004) 'The legitimacy of social enterprise', *Nonprofit Management and Leadership*, 14: 411–24.

Davies, I. A. (2009) 'Alliances and networks: creating success in the UK fair trade market', *Journal of Business Ethics*, 86: 109–26.

Davies, I. A. and Ryals, L. J. (2010) 'The role of social capital in the success of fair trade', *Journal of Business Ethics*, 96: 317–38.

Davies, I. A., Doherty, B. and Knox, S. (2010) 'The rise and stall of a fair trade pioneer: the story of Cafédirect', *Journal of Business Ethics*, 92: 127–47.

Dees, J. G. (1998) 'Enterprising nonprofits', *Harvard Business Review*, 76: 55–67.

Dees, J. G. (2007) 'Taking social entrepreneurship seriously', *Society*, 44(3): 24–31.

Defourny, J. and Nyssens, M. (2006) *Defining Social Enterprise: Social Enterprise at the Crossroads of Market, Public Policies and Civil Society*. London and New York: Routledge.

Di Domenico, D. M., Haugh, H. and Tracey, P. (2010) 'Social bricolage: theorising social value creation in social enterprises', *Entrepreneurship Theory and Practice*, 34(4): 681–703.

Drayton, B. (2005) 'Where the real power lies', *Alliance*, 10(1): 29–30.

Emerson, J. (2003) 'The blended value proposition: integrating social and financial returns', *California Management Review*, 45: 35–51.

Evers, A., Laville, J. L., Borgaza, C., Defourny, J., Lewis, J., Nyssens, M. and Pestoff, V. (2004) 'Defining the third sector in Europe', in Evers, A. and Laveille, J. L. (eds), *The Third Sector in Europe*. London: Edward Elgar.

Foster, W. and Bradach, J. (2005) 'Should nonprofits seek profits?', *Harvard Business Review*, February: 92–100.

Golding, K. (2009) 'Fair trade's dual aspect: the communications challenge of fair trade marketing', *Journal of Macromarketing*, 29(2): 160–71.

Grant, R. M. (2004) *Contemporary Strategy Analysis*, Fifth Edition. Oxford: Blackwell.

Gronroos, C. (2006) 'On defining marketing: finding a new roadmap for marketing', *Marketing Theory*, 6(4): 395–417.

Gupta, A. K., Sinha, R., Koradia, D. and Patel, R. (2003) 'Mobilizing grassroots' technological innovations and traditional knowledge, values and institutions: articulating social and ethical capital', *Futures*, 35(9): 975–87.

Haugh, H. (2006) 'A research agenda for social entrepreneurship?', *Social Enterprise Journal*, 1(1): 1–12.

Haugh, H., (2007) 'Community-Led Social Venture Creation', *Entreprenuership Theory and Practice*, 31(2): 161–182.

Hockerts, K. (2006) 'Entrepreneurial opportunity in social purpose ventures', in Mair, J., Robinson, J. and Hockerts, K. (eds), *Social Entrepreneurship*. Basingstoke: Palgrave Macmillan.

Hodgson, G. M. (1993) *Economics and Evolution*. Ann Arbor, MI: University of Michigan Press.

Hudson, M. (2002) *Managing Without Profit*, Second Edition. London: Penguin.

Hunt, S. D. (1997) 'Competing through relationship marketing in Resource-Advantage theory', *Journal of Marketing Management*, 13: 431–45.

Hunt, S. D. (2001) 'A general theory of competition: issues, answers and an invitation', *European Journal of Marketing*, 35(5/6): 524–48.

Hunt, S. D. (2002) 'Resource-Advantage theory and Austrian economics: toward an Austrian theory of competition?' in Foss, N. J. and Klein, P. G. (eds), *Entrepreneurship and the Firm: Austrian Perspectives on Economic Organisation*. Cheltenham, UK: Edward Elgar.

Hunt, S. D. and Arnett, D. B. (2003) 'Resource-Advantage theory and embeddedness: explaining R-A theory's explanatory success', *Journal of Marketing*, 11(1), Winter: 1–17.

Hunt, S. D. and Arnett, D. B. (2005) 'Toward a general theory of marketing: resource-advantage theory as an extension of Alderson's theory to market process', in Wooliscroft, B., Tamilia, R. and Shapiro, S. J. (eds), *A Twenty-First Century Guide to Aldersonian Marketing Thought*. New York: Springer Science and Business Media, pp. 453–71.

Hunt, S. D. and Derozier, C. (2004) 'The normative imperative of business and marketing strategy: grounded strategy resource-advantage theory', *Journal of Business and Industrial Marketing*, 19(1): 5–22.

Hunt, S. D. and Morgan, R. E. (1995) 'The comparative advantage theory of competition', *Journal of Marketing*, 59: 1–15.

Hunt, S. D. and Morgan, R. E. (1997) 'Resource-Advantage theory: a snake swallowing its tail or a general theory of competition?', *Journal of Marketing*, 61: 74–82.

Kerlin, J. (2006) 'Social enterprise in the United States and Europe: understanding and learning from the differences', *Voluntas*, 17: 246–62.

Laville, J. L. and Nysenns, M. (2001) 'Towards a theoretical socio-economic approach', in Borzaga, C. and Defourny J. (eds), *The Emergence of Social Enterprise*. London: Routledge, pp. 312–32.

Low, C. (2006) 'A framework for the governance of social enterprise', *International Journal of Social Economics*, 33(5/6): 376–85.

McDonagh, P. (2002) 'Communicative campaigns to effect anti-slavery and fair trade: the cases of Rugmark and Cafédirect', *European Journal of Marketing*, 36(5/6): 642–66.

Mair, J. and Martì, I. (2006) 'Social entrepreneurship research: a source of explanation, prediction, and delight', *Journal of World Business*, 4: 36–44.

Mair, J., Robinson, J. and Hockerts, K. (eds) (2006) *Social Entrepreneurship*. Basingstoke: Palgrave Macmillan.

Mann, S. (2008) 'Analysing fair trade in economic terms', *The Journal of Socio-Economics*, 37(5): 2034–42.

Meehan, J. (2009) 'Strategic management in social enterprise', in Doherty, B., Foster, G., Mason, C., Meehan, J., Rotheroe, N. and Royce, M. (eds), *Management for Social Enterprise*. London: Sage Publications.

Meyskens, M., Colleen, R., Stamp, J., Carsurd, A. L. and Reynolds, P. D. (2010) 'Social ventures from a resource-based perspective: an exploratory study assessing global Ashoka fellows', *Entrepreneurship Theory and Practice*, 34(4): 661–80.

Moizer, J. and Tracey, P. (2010) 'Strategy making in social enterprise: the role of resource allocation and its effects on organisational sustainability', *Systems Research and Behavioural Science*, 27: 252–66.

Morgan, M. R. and Hunt, D. S. (1994) 'The commitment-trust theory of relationship marketing', *Journal of Marketing*, 58: 20–38.

Morgan, M. R. and Hunt, D. S. (1999) 'Relationship-based competitive advantage: the role of relationship marketing in marketing strategy', *Journal of Business Research*, 46(3): 281–90.

Mort, G. S., Weerawardena, J. and Carnegie, K. (2003) 'Social entrepreneurship: towards conceptualization', *International Journal of Nonprofit and Voluntary Sector Marketing*, 8(1): 76–89.

Moss, W. T., Short, C. J., Payne, T. G. and Lumpkin, G. T. (2011) 'Dual identities in social ventures: an exploratory study', *Entrepreneurship Theory and Practice*, 35(4): 805–30.

Murphy, E. P., Laczniak, R. G. and Wood, G. (2007) 'An ethical basis for relationship marketing: a virtue ethics perspective', *European Journal of Marketing*, 41(1/2): 37–57.

Nicholls, A. (2006) *Social Entrepreneurship: New Models of Sustainable Social Change*. Oxford: Oxford University Press.

Nicholls, A. and Opal, C. (2005) *Fair Trade: Market-driven Ethical Consumption*. London: Sage Publications.

Paton, R. (2003) *Managing and Measuring Social Enterprise*. London: Sage Publications.

Peattie, K. and Morley, A. (2008) 'Eight paradoxes of the social enterprise research agenda', *Social Enterprise Journal*, 4(2): 91–107.

Peredo, M. A. and Chrisman, J. J. (2006) 'Towards a theory of community-based enterprise', *Academy of Management Review*, 31: 309–28.

Porter, M. E. (1996) 'What is strategy?', *Harvard Business Review*, November/December: 61–78.

Ridley-Duff, R. and Bull, M. (2011) *Understanding Social Enterprise: Theory and Practice*. London: Sage Publications.

Sarasvathy, S., Dew, N., Velamuri, S. R. and Venkataraman, S. (2003) 'Three views of entrepreneurial opportunity', in Acs, Z. J. and Audretsch, D. B. (eds), *Handbook of Entrepreneurship*. Norwell, MA: Kluwer Academic Publishers, pp. 141–60.

Schlegelmilch, B. B. (2002) 'Special symposium on Shelby D. Hunt's "A General Theory of Competition: Resources, Competences, Productivity Economic Growth" Part 1', *Journal of Marketing Management*, 18: 221–7.

Seelos, C. and Mair, J. (2005) 'Social entrepreneurship: creating new business models to serve the poor', *Business Horizons*, 48(3): 241–6.

Shaw, E. and Carter, S. (2007) 'Social entrepreneurship: theoretical antecedents and empirical analysis of entrepreneurial processes and outcomes', *Journal of Small Business and Enterprise Development*, 14(3): 418–34.

Short, J. C., Todd, W. M. and Lumpkin, G. T. (2009) 'Research in social entrepreneurship: past contributions and future opportunities', *Strategic Entrepreneurship Journal*, 3: 161–94.

Smith-Hunter, A. E. (2008) 'Toward a multidimensional model of social entrepreneurship: definitions, clarifications, and theoretical perspectives', *Journal of Business and Economics Research*, 6: 93–110.

Speckbacher, G. (2003) 'The economics of performance management in nonprofit organizations', *Nonprofit Management and Leadership*, 13(3): 267–81.

Strong. C. (1996) 'Features contributing to the growth of ethical consumerism – a preliminary investigation', *Marketing Intelligence and Planning*, 14: 5–9.

Strong, C. (1997) 'The problems of translating fair trade principles into consumer purchase behaviour', *Marketing Intelligence and Planning*, 15(1): 32–7.

Thompson, J., Alvy, G. and Lees, A. (2000) 'Social entrepreneurship – a new look at people and potential', *Management Decision*, 38: 328–38.

Tiffen, P. (2002) 'A chocolate-coated case for alternative international business models', *Development in Practice*, 12: 383–97.

Vargo, S. L. and Lusch, R. F. (2004) 'Evolving to a new dominant logic for marketing', *Journal of Marketing*, 68: 1–17.

Wagner-Tsukamoto, S. (2007) 'Moral agency, profits and the firm: economic revisions to the Friedman theorem', *Journal of Business Ethics*, 70(2): 209–20.

Westall, A. (2001) *Value-led, Market Driven*. London: Institute Public Policy Research.

Westall, A. and Chalkley, D. (2007) *Social Enterprise Futures*. London: The Smith Institute.

Whetton, D. A. (2006) 'Albert and Whetten revisted: strengthening the concept of organisational identity', *Journal of Management Inquiry*, 15: 216–34.

Yin, K. Y. (1994) *Case Study Research: Design and Methods*, Second Edition. London: Sage Publications.

Zadek, S., Lingayah, S. and Forstater, M. (1998) *Social Labels: Tools for Ethical Trade*. Final Report. Luxembourg: European Commission.

Zahra, S. A., Gedajlovic, E., Newbaum, D. O. and Shulman, J. M. (2009) 'A typology of social enterprise: motives, search processes and ethical challenges', *Journal of Business Venturing*, 24: 519–32.

4

IT'S NOT YOU, IT'S ME!

Breaking up social entrepreneurship identity

Chris Mason

[A]ll these ideas, half formed and half digested and half correct, mix up with other half-cooked ideas in your head ... Entrepreneurs are made from half-baked clay.
(Aravind Adiga, *The White Tiger: A Novel*, 2008)

Introduction

Social entrepreneurship (SE), as a field of practice that is widely endorsed and supported by political institutions, has come a long way in mainstreaming from the margins in recent decades (Morrin et al. 2004). Yet SE exists in a state of highly contested discourse, i.e. capable of forging social cohesion as well as shattering existing boundaries between state and society. Difficult and ambiguous to agreeably define, the optimistic rush to (re)invent and promote SE has faded somewhat as politicians, citizens and social entrepreneurs try to suitably reframe SE in a post-global financial crisis (GFC) environment. In the United Kingdom, political support has been maintained because SE offers a way to engage so-called 'third sector' organizations more efficiently with state processes and requirements (Aiken and Bode 2009; Haugh and Kitson 2007; Kelly 2007; Office of the Third Sector 2009). General publics have been both interested but also sceptical about SE – how is it different to the work done by voluntary and community organizations? What does one 'look' like and what are the benefits at local levels of social action? While we might expect that these questions have been already suitably answered, recent research shows that they have not (Curtis 2008; Haugh 2012; Steyaert and Dey 2010).

Instead of theorizing SE as a conceptual whole, I adopt a critical view which tolerates both the contradictory multiplicities in SE identities, and the centrality of fractured power relations in the SE construct and its discourses (Sharp and Richardson 2001; Tomlinson and Schwabenland 2010). In doing so, I draw from some key research dealing with SE identity, especially that which centres on articulation of the self and the suppressed-self (Jones et al. 2008; Parkinson and Howorth 2008). Following this, I develop an account of the contemporary importance of conceptual 'fault-lines' in SE discourse, which bears testament to the diverse histories and cultural legacies that have produced socially enterprising organizations. Building on this, I seek to further problematize SE discourse with reference to the current critical turn in SE research, especially in terms of the type of power relations in discourse. This assists current knowledge by acknowledging the necessary incompleteness of the SE idea and identities, and shows that political discourse overlooks this reality, creating a false consensus that SE offers a 'whole' solution. Indeed, I argue that it is perhaps less than necessary for a full 'mainstreaming' of SE when there seems to still be a great deal of value inhabiting the margins where corporations and the state cannot make sustainable impact.

Contextualising SE discourses

Current SE research is making bold steps into more critical terrain, as global communities continue to deal with the fall-out from the GFC. For some, SE has an important and intriguing place in the re-emergence of communities hardest hit by this moment of economic turmoil. For example, political actors and institutions are often supported by activists, lobbyists, academics and practitioners in pushing forward deeper engagement between private, public and third sectors (Lyon et al. 2010). In unison, these stakeholders are broadly in agreement that SEs (social entrepreneurs *and* social enterprise organizations [SEOs]) can successfully encourage community-led and privately financed economic solutions to social malaise. In essence, they (and we) have every cause to be optimistic, too. We know that there are countless, high (and low) profile case studies of successful SEOs across the globe, and each month witnesses new SE start-ups and a groundswell of local support.

Yet, for others (and often concurrently with the above), we are also dealing with a field of study still in its relative infancy (Dacin et al. 2010). As such, the best-case scenario is set off against the reality that we are grappling with significant conceptual, empirical, political and practical problems that shape the development of nascent fields and their organizations (Nicholls 2010b; Teasdale 2012). Thus the overtly positive rhetoric that accompanies SE is tempered by a looming critical turn in SE research. This coming mood of critique is perhaps the consequence of three, gradually converging factors.

First, at the *practitioner* level, there is a growing body of anecdotal evidence that both existing and new constraints are holding back individuals and groups seeking to establish and run SEOs. Engagement with political and academic partners should mitigate many of the barriers that often restrict SEOs' ability to carry out their social mission. However, although some good work has been achieved in doing this, especially in providing access to financial capital for start-up SEOs, new challenges arise in their place (Haugh 2012; Hynes 2009). One such example is the exogenous drive to 'scale up' social impact (Bloom and Chatterji 2009; Perrini et al. 2010). This, as with much in the SE movement, is laudable but also presents the burden of unrealistic expectations: only the most well designed and fortunately resourced SEs would be capable of scaling their organizations to this extent. Also this drive perhaps distorts the rationale that underscores most SEs and SEOs; many expect to serve their missions locally, with little desire to develop beyond their regional area. While acknowledging the success stories, more attention needs to focus on working with practitioners to address real operational problems. Understanding the interplay of the articulation of these issues is one of the main goals of this chapter.

Second, the *political* landscape within which SE develops is less of a cohesive and supportive environment, more of a fractured, unstable testing ground. Of course, such a position puts politics at the heart of discourse, thus it concerns issues of asymmetrical power relations, discourse opacity and discursive dominance and resistance. This view of discourse (and the relations of participants in it) draws largely from post-Marxist theory (Butler et al. 2000; Laclau 1977, 1996; Laclau and Mouffe 2001; Zizek and Laclau 1994). With regard to discourse contestation, this approach asserts the reality of distorted state relations with other participants in a given discourse. The mechanisms of governing in the so-called 'modern state' involves a high degree of lateral coordination (Newman and Clarke 2009). This type of governance encourages participation from private sectors to engage and collaborate in a shared market space (Fyfe 2005). Where compacts exist between the state and the 'third' sector, new opportunities and resources become available to encourage new modes of deployment.

Recent evidence suggests that political support for SEO development is something of a double-edged sword: the state offers a resource-rich arena for engaging in new opportunities, but also creates an environment of compliance and conformity, in place of innovation and creativity (Carmel and Harlock 2008; Frumkin and Galaskiewicz 2004; Mason 2012). This is problematic, because the essence of SE is nearly always concerned with supporting social *innovation* of some form (Grant 2008; Nicholls 2010a). Of course, state interests would be served by supporting innovation in the public sphere, yet it would be naïve to suppose this would present no greater political mileage in doing so. Thus, we need to be more deeply aware that the state has significantly (distorting) vested and even conflicting interests in the managed growth and grooming of SE. These interests may not be mutually felt, and consequently the shape and content of SE discourse has become more clouded. At present, SEs and SEOs are managing within this state of discursive opacity, creating ambiguities that can hide political intention (whether they are well intended or otherwise). Recent studies have shown such manoeuvrings to have an inimical effect on perceptions of grooming SE in the public sphere (Carmel and Harlock 2008; Mason 2012; Teasdale 2012). We must seek to make this discourse a more realistic and diverse reflection of its core subject, and failing this, equalize the power-legitimacy status of participants therein (Kelly 2007; Lyons and Passey 2006; Taylor and Bassi 1998; Taylor and Warburton 2003).

Thirdly, *academic communities* are rapidly developing new insights into SE, as a concept and a practice. This, too, creates tensions that are in need of redress (Alcock and Kendall 2011). For example, researchers engage in a definition debate – ostensibly one that seeks to simply clarify a (relatively) universal agreement on the meaning of SE, and something Nicholls (2006) described as 'increasingly desperate and mis-placed' (ibid: 4). Jones and Keogh (2006: 13 *passim*) explored this issue of meaning further, noting that conceptual barriers could be set apart according to voluntary participation, independence from the state, the role of 'profit', and ownership and corporate management structures. Often, although textual clarifications have been made to distinguish between and with types of SE, 'distinction(s) can easily be lost in conversation with the range of people operating in the social economy' (ibid: 18). Such academic exercises have conceptual merit and are an agreed necessary com-ponent of developing a coherent body of SE knowledge (Peattie and Morley 2008). The problem is that these very academic debates also serve to baffle and frustrate other stakeholders as part of that same process of discovery and consolidation. Although practitioners may have interests in this debate, they would likely under-stand 'SE' as an active verb. Therefore in '*the doing*' of SE, practitioners reside primarily in the substantive rather than conceptual domain (Hamby et al. 2010).

A seemingly unifying research goal between many SE stakeholders is the push for more empirical evidence to enhance the reach and relevance of the discourse to larger public audiences (Haugh 2012; Thompson 2008). Due to comparisons against nonprofit and voluntary organizations, defining SE is a tautological nightmare. In a recent paper on the subject of SE meaning, Teasdale addressed the 'bewildering' nature of SE discourse by identifying a possible cause for the ambiguity and confu-sion. The 'looseness' of the SE definition was intentionally deployed by a key (and significantly powerful) discourse player, the state. By keeping conceptual parameters loose between SE-type organizations, this allowed for SE policy which addressed a 'grand narrative [downplaying] the agency of practitioners in construct-ing the meaning of social enterprise ... [neglecting] competing discourses which place a higher emphasis on the role of collective self-help' (ibid: 107). This might have clear benefits so far as communities are concerned, with an intended synergy between 'third sector' and SE policies producing a more coherent and concerted social impact. Whether the political contributions to SE discourse impact upon the development of SE meaning and identity is debatable (for a critical discussion of the UK discourse, see Mason 2012).

The present moment is one of many crucial stages in the field's development, but my central concern is how this evidence-building can progress the critical aims of scholars *and also* address the operational challenges facing practitioners (Curtis 2008). Fundamental to working towards resolution to these barriers is a deeper understanding of the contradictory messages within discourse, as well as the dual process of SE identification. Curtis (2008: 280) summarizes the two sides of this coin neatly: SEs might be classified as either 'state-sponsored' or 'self-emergent'. Thus, without agreeing that such divisions portray the whole SE landscape, it is notable that key social and enterprise ideas are at conflict (281, *passim*). On one hand, we have militant decency, social movements and post-liberalism, set against contractualism, agencification and managerialism. This is a useful illustration of the conflict inherent in the SE idea, and arguably identifies that competing ideas are both in unison and in conflict when we talk about what SE is, is not and cannot be. Arguably, SE also brings together the interface between practitioners and academics over matters of importance to the field, and also offers policymakers the kind of insight into the people that make SE work. Based on the prior discussion of tripartite factors above (practitioners, political and academic communities), I too address SE identity. However, my analysis concerns the impact of the inherently political dimension in SE, and the way that practice is played out among a diverse, multi-faceted and largely incoherent political milieu (Gioia *et al.* 2000; Hamby *et al.* 2010; Humphreys and Brown 2002). The definitional process itself is a fascinating aspect of the SE discourse, as much (if not more than) the achievement of a satisfactory and stable meaning.

Researching SE discourse/identity

This leads us to consider more deeply the possibility of the idea of SE identity, which has been one of the more fruitful lines of enquiry for SE researchers. Identity is defined in a large number of ways, depending on the focus of analysis (individual/ organizational or personal/social). For this discussion, I am more concerned about the interplay between personal identity and the social process of identification (Cerulo 1997). This process, which informs personal identity and is honed and resisted in varying degrees, is appropriated through discourse (Hardy *et al.* 2005). Thus, a sense of 'meaning' attached to identity is imbued in the way that we talk and write about, for example, a concept or an idea (Benwell and Stokoe 2006; Kuhn 2006). The identification of the subject is part of a reflexive process, involving the synthesis and decomposition of former, existing and possible new identities (Sveningsson and Alvesson 2003).

The concept of identity seems to have become a useful counterpoint in SE research because it confronts the inherent paradox at the heart of the SE concept. Often, SE is articulated by what it *means* to work in a SEO, and the cognitive frameworks that portray the socially enterprising individual and organization. The challenges inherent in this meaning have been described as both lacking in a common metaphor and as fragmentary (Seanor and Meaton 2007: 98, *passim*). Thus SE identity may well produce a coherent but simultaneously conflicting sense of meaning. As part of an emerging change of mood in SE research, there has been a degree of unity in those trying to move away from the definition debate. Undoubtedly, it is common in social research to proceed from defined origins, but consideration is needed for nascent concepts that are highly contested. This contestation is also common, concerning new or changeable ideas – and SE is one such idea. Part of the benefit of a unifying SE definition is the stability it offers researchers entrenched in the 'field', and its offer of an easily communicable way of learning about an idea. SE has been notoriously tricky to define, as well as explaining how SE differs from other (very similar) organizations, such as non-profits and voluntary/ community entities.

Additionally, as scholars have embarked on a phase of theoretical exploration, we have begun to see a redevelopment and analytical critique signifying SEs' growing conceptual maturity. A key aspect of this critical research stream has been work concerning SE identity, identification and discourse (Eikenberry 2009; Seanor and Meaton 2007; Teasdale 2012). Naturally, this research focus has contributed significantly to how SE is articulated, recognizing the difficulties in trying to neatly capture SE meaning (especially one that is cross-culturally relevant). This combination of identification, articulation and the role of discourse is important because it encourages an interrogation of this composite SE identity, especially the ideational and political influences upon it.

Two of the most instructive recent works connecting SE discourse and identity are Parkinson and Howorth (2008) and Jones *et al.* (2008). The former dealt with the re-articulation of social entrepreneurship discourse by practitioners, placing the micro-discourses against social enterprise policies. Specifically, they highlighted the complexities inherent in converging entrepreneurship and social enterprise discourses. The major issue arising from these messy discourses is the selective 'couching' of entrepreneurship discourses alongside more recognizable traces of SE, i.e. local and social legitimacy. Thus, we are continually seeking to redetermine the balance of competing discourses, and understand how this infers 'something' about SE identity. The 'text' and 'talk' that provide a socio-linguistic basis for understanding discourses is instructive in linking together micro-level utterances, as reported in Parkinson and Howorth (2008), with the discursive interplay at the macro-level (Blommaert and Bulcaen 2000; Van Dijk 1980, 1993). Such analysis is fundamental to furthering our insights into the particularity of SE identity, as a distinct domain, even acknowledging its various histories and origins. Importantly, SE discourse appears heavily weighed down with text – predominantly policies and academic writing. Government policies directly and indirectly influence discourses (Fairclough 1995), and current research has shown how UK policy has subverted SE discourse (Mason 2012). Consequently, we are still searching for more evidence of multiple voices 'from the field', based on the assertion that speech is both privileged over text, and also more directly correlated to meanings of what is real (Derrida 1967 [1997]). This provides the rationale for one of the goals of this chapter – to re-examine the spoken articulations of SE identity in order to expose their inherent and necessary incompleteness.

A second recent piece of research (by Jones *et al.* 2008) has also been influential on this chapter, and I adopt a view of identity and identification that accepts a variety of exogenous and endogenous influences. In so doing, this position infers that identity is dynamic, fragmentary and particularly unstable, and thus I propose to show that articulations of social entrepreneur self-identity also have a distinctive political dimension. In seeking a stable definition of what SE is, some researchers have collected and analyzed empirical data to illustrate quite how individuals articulate their sense of SE (Young 2001). Jones *et al.* (2008) attempt this with a constructivist analysis of a SE case study, and argue that the narration of this individual's self-identity provides insight into how SE is portrayed. They applied the triad of Me, Not-Me and Suppressed-Me to the narrative to show how SEs utilize language to convey and compartmentalize the self. As a contribution to the literature on the meaning of SE, as well as to the process of forming SE identity, this work is very useful. Principally, this encourages researchers to examine discursive domains that are included, or excluded, from individual approximations of their sense of self. Although the Me and Not Me categories offer more simple (although interesting) accounts of this phenomena, it is the Suppressed-Me which provides the more tempting angle for further exploration. The former pair are relatively clear, opposite values, such as (hypothetically): 'We operate to maximize its social impact', opposed to 'Corporate and public sectors solutions have failed to deliver suitable local impact'. The first indicates alignment with our collective understanding of SE, the second explains a belief against the viability of non-SE activities in a given community. Identity is therefore articulated as one of difference, a descriptive account of what does not classify as self by virtue of its lacking the ideological and/ or instrumental criteria to associate with Me. Of course, this 'oppositeness' can actually cause there to be less accurate interpretations of the Me identity. We cannot identify a SE by consequence of not being seemingly like a corporation, because it does little to distinguish the sufficiently unique characteristics of either. The fact is, SE and SEOs are in some way similar to corporations (and other organizations), and they possess many similar characteristics. These include generic board structures, managerial roles and hierarchies, reporting requirements to legislative and regulatory bodies (including financial disclosures), even in terms of product/ service development and branding.

However, the Suppressed Me is the narrative that emerges from 'discursive suppression', where individuals deal with competing discourses through silencing them in their narrative. As Jones *et al.* put it: 'in painting (an) ideological narrative the notion of putting social welfare first whilst still being a profitable business can be both counterintuitive and painful' (2008: 341). Utilizing the work on organizational and entrepreneurial identity by Cohen and Musson (2000), the authors determined that Me and Not-Me are present in SE narratives as a method of 'divisioning' opposite discourses by way of signifying the Me identity. Yet, the Suppressed Me is actually a mechanism for deferral – constructing a narrative of identity that is never whole because it must deny (or suppress) inherently conflicting discourses. Of course, we know that the SE concept contains a plethora of conflicting discourses. Importantly, these suppressed discourses form a key part of SE identity, knowledge that must be eschewed. In addition, an additional element to this tripartite structure could be 'Suppressed Not-Me' – a cognitive, individual response where SEs defer conflicting identities that do not need to be articulated, but need to be gently suppressed. For example, the implicit similarity between the different types of SEOs – say cooperatives and Social Firms – are not ideologically opposite, rather they are just different forms within a category. Thus, it becomes less important for SEs to articulate their differences within types, instead focusing on ideas and/or identities that belong to different categories. Nevertheless, both of the 'suppressed' divisions refer to conflicting discourses that the SE seeks to silence when articulating its Me-identity.

If we never truly capture identity through Me and Not-Me, we are forced to postpone certainty over both. The identity knowledge that is hidden from view means that, as with defining SE, we are forever trying to capture an elusive meaning. Exploring and analyzing the Suppressed Me is therefore highly important – it allows us to at least ascertain the missing pieces from individual SE identity. However, as Jones *et al.* (2008) mention, this process is made more difficult by the imposed influence of political discourses on individual actors. Indeed, the importance of the political dimension to SE discourse has not been overlooked by research, and has done well to recognize the inherently (sometimes fervent) political elements with SEs themselves. Importantly, there must be a stage in discourse, albeit fleetingly, where ideas take on a level of determinacy. At this point, (re)definitions emerge and are diffused across actors, and the re-engagement in conflict and debate ensures the fragility of meaning. SEs identities form and re-form during this fractious process, drawing from the broader political discourse as well as between articulations of suppressed (and not suppressed) self-identities. Naturally, this frames SE identification as a disjointed and contradictory process producing ambiguous and shifting senses of what SEs are.

Positioning différance and supplementarity in SE discourse

Central to this issue of discursive meaning and identity, and hence counter-discourse, resistance or suppression of alternative identities, is the taken-for-granted nature of stable, definite values of what constitutes (or not) a social entrepreneur. This view is a relic of the modernist worldview, that there lingers an (unachievable) ideal, i.e. there somewhere exists a suitable and stable SE construct which we slowly negotiate towards. Postmodernist views on the viability of such an ontological position are, by and large, heavily *critical* by nature (Graham 1988). Such an orientation supposedly blows apart the myth of the supremacy of rationality and logic in the production of 'facts'. For writers such as Jacques Derrida, the mediation of these facts is through the text, and a suitable deconstruction of texts exposes the frailty of logocentric thought and the misrepresentation of symbolic forms of language (Cooper 1989; Derrida 1967 [1997]). Thus part of the problem for discourse participants in determining this meaning is trying to pin down values that are inherently ambiguous and indefinite, and drawn from discourses that are invariably opaque. For these reasons, in the postmodern view it becomes necessary to stop seeking a modernist determinism from such a messy and contentious debate of meaning. Instead, I suggest recourse to examining the processes that produce an indeterminate understanding of the term 'social entrepreneurship'. To do this, I utilize Derrida's concepts of *différance* and *supplementarity*, emphasizing the importance of *process* in place of structure (Cooper 1989). In so doing, I wish to emphasize that these meaning-making processes are political, discursive, incomplete, asymmetrical and most importantly open-ended. Thus, closure of such a debate limits the enthusiasm across a wide field of interest in SE. In place of closure, we should welcome the openness of SE debate but also be mindful of the challenges inherent in the discursive process.

Différance

Based loosely on Ferdinand de Saussure's work on linguistic signs (Holdcroft 1991; Saussure 1916 [1996]), *différance* forms part of Derrida's *deconstruction*, and seems to offer a suitable way out of this SE definitional dilemma. Derrida invented this term as a way of explaining that words cannot ever truly symbolize either what is, or what is not. As soon as we try to articulate a given 'reality', we actually fail to accurately describe the item, or concept, itself. In *On Grammatology*, Derrida offered one (of many) explanations:

> signification can only describe the work and the fact of *différance*, the determined differences and the determined presences that they make possible. *Différance* is therefore the formation of form. But it is on the other hand the being-imprinted of the imprint.
>
> (Derrida 1967 [1997]: 63)

Reality is 'as it is', and cannot be truly reproduced using words, or texts, or other forms of written language – the act of writing subverts meaning. We try to provide a closure or ending to the efforts of symbolizing the subject under description. However, it is not possible to provide a written expression of an idea, concept or tangible item without trying to position it against its opposite – and also within itself – thus defining something by what it cannot be. Such binary oppositions are central to *différance*, as is the notion that these differences also fuse ideas together, creating an 'undecidable' whole (Cooper 1989).

Hence we embark on a process of trying (and often failing) to define and redefine concepts through our perception of intelligible alternatives. Following this line of argument underlines the key problem in the SE definitional debate: the words we use to describe the essence of a concept, such as SE, cannot be done without reference to oppositional symbols, such as non-social enterprises. In relation to the axiology of the SE concept, we find a problematical (and inherent) conflict within the term itself – *social* and *enterprise/entrepreneurship*. As Cooper notes: 'one of the two terms governs the other … or has the upper hand' (1989: 483). Our definitional problem is: which of the ideas with the SE term has the 'upper hand' over the other? Seemingly, it entirely depends on the beholder, and is therefore subjectively defined. As a field of practice, SEs and SEOs are simultaneously both pro-social, pro-enterprise and variations of emphasis in-between. Identification with one or other depends on the type and context of individual and organization, or frame of analysis (Jeffcutt 1994) Therefore, the real issue is not the lack of a generic definition, but the *process* of defining SE. This debate that I alluded to earlier involves any number of 'players' – from the political, practitioner and academic fields of interest (although not always from social beneficiary groups). Thus the dynamic between these players is one of competition: to try to assert a more legitimate understanding of SE, to provide more certain knowledge of it. Of course, the problem here is that in such a politically charged arena with difficult external circumstances (i.e. the

GFC), certainty is actually not realistic, or feasible. The ambiguity of difference (as part of *différance*) muddies the conceptual waters too readily and too much – there are so many similar yet oppositional concepts, with diverse histories to find sufficient clarity.

The other side to *différance* is 'to defer or delay', as a way of explaining how literal interpretations of reality are forever postponed, with deference to meta-level concepts instead. Describing the process of uncovering the 'real' is impossible since we always seek a closure to our definitions, and this closure is forever denied by the inaccessibility of a larger concept or idea that is signified. Without the ability to affirm or consolidate a meaning, the deferral element of *différance* ensures that we can never actually settle on a certainty of meaning (Derrida 1978). Our attempts to consolidate SE meaning are difficult precisely because 'no utterance, writing or text can guarantee its own truth and must necessarily resort to a meta-level or reference in order to derive its authority' (Linstead 1993: 56). The continual search for SE meaning is quite consistent with this process of *différance:* the meaning is never static, always changing, forever debatable and always inaccurate.

Supplementarity

The second key element to Derrida's deconstruction of texts is *supplementarity*. The essence of this idea is that meaning of terms is always incomplete, thus we are always trying to supplement with further information to make the idea whole. As part of the erratic ebb and flow of SE discourse, the meaning-making process forms part of the supplementarity of meaning itself. Also supplementarity refers to a *disruptive* process of identification through additional reference, where self-identification might link back to the Suppressed Me. According to Linstead (ibid: 57, italics in original): 'It is a *human* response to the self-destructive quality of sup-plementarity *within the term itself*. The combination of the 'social' with enterprise/ entrepreneurship is illustrative of supplementarity. Both terms are used as a signifier for the same real thing, and are used positively (in other words, their presence negates other words that could be used to also describe the same phenomenon). Of course, the problem that many people recognize is the apparent tension (rather than harmony) between conceptions of social *and* enterprise/entrepreneurship. This forces us to (re)justify their presence as an accurate *signifier* of SE-type organizations. Furthermore, it must also act as a suitable *replacement* for the existing SE-type organ-izations. In actuality, many discourse participants are uncomfortable with the tension between the two words (social and enterprise/entrepreneurship). This highlights Derrida's main claim that oppositional tensions force us to seek further supplementation to clarify our ideas. This causes the initial symbol or term to be rendered nothing more than an inaccurately composed deferential subject.

In relation to this elusive SE definition, the discourse players attempt sense-making through their written texts – academic papers (and book chapters!), policies, position papers, practitioner case studies, and more. Through our interpretation of these texts we, perhaps unknowingly, contribute to discourse contestation – when our 'knowledge' of SE becomes in conflict. In so doing, these participants engage in supplementing SE meaning: a continuous evolution and decomposition of the concept. We still seek clarity from a clouded idea that simultaneously means something, yet verifying this meaning always slips away from us. Participants in this discursive process seek to add depth by adding more words by way of explanation, when the variety of texts always demand further supplementation.

Concluding remarks

In this chapter I have tried to coherently address the problematical nature of the SE definition process. In so doing, I propose that part of the difficulty in settling upon a definition may be the result of *différance* and *supplementarity*. SE is inherently ambiguous and contradictory within itself, meaning that defining by its opposite (whatever that object might be) is nonsensical and difficult. We also cannot help but seek out further reference to add more detail to this meaning, yet SE is not a complete and cohesive whole. Thus our continued fascination with it is all the more interesting. Although some have called for a move on from the meaning debate (Dacin et al. 2011), there seems no end to our engagement in the process of SE identification. The current stream of critical SE research is uncovering new insights into this phenomenon, be it practitioner, political/policy related or scholarly. This new ground provides/exposes different motives behind and experiences of SE in a multitude of contexts. However, within this accumulative discursive process of discovery and disputation, we still seek to consolidate what SE *means*/what SEOs *do*. As something of an addendum to this debate, the contribution of this chapter is to reconsider the reason for the existence of the definitional process, and to consider what it adds. Current literature highlights the core and interlinked roles of discourse/meaning/identity within a loosely configured SE construct. The discursive perspective on SE meaning-making is, in one view, an endemically political process where 'players' (or participants) seek to assert more power and thus acquire legitimacy over each other (Griffith 2012; Mason 2012). The sedimentation of this discursive power-play filters down into other areas of SE identification, and exposes the presence of *différance* at play upon this process. Yet, this debate is a necessary feature in our rearticulating of what SE is, even if it is a messy, confusing and ambiguous process. In pinning down how these understandings come about, specifically the influence of political actors on the shape of discourse, we fundamentally seek to uncover more about SE identification as externally driven as well as internally processed. This link is important, but so too is recognition that the interface between these varied factors oscillates, possibly in a way similar to that shown by Jones *et al.* (2008). While I have recognized the more prominent contributors to SE discourse from the academic arena, an exploration of the 'verbal texts' as articulated by practitioners would benefit further research. For example, the presence and influence of Me, Not-Me and Suppressed-Me/Suppressed Not-Me might be effectively shown through action research methodologies. Thus, SE research can continue to play its part in illustrating the open-ended nature of our understanding, and how 'knowledge' is made more opaque through our over-reliance on texts to enhance the clarity of our knowledge. Although Derrida's is a controversial terrain, the two components of deconstruction that I have addressed offer an extra analytical angle that serves the interests of a number of discourse participants, principally academics and practitioners. The ebb and flow of SE discourse and identification processes seem set to offer more intriguing interactions between these groups for the foreseeable future, keeping SE meaning and identity at the front of the research agenda.

References

Adiga, A. (2008) *The White Tiger: A Novel*. London: Free Press.

Aiken, M. and Bode, I. (2009) 'Killing the golden goose? Third sector organizations and back-to-work programmes in Germany and the UK', *Social Policy and Administration*, 43(3): 209–25.

Alcock, P. and Kendall, J. (2011) 'Constituting the third sector: processes of decontestation and contention under the UK Labour governments in England', *Voluntas: International Journal of Voluntary and Nonprofit Organizations*, 22(3): 450–69.

Benwell, B. and Stokoe, E. (2006) *Discourse and Identity*. Edinburgh: Edinburgh University Press.

Blommaert, J. and Bulcaen, C. (2000) 'Critical discourse analysis', *Annual Review of Anthropology*, 29: 447–66.

Bloom, P. N. and Chatterji, A. K. (2009) 'Scaling social entrepreneurial impact', *California Management Review*, 51(3): 114–33.

Butler, J., Laclau, E. and Zizek, S. (2000) *Contingency, Hegemony, Universality: Contemporary Dialogues on the Left*. London: Verso Books.

Carmel, E. and Harlock, J. (2008) 'Instituting the "third sector" as a governable terrain: partnership, procurement and performance in the UK', *Policy and Politics*, 36(2): 155–71.

Cerulo, K. A. (1997) 'Identity construction: new issues, new directions', *Annual Review of Sociology*, 23: 385–409.

Cohen, L. and Musson, G. (2000) 'Entrepreneurial identities: reflections from two case studies', *Organization*, 7(1): 31–48.

Cooper, R. (1989) 'Modernism, post modernism and organizational analysis 3: The contribution of Jacques Derrida', *Organization Studies*, 10(4): 479–502.

Curtis, T. (2008) 'Finding that grit makes a pearl – a critical re-reading of research into the development of social enterprises by the public sector', *International Journal of Entrepreneurial Behaviour and Research*, 14(5): 276–90.

Dacin, P. A., Dacin, M. T. and Matear, M. (2010) 'Social entrepreneurship: why we don't need a new theory and how we move forward from here', *The Academy of Management Perspectives*, 24(3): 37–57.

Dacin, M. T., Dacin, P. A. and Tracey, P. (2011) 'Social entrepreneurship: a critique and future directions', *Organization Science*, 22(5): 1203–13.

Derrida, J. (1967 [1997]) *Of Grammatology*, Baltimore, MA: Johns Hopkins University Press.

Derrida, J. (1978) *Writing and Difference*. Chicago, IL: University of Chicago Press.

Eikenberry, A. (2009) 'Refusing the market: a democratic discourse for voluntary and nonprofit organizations', *Nonprofit and Voluntary Sector Quarterly*, 38(4): 582–96.

Fairclough, N. (1995) *Critical Discourse Analysis: The Critical Study of Language*. London: Pearson.

Frumkin, P. and Galaskiewicz, J. (2004) 'Institutional isomorphism and public sector organizations', *Journal of Public Administration Research and Theory*, 14(3): 283–307.

Fyfe, N. (2005) 'Making space for "neo-communitarianism"? The third sector, state and civil society in the UK', *Antipode*, 37(3): 536–57.

Gioia, D., Schultz, M. and Corley, K. (2000) 'Organizational identity, image, and adaptive instability', *Academy of Management Review*, 25(1): 63–81.

Graham, J. (1988) 'Postmodernism and Marxism', *Antipode*, 20(1): 60–6.

Grant, S. (2008) 'Contextualising social enterprise in New Zealand', *Social Enterprise Journal*, 4(1): 9–23.

Griffith, J. (2012) 'Social enterprise under New Labour and beyond: many good ideas with the potential to become a disaster', Speech at University of East London, Centre for Institutional Studies.

Hamby, A., Pierce, M. and Brinberg, D. (2010) 'A conceptual framework to structure research in strategic and social entrepreneurship', *Journal of Asia-Pacific Business*, 11(3): 166–78.

Hardy, C., Lawrence, T. B. and Grant, D. (2005) 'Discourse and collaboration: the role of conversations and collective identity', *The Academy of Management Review*, 30(1): 58–77.

Haugh, H. (2012) 'The importance of theory in social enterprise research', *Social Enterprise Journal*, 8(1): 7–15.

Haugh, H. and Kitson, M. (2007) 'The third way and the third sector: New Labour's economic policy and the social economy', *Cambridge Journal of Economics*, 31(6): 973–94.

Holdcroft, D. (1991) *Saussure: Signs, System, and Arbitrariness*. Cambridge: Cambridge University Press.

Humphreys, M. and Brown, A. D. (2002) 'Narratives of organizational identity and identification: a case study of hegemony and resistance', *Organization Studies*, 23(3): 421–44.

Hynes, B. (2009) 'Growing the social enterprise: issues and challenges', *Social Enterprise Journal*, 5(2): 114–25.

Jeffcutt, P. (1994) 'From interpretation to representation in organizational analysis: postmodernism, ethnography and organizational symbolism', *Organization Studies*, 15(2): 241–74.

Jones, D. and Keogh, W. (2006) 'Social enterprise: a case of terminological ambiguity and complexity', *Social Enterprise Journal*, 2(1): 11–26.

Jones, R., Latham, J. and Betta, M. (2008) 'Narrative construction of the social entrepreneurial identity', *International Journal of Entrepreneurial Behaviour and Research*, 14(5): 330–45.

Kelly, J. (2007) 'Reforming public services in the UK: bringing in the third sector', *Public Administration*, 85(4): 1003–22.

Kuhn, T. (2006) 'A "demented work ethic" and a "lifestyle firm": discourse, identity, and workplace time commitments', *Organization Studies*, 27(9): 1339–58.

Laclau, E. (1977) *Politics and Ideology in Marxist Theory: Capitalism, Fascism, Populism*. London: NLB.

Laclau, E. (1996) *Emancipation(s)*. London: Verso Books.

Laclau, E. and Mouffe, C. (2001) *Hegemony and Socialist Strategy: Towards a Radical Democratic Politics*. London: Verso Books.

Linstead, S. (1993) 'From postmodern anthropology to deconstructive ethnography', *Human Relations*, 46(1): 97–120.

Lyon, F., Baldock, R. and Teasdale, S. (2010) 'Approaches to measuring the scale of the social enterprise sector in the UK', Birmingham, UK: University of Birmingham.

Lyons, M. and Passey, A. (2006) 'Need public policy ignore the third sector? Government policy in Australia and the United Kingdom', *Australian Journal of Public Administration*, 65(3): 90–102.

Mason, C. (2012) 'Up for grabs: a critical analysis of social entrepreneurship discourse in the United Kingdom', *Social Enterprise Journal*, 8(2): 123–40.

Morrin, M., Simmonds, D. and Somerville, W. (2004) 'Social enterprise: mainstreamed from the margins?', *Local Economy*, 19(1): 69–84.

Newman, J. and Clarke, J. (2009) *Publics, Politics and Power: Remaking the Public in Public Services*. London: Sage.

Nicholls, A. (2006) 'Playing the field: a new approach to the meaning of social entrepreneurship', *Social Enterprise Journal*, 2(1): 1–5.

Nicholls, A. (2010a) 'Institutionalizing social entrepreneurship in regulatory space: reporting and disclosure by community interest companies', *Accounting, Organizations and Society*, 35(4): 394–415.

Nicholls, A. (2010b) 'The legitimacy of social entrepreneurship: reflexive isomorphism in a pre-paradigmatic field', *Entrepreneurship Theory and Practice*, 34(4): 611–33.

Office of the Third Sector (2009) *Real Help for Communities: Volunteers, Charities and Social Enterprises*. London: Cabinet Office/HMSO.

Parkinson, C. and Howorth, C. (2008) 'The language of social entrepreneurs', *Entrepreneurship and Regional Development*, 20(3): 285–309.

Peattie, K. and Morley, A. (2008) 'Eight paradoxes of the social enterprise research agenda', *Social Enterprise Journal*, 4(2): 91–107.

Perrini, F., Vurro, C. and Costanzo, L. A. (2010) 'A process-based view of social entrepreneurship: from opportunity identification to scaling-up social change in the case of San Patrignano', *Entrepreneurship and Regional Development: An International Journal*, 22(6): 515–34.

Saussure, F. D. (1916 [1996]) *Course In General Linguistics*. New York: McGraw-Hill Publishing.

Seanor, P. and Meaton, J. (2007) 'Making sense of social enterprise', *Social Enterprise Journal*, 3(1): 90–100.

Sharp, L. and Richardson, T. (2001) 'Reflections on Foucauldian discourse analysis in planning and environmental policy research', *Journal of Environmental Policy and Planning*, 3(3): 139–209.

Steyaert, C. and Dey, P. (2010) 'Nine verbs to keep the social entrepreneurship research agenda "dangerous"', *Journal of Social Entrepreneurship*, 1(2): 231–54.

Sveningsson, S. and Alvesson, M. (2003) 'Managing managerial identities: organizational fragmentation, discourse and identity struggle', *Human Relations*, 56(10): 1163–93.

Taylor, M. and Bassi, A. (1998) 'Unpacking the state: the implications for the third sector of changing relationships between national and local government', *Voluntas: International Journal of Voluntary and Nonprofit Organizations*, 9(2): 113–36.

Taylor, M. and Warburton, D. (2003) 'Legitimacy and the role of UK third sector organisations in the policy process', *Voluntas: International Journal of Voluntary and Nonprofit Organisations*, 14(3): 321–38.

Teasdale, S. (2012) 'What's in a name? Making sense of social enterprise discourses', *Public Policy and Administration*, 27(2): 99–119.

Thompson, J. (2008) 'Social enterprise and social entrepreneurship: where have we reached?: A summary of issues and discussion points', *Social Enterprise Journal*, 4: 149–61.

Tomlinson, F. and Schwabenland, C. (2010) 'Reconciling competing discourses of diversity? The UK non-profit sector between social justice and the business case', *Organization*, 17(1): 101.

Van Dijk, T. (1980) *Macrostructures: An Interdisciplinary Study of Global Structures in Discourse, Interaction, and Cognition*. Hillsdale, NJ: Lawrence Erlbaum Associates.

Van Dijk, T. (1993) 'Principles of critical discourse analysis', *Discourse and Society*, 4(2): 249–83.

Young, D. R. (2001) 'Organizational identity in nonprofit organizations: strategic and structural implications', *Nonprofit Management and Leadership*, 12 (2): 139–57.

Zizek, S. and Laclau, E. (1994) *The Sublime Object of Ideology*. London:Verso.

PART III
Evaluating social enterprise: international research studies

5

WORKING FOR A SOCIAL ENTERPRISE

An exploration of employee rewards and motivations

Belinda Bell and Helen Haugh

Introduction

The twenty-first century has witnessed growth of the social enterprise sector in the developed world and increased discussion about the potential of such organizations to expand their size, scale and impact (Pearce 2003; Doherty *et al.* 2009; SEC 2009, 2011). Although an internationally agreed definition of social enterprise has yet to be produced it is generally positioned as a subset of the wider social economy or non-profit sector, i.e. organizations that are neither privately nor publicly owned. The social economy comprises organizations that range from small, informal community and voluntary groups that operate locally, to large, charitable organizations with an international presence. These organizational forms share in common the pursuit of social and environmental goals. Social enterprises are included in the social economy yet they are distinctive in that they aim to achieve financial sustainability from pursuing strategies to generate income from the sale of goods and services, i.e. they are 'businesses trading for social and environmental purposes' (SEC 2009: 3).

Income generation is an important and longstanding strategy for many non-profit sector organizations, for instance in the UK the first charity shops appeared during the 1940s. However, the regulations concerning charitable status in the UK, IRS 501(a) in the US and similar internationally, are often onerous and require for instance that much trading is conducted by a separate legal entity and place constraint upon the use of surplus revenues (Framjee 2010). In contrast, social enterprises adopt legal forms constructed expressly for the purpose of income generation. In this way social enterprise business models directly link trading activity to the pursuit of social and/or environmental goals. Revenue generation from trading may be the primary source of income in association with other sources of finance, such as grants and donations. In 2009, 72 per cent of UK social enterprises earned more than 50 per cent of their income from trading, and dependence on grants decreased in organizations such more than £1 million turnover (SEC 2009). The reinvestment of profits to further the goals of the social enterprise might be achieved through either underwriting or cross-subsidising other activities. In 2009, 70 per cent of UK social enterprises reinvested profits by expanding services or providing new services to their beneficiaries (SEC 2009). Social enterprises hence combine the pursuit of social goals with the establishment and management of a viable business venture.

The size and scale of social enterprise activity in the UK has yet to be precisely defined. In 2005 it was estimated that there were 15,000 social enterprises in the UK (IFF 2005), however this figure was substantially revised upwards to 55,000 (OTS 2006). In addition, the IFF survey (2005) estimated that more than 475,000 people worked for social enterprises, of whom 66 per cent were employed full time (IFF 2005). This equates to approximately 2.5 per cent of all UK private sector employment. By 2009 the number of social enterprises had increased to 62,000 with a collective contribution of more than £24 billion to the economy (SEC 2011: 5). However, despite the increasing importance of social enterprises in terms of employment opportunities (SEC 2011) we know little about social enterprise employee remuneration and motivation.

In the UK, social enterprises operate in many different industry sectors and have created employment opportunities in a range of business ventures. Employment opportunities extend from recruiting individuals new to the workforce, those already employed and who seek to change employer, and those returning to work after a break. Some social enterprises such as Social Firms or Work Integration Social Enterprises aim to provide integrated employment and training opportunities for people with a disability (or other labour market disadvantage) (Nyssens 2006; Doherty et al. 2009). Other social enterprises aim to encourage entrepreneurs to create their own employment opportunities through strategies to stimulate new venture creation. In this domain, a key group of social enterprises in both the UK and the US are community development finance institutions (CDFIs). CDFIs provide services similar to those provided by microfinance institutions in that they offer loans to entrepreneurs who do not satisfy the lending criteria of mainstream financial institutions (primarily the retail banks). In the wake of the 2008 economic crisis the CDFI sector continues to receive strong support from central governments as it seeks to fill market gaps in financial services provision (BIS 2010).

The research presented in this chapter examines the remuneration, motivation and job satisfaction of employees who currently work for CDFIs in the UK and who had previously been employed in the financial services industry in the private sector. This was achieved by gathering data from informants from seventeen CDFIs. We compare their remuneration in previous and current employment, examine their reasons for leaving the private sector, the factors that influenced their decision to work for a social enterprise, and their satisfaction with their current employment.

Knowledge about why employees move between economic sectors, and the factors that influence choice of employer and job satisfaction is important for increasing our understanding about the attractiveness of working for a specific type of organization. The study also has practical implications in that awareness of the motivations and satisfaction of those working for CDFIs can be used to inform recruitment policies and develop strategies to attract the best talent to the increasingly important social economy.

Our chapter is laid out as follows: to begin, we review the key constituents of employee motivation and job satisfaction, and summarize employment in the non-profit sector. This is followed by an explanation of our methodology, results and analysis of the in-depth interviews with informants. In our conclusion we consider how our results provide an insight into the role of altruism in employee motivation and suggest further research possibilities.

Employee motivation

Motivation relates to action needed to fulfil human needs and in general refers to the processes that elicit, control and sustain behaviour. Since a highly motivated employee is more likely to be productive and content, there is a long history of scholarly and practitioner interest in employee motivation. Early theoretical work began with content theories that sought to identify factors that produced motivation in employees (Maslow 1943; Alderfer 1972; Herzberg *et al.* 1959). Content theories differentiate between motivation arising from extrinsic factors, for example, pay, opportunities for training, learning and promotion, and intrinsic motivation arising from, for example, interest and enjoyment of the task itself such as achievement of self-fulfilment through work. Thus, the more interesting the tasks and greater social and relational opportunities at work, the higher the intrinsic motivation for an employee to perform well (Frey 1997a; Handy and Katz 1998). Content theories present useful ways of thinking about what motivates employees to work and how they might achieve satisfaction from work, however they take a universal, generic approach that overlooks the potentially subtle differences between individuals and, relevant to our research, the impact of external factors, such as social context, on employee motivation.

Content theories were followed by process theories that sought to explain how motivation and employee behaviour were related (Vroom 1964; Adams 1965; Porter and Lawler 1968; Fehr and Fischbacher 2002). Process theories aim to examine how work satisfies the needs of an employee and links expectations about future rewards to motivation. Expectancy theory, first developed by Vroom and advanced by Porter and Lawler, examines the relationship between the anticipation of future rewards (e.g. promotion, recognition) and employee effort and performance (e.g. hours worked) (Vroom 1964; Porter and Lawler 1968). In contrast, equity theory (Adams 1965) draws on the assumption that employees make judgements about fairness by comparing themselves with others; they will compare their relative inputs and outputs with other employees and if they judge their relative treatment to be unfair they will make changes to inputs (effort), outputs (performance) or their comparison group (employer). Equity theory has been useful for understanding why employees become dissatisfied at work and why they might be motivated to make changes to their employment in that inequity-averse individuals might seek to change their employer to find a different comparison group (Fehr and Fischbacher 2002).

Job satisfaction has a long association with employee motivation to join, stay and work hard and well within the organization (Barnard 1938) and scholarly interest in explaining employee motivation was followed by research that investigated job satisfaction and employee engagement. Job satisfaction is the 'pleasurable or positive emotional state resulting from the appraisal of one's job or job experience' (Locke 1976: 1300) and has been found to be associated with the extent that work is interesting, i.e. that work provides opportunities for training and learning, task variety, autonomy and control (Barling *et al.* 2003; Bond and Bunce 2003). High employee engagement is associated with opportunities to learn, meaningful work and opportunities for social interaction in the workplace (Vance 2006). Positive attitudes towards work have been found to be associated with psychological empowerment, i.e. arising from meaningful work, competences, perceived autonomy at work and perceived control over one's environment (Thomas and Velthouse 1990; Spreitzer 1995).

The brief review of motivation and job satisfaction presented above is important for the context of our study. However, concerns about the extent of fundamental differences between economic sectors (Fottler 1981; Perry and Rainey 1988; Mirvis 1992; Cheverton 2007) have led to the suggestion that employee motivation and job satisfaction varies by sector. Commitment to values is said to differentiate non-profits from organizations in the private and public sectors (Cheverton 2007) and they are thus hypothesized to function quite differently from organizations in other sectors (Leete 2001). Previous research has examined motivation to work and job satisfaction in the non-profit sector and, in the absence of studies specifically focused on social enterprises, we draw on this research to present the context of our work. Within this context the relatively recent emergence of social enterprise as a distinct organizational form may explain the lack of research to date that examines the motivation to work for a social enterprise. Whilst there is a growing body of research that examines the processes of social entrepreneurship (Dearden-Phillips 2008; Clark 2009), this phenomenon is quite different from actively seeking employment in an established social enterprise.

Our research thus presents an opportunity to investigate the extent that three conventional wisdoms regarding the social economy are related to the experiences of those that work in the sector: (1) that wages are lower than for comparable employment in the private sector; (2) that employees are motivated by factors other than economic motivation to work in the social economy; and (3) that employees are motivated by altruism to work in the social economy.

Remuneration in the non-profit sector

Several studies from the UK and the US have found that remuneration for comparable work in the non-profit sector is lower than in the private sector (Mirvis and

Hackett 1983; Weisbrod 1983; Preston 1989; Leete 2000; Almond and Kendall 2001; ACEVO 2005). Mirvis and Hackett (1983) found that non-profit employees earned etween 67.5 and 68.1 per cent of that earned by those working in the private sector (1983: 7). A study by Weisbrod (1983) compared US lawyers employed by non-profit law firms (i.e. public interest lawyers) with those working in private practice and calculated that public interest lawyers received wages that were approximately 20 per cent lower than lawyers in private practice (1983: 253). A large-scale research project analyzed data gathered in the 1979 Current Population Survey to examine remuneration in the non-profit sector (Preston 1989). Multivariate analysis of the dataset calculated that employees in non-profit organizations earned up to 20 per cent less than those in the private sector (1989: 439). More recently, Barbian (2001) found that employees would rather earn less than work for an organization with a poor reputation for social responsibility. A survey of remuneration in non-profit organizations in the UK found that between 2000 and 2005 there was a narrowing negative wage differential between non-profit and other organizations (ACEVO 2005). The ACEVO study identified a wage differential of between 75 and 84 per cent in 2000 and between 85 and 87 per cent in 2005 (ACEVO 2005). In contrast, Leete (2001) found a range of both positive and negative wage differentials that varied by occupation and industry but that averaged zero across the economy. Ruhm and Borkoski (2001) also found that when a limited set of job characteristics was controlled for (size of organization and industry sector) employees in non-profit organizations received approximately the same pay that they would have received had they been employed in equivalent profit-seeking organizations. On balance we conclude that there is a negative wage differential for employees in the non-profit sector when compared with the private sector. We therefore propose that:

P1 Social enterprise employees are paid less than in the private sector for the same type of work.

Motivation and job satisfaction in the non-profit sector

Several explanations for the pay differential between for-profit and non-profit organizations have been proposed: (1) employees accept lower pay in return for work that they find intrinsically rewarding (Mirvis and Hackett 1983; Preston 1989; Rose-Ackerman 1996); (2) employees are motivated by the social purpose of their employer (Weisbrod 1983; Preston 1989); and (3), the wage differential reflects fundamental differences in conditions (e.g. size, structure and governance) between the two types of organizations (Leete 2001).

Mirvis and Hackett (1983) assessed 'whether employee attitudes, work orientations, job characteristics and motivations and satisfactions differ across the sectors' (1983: 4) and revealed three important insights concerning non-profit employee remuneration and motivation. First, that '[n]onprofit employees are more likely to report that their work is more important to them than the money they earn'; second that non-profit employees 'bring a stronger commitment to their jobs [and] may make and sustain their choices on an ideological basis'; and third that, despite the wage differential, non-profit employees did not consider their compensation to be unfair (Mirvis and Hackett 1983: 7). This suggests that employees in the non-profit sector are fully aware of the differences in remuneration for comparable work in the private sector, and that in accepting this difference, they are motivated to work by factors other than maximising remuneration. Mirvis and Hackett concluded that non-profit employees 'bring to their jobs a greater commitment and non-monetary orientation and find more challenge, variety and autonomy in their jobs. Non-profit employees also find more intrinsic rewards in their jobs' (Mirvis and Hackett 1983: 10). Previous research has found that job satisfaction in non-profit organizations is higher than in other sectors (Benz 2005; Donegani *et al.* 2012) even when remuneration is lower (Mirvis 1992; Light 2002; Benz 2005; Borzaga and Depedri 2005; Borzaga and Tortia 2006).

Weisbrod (1983) found that the most significant non-wage rewards for public interest lawyers were (1) opportunities to work on cases that address novel legal issues, and (2) to be involved in pursuing social goals. However, the difficulty in identifying and defining social goals is not elaborated upon and 'the forms of non-pecuniary compensation are not clear' (Weisbrod 1983: 260).

Preston (1989) examined various explanations for the negative pay differential in the non-profit sector, e.g. industry sector, employee skills and non-wage characteristics of the jobs such as satisfaction of personal goals. Preston proposed that, in exchange for lower wages, non-profit employees have the 'opportunity to provide goods with positive social externalities' (1989: 438). Preston labels this supply of labour at below market rates as 'labour donation' in that there is a trade-off between wages and the perceived social benefits resulting from working for a non-profit organization. Although it is suggested that employee motivation is explained by positive social externalities, the precise nature of the externalities is not made explicit: 'empirical tests have not been able to pinpoint the force behind the differential' (Preston 1989: 453). Ultimately, Preston concludes that the wage differential 'may signal complex differences in motivations of workers' (Preston 1989: 460) but does not elaborate further.

The negative, but narrowing, wage differential found by ACEVO (2005) could be explained by the demand for senior personnel with the requisite management and leadership skills. It is not unreasonable to propose that senior level skills are transferable between sectors and thus in order to attract new leaders, non-profit organizations might have been pushed into paying higher salaries typical of the private sector.

Finally, Leete (2001) summarizes two explanations for wage differentials between for-profit and non-profit organizations in comparable occupations and industries. First, that non-profit firms produce a different type/quality of good or service than their counterparts in the private sector and that non-profit employees derive satisfaction from the type of goods or services that they produce and therefore will accept a lower (compensating) wage in exchange for their labour. Second, pay differences are attributed to observable and unobservable differences between firms, employees and their jobs (Leete 2001). Thus we propose that:

P2 Employees are motivated to work in a social enterprise by factors other than monetary rewards.

Altruism and employment in the non-profit sector

The previous sections suggested that employees accept lower remuneration in return for non-wage benefits. One frequently occurring explanation, a conventional wisdom, is that the motivation to work in the non-profit sector is attributable to altruism (Borzaga 2009; Mirvis and Hackett 1983; Rose-Ackerman 1997).

The classical economic model of human behaviour assumes that individuals respond to incentives, in particular money. Indeed the price effect is 'the backbone of modern economic theory' (Frey 1997b: 105). If we consider the job market a market system in which wages are the exchange value of labour then employment decisions should be largely determined by wages. However, the previous section showed that this rational explanation of employment choice is not universal. The 'paradox at the heart of economics' (Monroe 1994: 869) is that although economists consider that 'rational individuals always choose the option that makes them better off as they see it' (Jensen 1994: 42), rationality does not explain much of observed human behaviour (Phelps 1975; Monroe 1994; Fehr and Fischbacher 2002).

A substantial body of work has examined the wider range of motivations that impact on job choice and has concluded that a combination of financial and non-financial factors affect employment decisions (Rupert 2004). In relation to non-profit organizations a potential motivation is the opportunity to create social value, and there is an underlying assumption that 'ideology and altruism are key to understanding the non-profit charitable sector' (Rose-Ackerman 1997: 120).

Three potential factors have been suggested to explain the motivation of employees to work in the non-profit sector.

1. The non-profit status of the organization provides a guarantee that any surplus generated from its activities will not be distributed to those with a controlling interest (Hansmann 1990). 'Committed employees may be easier to attract if the firm is a non-profit. The lack of equity holders is a signal to employees that their selflessness is not enriching someone else [...] High level professional employees may accept lower levels of pay in return for greater certainty that their efforts are actually helping to achieve their altruistic goals' (Rose-Ackermann 1996: 720).
2. The personal goals of the individual motivate them to seek work in a non-profit organization, for instance the view that employees in non-profit organizations 'are attracted by the ideals of selfless service and work fulfilment' (Mirvis and Hackett 1983: 3).
3. Employees might be motivated by the ideology of the organization – Oster refers to non-profits attracting their staff through the 'ideology of the enterprise' (Oster 1995: 67), and Almond and Kendall (2001) propose that low pay

in the sector could be a result of workers placing more emphasis on non-monetary rewards, including for instance their ideological goals (Almond and Kendall 2001: 52).

Individual behaviour is interpreted as displaying altruism when it is undertaken 'with the goal of benefiting another' (Piliavin and Charng 1990: 27) even when doing so 'may risk or entail some sacrifice to the welfare of the actor' (Monroe 1994: 862). Thus an act is altruistic if it benefits others more than the actor, and if the actor might have produced a better outcome for himself by acting differently (Margolis 1982). Altruism is notoriously difficult to observe, and in our study we use acceptance of a lower wage than could be earned coupled with the informant's expression of pro-social motivation as a proxy for altruism. This leads to proposition 3:

P3 Employees are motivated by altruism to work for a social enterprise.

Methodology

Our aim is to investigate why employees work for a social enterprise and the selection of industry and informants was guided by three criteria: (1) to reduce occupational effect on employee motivation we focused on one industry; (2) to discover the distinctive factors associated with social enterprise we wanted informants to be able to make comparisons between previous employment (not in a social enterprise) and their current employment; and (3) to investigate motivation for the same type of work, we sought an industry where it was likely that informants would use similar skills and knowledge as in their previous employment. All informants were employed by organizations in the UK.

The financial services sector satisfied our criteria. In the private sector, financial services are sold by retail and merchant banks, building societies, equity investors, insurance companies and doorstep lenders. In the non-profit sector financial services are sold by CDFIs and credit unions. The sale of financial services is tightly regulated and the skills and knowledge required by employees are industry-specific and likely to be transferable between sectors.

The methodology of the study is qualitative and interview data was gathered from informants from seventeen CDFIs that were based and operating in different locations across England. The decision to use semi-structured in-depth interviews was led by our aim to explore with informants the factors that influenced their decision to leave the private sector and secure employment in a social enterprise. Our intention was to collect thick and rich descriptions (Miles and Huberman 1994: 38) from each informant and the interview questions focused on finding out why they had left their previous employer, why they had moved between economic sectors, the extent to which different factors had influenced their decision, and the impact of their decision on themselves both now and in the future.

Altruism is a sensitive topic that is intimately linked to the individual and their attitudes and values, and, just like motivation, we cannot actually see or measure it. We must therefore rely on indirect constructs to deduce its presence. The interview method was considered appropriate to enable each informant to give a detailed and reflective account of the reasons for their employment choices. Although the method relies on honesty and post-event recall, the method was considered more appropriate than a survey for encouraging informants to talk more freely and to reflect more deeply on their employment decisions.

Previous research into motivation and job satisfaction was used to construct an interview schedule for the fieldwork. The first draft of the interview schedule was critically reviewed by one senior employee in a CDFI and one expert academic with knowledge of both the financial services sector and the social economy. The schedule was then refined and pilot tested with executives from two CDFIs. Further refinements were made to produce the final interview schedule. In-depth interviews were then conducted with informants from seventeen CDFIs.

The first author has extensive employment experience in social enterprises and the first eight informants were drawn from her networks. All eight were employees of CDFIs that were members of the Community Development Finance Association (CDFA). The CDFA is the professional trade association for CDFIs in the UK. In 2005 there were 44 members of the CDFA that together employed 233 staff (McGeehan 2006). The first eight informants thus represented 18 per cent of CDFA member organizations. The remainder of the sample were recruited through the networks of the first set of informants. This conceptually driven sampling process is similar to other qualitative studies where the samples 'are usually not wholly pre-specified but can evolve once fieldwork begins' (Miles and Huberman 1994: 27). On balance, the first author's advantages in terms of access to informants and securing informant cooperation (Flick 2002: 53) exceeded the disadvantages associated with habituation and over-familiarity with informants.

There are two limitations of the study: the informants included were selected to share their experiences and are not necessarily representative of all employees that work for social enterprises; and the study focuses on one sector. The scope of the chapter is thus to present an insight into remuneration, motivation and satisfaction in CDFIs and not to offer a conclusive account of the sector.

Results and analysis

The sample consisted of nine males (M) and eight females (F). The previous employment of informants was retail banking (R) (nine informants), investment banking (I) (six informants) and doorstep lending (D) (two informants) – see Table 5.1. The interviews lasted between 60 and 90 minutes and were recorded and transcribed after the interview, usually within 24 hours. The transcripts were analyzed independently by the authors by searching for key words and phrases related to remuneration and motivation. The analytical process of each author followed the principles of grounded theory in which key words and phrases are isolated and then grouped into first order codes, and subsequently second order categories (Strauss and Corbin 1990). Both authors then reviewed the analyses to produce one composite data structure – see Figure 5.1.

TABLE 5.1 Informants

Code	Male (M)/ Female (F)	Previous employer	Code	Male (M)/ Female (F)	Previous employer
1FR	F	Retail	10FI	F	Investment
2FI	F	Investment	11FR	F	Retail
3FR	F	Retail	12MR	M	Retail
4MR	M	Retail	13FI	F	Investment
5MI	M	Investment	14FR	MF	Retail
6MI	M	Investment	15MI	M	Investment
7MR	M	Retail	16MD	M	Doorstep lender
8FR	F	Retail	17MD	M	Doorstep lender
9MR	M	Retail			

Remuneration

Informants were asked to compare the salary they had been paid in the private sector with the current salary paid by a social enterprise. When compared to previous employment, two informants were paid more, two were paid about the same and thirteen (74 per cent) were paid less. Informants were also asked to express the difference in their salaries as a percentage. Of those paid less, the average wage differential was 50 per cent and the range extended from 10 per cent to 90 per cent less: 'My salary is probably about 85 per cent of my salary beforehand. My total income, because my last bonus before I left was two and half times my salary, my total income was less than a third' (2FI). The wage differential identified in our study was greater than those found in previous studies in the non-profit sector. This could be explained by the distorting effect of very high salaries paid to employees in private-sector financial services, for example by investment banks. Although four of our informants reported that their previous remuneration was either more or equal to their current salary, the majority were paid less. Thus there is support for our first proposition.

Motivation

Informants were asked to explain, in as much detail as possible, why they had sought employment in a CDFI and to specifically elaborate on their views about their remuneration. We analyzed the transcripts and noted all comments that related to explanations for working for a social enterprise. In line with the motivation theories discussed earlier, we use the label 'extrinsic' for personal factors related to the nature of work, e.g. acquiring new knowledge and skills, doing challenging work tasks. 'In terms of skills, it was challenging' (13FI), and 'It's taught me a lot about banking that I never had to learn' (12MR). We label opportunities

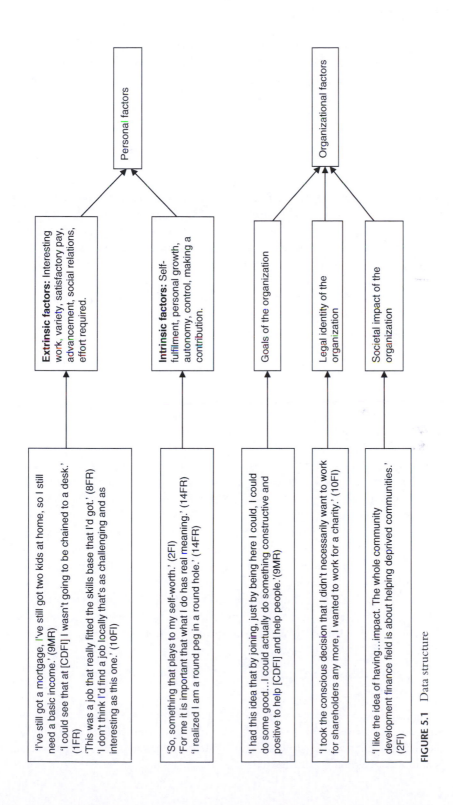

FIGURE 5.1 Data structure

for personal growth and personal feelings about work 'intrinsic', e.g. being in control at work, happiness, satisfaction. 'I was really excited by the prospect of, of the project, and I thought, yeah, I really want to do this' (3FR), and 'We all work in it because we believe what we are doing ... it is job satisfaction, whereas you work for some of the corporates and you don't necessarily get job satisfaction' (10FI).

Informants also referred to aspects of their employing organization, for example the non-profit status of the organization, the goals and values of their employer; and the impact that their employer had on society. Eight informants explicitly mentioned that they wanted to find work in the non-profit or voluntary sector. The reasons for doing so included finding a fit between their personal goals and the goals of the social enterprise. 'I figured out that I quite like being a banker, I just didn't like being that kind of banker. But I like working for an organization where we care about things, as opposed to just making money' (13FI). And, 'I had this idea that by joining, just by being here I could, I could do some good ... I could actually do something constructive and positive to help [CDFI] and help people' (9MR). Our informants were thus motivated by expectations about the benefits their employer would generate for themselves and for society. Thus there is support for our second proposition.

Altruism

When giving an account of their reasons for seeking employment in a social enterprise, informants used a variety of terms, phrases and expressions to explain their decisions. We found that all informants struggled to find words to articulate their reasons: they used phrases that alluded to their own personal goals and how their behaviour helped them achieve their goals, their support for the goals of their employer and what it was trying to do, and the contribution that their employer made to the general welfare of society.

Their reasoning indicates that the goals of the organization are aligned with the personal goals of the informant, i.e. they are socially motivated. When combined with accepting a lower wage, we interpreted this as evidence of altruism. Our data thus concurs with the findings of Mirvis and Hackett (1983) that employees in non-profit organizations find intrinsic rewards from the type of work and this is an incentive for employee motivation. Thus, when combined with a negative wage differential, there is some evidence to support proposition 3.

Employee satisfaction, engagement and psychological empowerment

In the second stage of analysis we reviewed the transcripts in relation to established theories related to motivation and job satisfaction (Barling *et al.* 2003; Bond and Bunce 2003), employee engagement (Vance 2006) and psychological empowerment (Thomas and Velthouse 1990; Spreitzer 1995).

Job satisfaction

Research in other sectors has found that employee job satisfaction is influenced by the extent to which work is interesting, i.e. work provides opportunities for training and learning, task variety, autonomy and control (Barling *et al.* 2003; Bond and Bunce 2003). In our study nine informants specifically mentioned that their work provided opportunities to learn; eight referred to their work as interesting, varied or challenging; five commented on having freedom at work, making their own choices and decisions, and working independently; and three mentioned having more control, for example over their workplace and managing their work–life balance.

Informants also described how their satisfaction with their current job would impact on their future career aspirations and had led to a preference to continue working for an organization that pursues social goals: 'It is very difficult for me to think of ever going back to a job that has no social dimension' (13FI). Thus, although not conclusive, this suggests that working for a social enterprise is associated with job satisfaction.

Employee engagement

High employee engagement is associated with opportunities to learn, meaningful work and opportunities for social interaction in the workplace (Vance 2006). In our data nine informants mentioned that their work was challenging, provided opportunities to learn new skills, and enhanced their own personal development; three informants described their work as meaningful; and seven talked positively about their relationships with colleagues. This suggests that, when compared with previous employment in the private sector, working for a social enterprise has greater potential for employee engagement.

Psychological empowerment

Previous research in other sectors has identified that psychological empowerment is associated with positive attitudes towards work. Psychological empowerment is a collective construct composed of meaningful work, competences, perceived autonomy at work and control over one's environment (Thomas and Velthouse 1990; Spreitzer 1995). In the interviews eight informants referred to alignment of their own values with those of their employer; ten commented on having the skills and ability to do their work; eight referred to freedom, autonomy and control; and two referred to being able to influence their work environment. The data suggest that for some employees, working for a social enterprise is associated with positive attitudes towards work.

Conclusion

This chapter has presented the results from a qualitative investigation into the remuneration and motivation of employees who work for CDFIs. On balance, our empirical data supports the proposition that employees in the financial services sector are paid less by a social enterprise than a private organization. However, the evidence does not present an uncontested account as four informants (16 per cent) earned either the same or more. This variation may be explained by the different types of financial services organizations (and hence remuneration policies) in which the informants were previously employed that included retail banks, investment banks and doorstep lenders. All informants were aware of the financial impact of their decision to work in a social enterprise and therefore this suggests that their decisions were both informed and intentional.

Our informants offered several explanations for accepting lower wages from which we identified two thematic categories. These categories relate to extrinsic and intrinsic factors noted in motivation theories; and the legal goals, identity and societal impact of their employer. The combination of negative wage differential and social value creation provides some evidence of the trade-off between monetary and non-monetary rewards. Thus we have demonstrated that our informants were aware that they accepted lower remuneration for their work and an important factor in their job choice was their desire to work for an organization that created benefits for society. We therefore tentatively conclude that informants' acceptance of lower wages in exchange for the opportunity to create social value is evidence of altruistic behaviour.

Our investigation also sheds light on the relationship between social enterprise employee motivation and job satisfaction. The alignment of goals between employer and employee has the potential to reduce conflict and thereby generate additional benefits in terms of reducing the need to put in place mechanisms to control and restrain employee behaviour. Thus, aspects of organizational stewardship, in which the interests of principals and agents are perfectly aligned, might be brought into our understanding of employee motivation.

Our study also has practical implications in that the high levels of job satisfaction reported by informants could be used to raise the skills levels of social enterprises through enhancing the attractiveness of careers in the non-profit sector to attract applicants with suitable financial experience to financial services social enterprises. Employees who rate job satisfaction more highly than other employment characteristics might also potentially be attracted by increasing the visibility of employment in social enterprise as a purposive choice for highly qualified individuals. Presenting CDFI employment in this context could facilitate the recruitment of highly qualified professionals from private sector financial services organizations into social enterprises and the non-profit sector more generally.

In the context of the post-2008 global economic crisis financial services organizations in the for-profit sector have been heavily criticized and this may lead employees to seek new employment in the value-driven social economy. Although these individuals may be attracted to CDFIs, there is no assurance that they are altruistically motivated. CDFIs would be well advised to ensure new employees share the values of the social enterprise and not those espoused by many elements of private sector financial service providers.

Our study has provided an in-depth view of the remuneration and motivation of a small group of CDFI employees and three avenues for research follow directly from our results. First, the findings could be used to design a questionnaire to survey remuneration and motivation in a larger sample of CDFI employees. This would enable the validity and reliability of the results to be tested. This might also be extended to survey remuneration and motivation of employees in a wider range of social enterprises, extending beyond financial services. This would need to be pilot-tested to ensure that the motivating factors were applicable to non-financial services social enterprises. The data could then be interrogated to determine the relationship between age, work experience, gender and remuneration and motivation.

A second stream of research would extend qualitative enquiry to examine the concept of social value. Although central to definitions of social enterprise, we still know little about how to define and measure social value. Content and process motivation theories distinguish between intrinsic and extrinsic motivation and we have found that satisfaction from working for a social enterprise combines both these motivations and goes further to include benefits that extend beyond the individual. Future studies could include firms in the private sector and the non-profit sector and investigate the relationship between legal status and perceived social value creation. The results would have practical benefits for the social enterprise sector in terms of designing appropriate recruitment policies and strategies.

Finally, building on the two themes, theory could be advanced by developing understanding about why and when employees elect to move from employment in the private sector to the non-profit sector. Does working in a social enterprise only become an option when individuals are financially secure and can afford to accept a lower wage? Or is choice based on the pursuit of job satisfaction that may arise from a working environment in which the goals of the individual are aligned with those of the organization? At what point does a negative wage differential become a constraint on recruitment and prevent individuals from accepting employment, and does this differ according to the financial status of the employee and the availability of alternative employment opportunities? Working for a social enterprise might be a very attractive and intrinsically rewarding opportunity, but perhaps only for those who can afford it.

References

ACEVO (2005) *Making a Difference*, Acevo remuneration survey 2005/06. London: ACEVO.

Adams, J. S. (1965) 'Inequity in social exchange', in Berkowitz, L. (ed.), *Advances in Experimental Psychology*. New York: Academic Press, pp. 267–99.

Alderfer, C. P. (1972) *Existence, Relatedness and Growth*. New York: Free Press.

Almond, S. and Kendall, J. (2001) 'Low pay in the UK: the case for a three sector comparative approach', *Annals of Public and Cooperative Economics*, 72(1): 45–76.

Barbian, J. (2001) 'The charitable worker', *Training*, 38(7): 50–5.

Barling, J., Kelloway, E. K. and Iverson, R. D. (2003) 'High quality work, job satisfaction and occupational injuries', *Journal of Applied Psychology*, 88(2): 276–83.

Barnard, C. (1938) *The Functions of the Executive.* Cambridge, MA: Cambridge University Press.

Benz, M. (2005) 'Not for profit, but for the satisfaction? Evidence on worker well-being in non-profit firms', *Kyklos*, 58(2): 155–76.

BIS (Department of Business, Innovation and Skills) (2010) *The National Evaluation of Community Development Finance Institutions (CDFIs): An Action-orientated Summary for the Sector.* London: Cabinet Office.

Bond, F. W. and Bunce, D. (2003) 'The role of acceptance and job control in mental health, job satisfaction and work performance', *Journal of Applied Psychology*, 88(6): 1057–67.

Borzaga, C. (2009) 'A comprehensive interpretation of voluntary and under-remunerated work', in S. Destefanis and M. Musella (eds), *Paid and Unpaid Labour in the Social Economy.* AIEL Series in Labour Economics, 11–32.

Borzaga, C. and Depredi, S. (2005) 'Interpersonal relations and job satisfaction: some empirical results in social and community care services', in B. Gui and R. Sugden (eds), *Economics and Social Interaction: Accounting for Interpersonal Relations.* Cambridge: Cambridge University Press, pp. 132–53.

Borzaga, C. and Tortia, E. (2006) 'Worker motivations, job satisfaction and loyalty in public and non-profit social services', *Non-profit and Voluntary Sector Quarterly*, 35: 225–48.

Cheverton, J. (2007) 'Holding our own: value and performance in non-profit organizations', *Australian Journal of Social Issues*, 42: 427–36.

Clark, M. (2009) *The Social Entrepreneur Revolution.* London: Marshall Cavendish.

Dearden-Phillips, C. (2008) *Your Chance to Change the World.* London: Directory of Social Change.

Doherty, B., Foster, G., Mason, C., Meehan, J., Meehan, K., Rotheroe, N. and Royce, M. (2009) *Management for Social Enterprise.* London: Sage.

Donegani, C. P., McKay, S. and Moro, D. (2012) 'A dimming of the "warm glow"? Are non-profit workers in the UK still more satisfied with their jobs than other workers?', Working Paper 74, ESRC Third Sector Research Centre.

Fehr, E. and Fischbacher, U. (2002) 'Why social preferences matter – the impact of non-selfish motives on competition, cooperation and incentives', *The Economic Journal*, 112: C1–C33.

Flick, U. (2002) *An Introduction to Qualitative Research.* London: Sage.

Fottler, M. D. (1981) 'Is management really generic?', *Academy of Management Review*, 6(1): 1–12.

Framjee, P. (2010) *The Tax Implications of Charity Trading.* London: ACEVO.

Frey, B. S. (1997a) 'On the relationship between intrinsic and extrinsic work motivation', *International Journal of Industrial Organization*, 15: 427–39.

Frey, B. S. (1997b) *Not Just for the Money: An Economic Theory of Personal Motivation.* Cheltenham: Edward Elgar.

Handy, F. and Katz, E. (1998) 'The wage differential between non-profit institutions and corporations: getting more by paying less?', *Journal of Comparative Economics*, 12: 246–61.

Hansmann, H. (1990) 'The role of non-profit enterprise', *Yale Law Review*, 89(5): 835–902.

Herzberg, F., Mausener, B. and Snyderman, B. B. (1959) *The Motivation to Work.* London: Wiley.

IFF (2005) *A Survey of Social Enterprises Across the UK.* London: Department of Trade and Industry.

Jensen, M. C. (1994) 'Self-interest, altruism, incentives and agency theory', *Journal of Applied Corporate Finance*, 7(2): 40–5.

Leete, L. (2000) 'Wage equity and employment motivation in non-profit and for-profit organizations', *Journal of Economic Behaviour and Organization*, 34: 423–46.

Leete, L. (2001) 'Whither the non-profit wage differential? Estimates from the 1990 Census', *Journal of Labor Economics*, 19(1): 136–71.

Light, P. (2002) 'The content of their character: the state of the non-profit worker', *Non-Profit Quarterly*, 9(3): 6–19.

Locke, E. A. (1976) 'The nature and causes of job satisfaction', in M. D. Dunette (ed.), *Handbook of Industrial and Organizational Psychology*. Chicago: Rand McNally, pp. 1297–349.

McGeehan, S. (2006) Community Development Finance Association. Private correspondence.

Margolis, H. (1982) *Selfishness, Altruism and Rationality*. Cambridge: Cambridge University Press.

Maslow, A. H. (1943) 'A theory of human motivation', *Psychological Review*, 50: 370–96.

Miles, M. B. and Huberman, A. M. (1994) *An Expanded Sourcebook: Qualitative Data Analysis*. London: Sage.

Mirvis, P. H. (1992) 'The quality of employment in the non-profit sector: An update on employee attitudes in non-profit versus business and government', *Non-Profit Management and Leadership*, 3(1): 23–41.

Mirvis, P. H. and Hackett, E. J. (1983) 'Work and work force characteristics in the non-profit sector', *Monthly Labor Review*, 106(4): 3–12.

Monroe, K. F. (1994) 'A fat lady in a corset: altruism and social theory', *American Journal of Political Science*, 38: 861–93.

Nyssens, M. (ed.) (2006) *Social Enterprise, At the Crossroads of Market, Public Policies and Civil Society*. Oxon: Routledge.

Oster, S. M. (1995) *Strategic Management for Non-profit Organizations: Theory and Cases*. Oxford: Oxford University Press.

OTS (2006) *Social Enterprise Action Plan: Scaling New Heights*. London: Office of the Third Sector.

Pearce, J. (2003) *Social Enterprise in Anytown*. London: Calouste Gulbenkian Foundation.

Perry, J. L. and Rainey, H. G. (1988) 'The public-private distinction in organization theory: a critique and research strategy', *Academy of Management Review*, 13(2): 182–201.

Phelps, E. S. (ed.) (1975) *Altruism, Morality, and Economic Theory*. New York: Russell Sage Foundation.

Piliavin, J. A. and Charng, H. W. (1990) 'Altruism: a review of recent theory and research', *Annual Review of Sociology*, 16: 27–65.

Porter, L. W. and Lawler, E. E. (1968) *Managerial Attitudes and Performance*. London: Irwin.

Preston, A. E. (1989) 'The non-profit worker in a for-profit world', *Journal of Labor Economics*, 7(4): 438–63.

Rose-Ackerman, S. (1996) 'Altruism, non-profits, and economic theory', *Journal of Economic Literature*, 34: 701–28.

Rose-Ackerman, S. (1997) 'Altruism, ideological entrepreneurs and the non-profit firm', *Voluntas*, 8(2): 120–34.

Ruhm, C. J. and Borkoski, C. (2001) 'Compensation in the non-profit sector', NBER Research Paper.

Rupert, P. (2004) *Wage and Employer Changes Over the Life Cycle*. Federal Reserve Bank of Cleveland.

SEC (2009) *State of Social Enterprise Survey 2009*. London: Social Enterprise Coalition.

SEC (2011) *Enjoy What You Do, Work in Social Enterprise*. London: Social Enterprise Coalition.

Spreitzer, G. M. (1995) 'Psychological empowerment in the workplace: dimensions, measurement and validation', *Academy of Management Journal*, 38(5): 1442–65.

Strauss, A. and Corbin, J. (1990) *Basics of Qualitative Research: Grounded Theory Procedures and Techniques*. Thousand Oaks, CA: Sage.

Thomas, K. W. and Velthouse, B. A. (1990) 'Cognitive elements of empowerment', *Academy of Management Review*, 15: 666–81.

Vance, R. J. (2006) *Employee Engagement and Commitment. A Guide to Understanding, Measuring and Increasing Engagement in your Organization*. Alexandria, VA: Society for Human Resources and Management Foundation.

Vroom, V. H. (1964) *Work and Motivation*. New York: John Wiley & Sons.

Weisbrod, B. A. (1983) 'Non-profit and proprietary sector behaviour: wage differentials among lawyers', *Journal of Labor Economics*, 1: 246–63.

6

WHEN SOCIAL ENTERPRISES DO IT BETTER

Efficiency and efficacy of work integration in Italian social cooperatives

Carlo Borzaga and Sara Depedri

Introduction

In market economies, where most income is derived through work, the labour market should guarantee the employment of all or at least of the largest number of job seekers. Instead, the labour market is characterized by some imperfections, informational asymmetries,[1] and rigidities, which impact upon the probability of being employed in general and especially affects people classified as disadvantaged. This last concept refers to all workers who are not able to guarantee productivity at least equal to the market wage and more specifically to vulnerable people (i.e. people with mental disorders or physical disabilities, but also people with low educational levels and poor social skills).

While a perfect labour market, by definition, should tend to efficiently exclude only those workers who do not deliver sufficient productivity in their work, market imperfections tend to fail to produce the required alignment. Due to informational asymmetries, firms tend to exclude many workers who are otherwise able to guarantee the expected level of efficiency at least in one job. In fact, firms frequently underestimate the real skills of workers who fall into the class of 'the disadvantaged'. Incomplete and asymmetric information makes worker selection a costly process (Spence 1974). With good levels of productivity and costs coverage achievable only in the long run and exposed to some risks (Ritzen 1991) firms should initially invest not only in training (Mincer 1991) but also in the selection process in order to overcome informational asymmetries concerning employees' abilities (Spence 1974). These costs are often reduced by adopting statistically discriminative practices based on easy-to-collect information (Borzaga *et al.* 1998). As a consequence, disadvantaged workers are often excluded from the labour market and this problem increases in periods of economic crisis and high unemployment rates.

Since the labour market does not have the tools to address the needs of disadvantaged workers, alternative solutions have been developed in several countries. They have taken – alternatively or concurrently – the form of public policies or of non-profit organizations. Public institutions have firstly aimed at defining the notion of 'disadvantage'.[2] With this conceptual definition in hand, public authorities thereafter developed policies aimed at facilitating the access of vulnerable people to employment: regulatory policies and 'quota systems', which oblige firms to employ vulnerable people; compensatory policies, by which the government provide firms with some money to cover part of the costs related to the underproductivity or the training of disadvantaged workers; substitutive policies, by which the government promotes directly the employment of vulnerable people in the public sector or in non-profit entities such as 'sheltered employment shops' or enterprises created ad hoc; and finally 'supported employment', which reassures the businesses that hire vulnerable people by providing a case worker to follow a disadvantaged employee and help the recipient achieve a normal degree of productivity. Given their high costs and their limited effectiveness, all of these state-based interventions have progressively declined over the years, with the result of excluding a significant swathe of disadvantaged persons from participating. This is why, alongside the decline of public policies, an alternative solution has been the emergence of private and independent work placement initiatives which have been totally self-financed or supported, to a certain extent, by public subsidies.

Both public policies and non-profit organizations have assumed different traits and managerial practices with regard to assisting the emergent needs of the disadvantaged in different countries. In this evolution, Italy represents an interesting example. Since the 1980s it has witnessed the emergence of a particular form of cooperative aimed primarily at employing disadvantaged workers: the so-called *work integration social cooperatives*. These organizations initially stemmed from groups of individuals who noticed and sought to address the shortfalls of public programs, especially toward those categories of people that at the time were not considered 'in need' by the normative definition of 'disadvantage': for instance, people with drug or alcohol abuse issues, immigrants, ex-convicts, people with a psychiatric disability, and youngsters with low levels of education. Italian legislation formally recognized these types of social cooperatives in 1991 with Law 381.[3] Since the introduction of this legislation, work integration social cooperatives have grown progressively in number and have, over time, developed complex and refined tools to achieve their mission of supporting training and skills development for vulnerable people, often giving them an opportunity to be subsequently employed in the open labour market.

As demonstrated by a large research project on 'The Socio-Economic Performance of Social Enterprises in the Field of Integration by Work' (named PERSE), which covered eleven European countries in 2001–04 in order to measure the social and economic performance of work integration social enterprises, organizational types similar to the Italian work integration social cooperatives have emerged over the years in different countries, including a variety of organizational models for work integration. National policies have progressively recognized and supported these models in different ways. Nevertheless, deeper knowledge of the efficiency of work integration objectives in social enterprises is still lacking, especially when compared to other policies of income support or work integration of vulnerable people geared towards for-profit enterprises or delivered via public agencies. In the light of these limitations, the evaluation of the efficiency and the efficacy of work integration is particularly interesting and especially important when public funding is significantly decreasing.

This chapter seeks to propose a comprehensive and multi-step model of interpreting the advantages of work integration social enterprises (WISEs hereafter) by investigating the Italian experience, where the organizational model assured the legal form of social cooperatives (WISCs, hereafter). In order to understand the main traits that distinguish the Italian model of WISCs from other European experiences of work integration by private institutions, the chapter begins with a short presentation of the evolution of Italian WISCs in the legal system and in their management. The second section then presents the first stage of the evaluation of WISCs, which consists of the quantitative analysis of the phenomenon and the WISCs' advantages. The third section represents the core of the evaluation since it assesses the efficiency of WISCs and of their practices by implementing a comparison between costs and benefits for the public administration generated by the integration of vulnerable people into social cooperatives. The chapter will therefore help students and researchers define the guidelines to be followed when conducting an evaluation of the WISCs' activity, but will also allow the identification of the main traits that set them apart from other solutions adopted in other countries both in and outside of Europe.

The Italian experience

The presence of WISEs is today quite widespread over many countries. The recent contributions of the EMES Network (European Research Network on 'the emergence of social enterprises in Europe') have defined three main types of WISEs that have been developed in Europe (Nyssens 2006): (i) institutions that use productive activities as secondary outcomes to the main aim of supplying vulnerable people social, rather than worker, integration opportunities; disadvantaged workers are often not paid, but they are assigned public benefits and subsidies, and the percentage of disadvantaged workers to the total is very high; (ii) enterprises that principally produce some goods and services for the public administration at prices over the market level or are partially subsidized by public contributions, so that the government indirectly supports the expenses of the social enterprise for the training and the integration of the vulnerable person; in these enterprises, disadvantaged workers are usually paid regular salaries and offered regular open-ended contracts; (iii) enterprises that deliver their goods and services on the ordinary market, by selling them at market prices to citizens, other firms, or the public administration; these social enterprises therefore are more similar to ordinary firms than type (i) and (ii) described, while they have an explicit social aim; they are sometimes awarded temporary subsidies in order to cover most of the expenses for the integration process; disadvantaged workers are supplied regular salaries and offered concrete opportunities to have access to the open labour market; disadvantaged workers usually do not represent a very high percentage of people employed by the organization.

The descriptions of the three models clearly show that the last is the most innovative one, since these organizations emerged as bottom-up phenomena thanks to the self-organization of citizens, they are quite autonomous, and their activities can be aligned with that of ordinary enterprises. Furthermore, they supply concrete job opportunities to their disadvantaged workers, some of them providing transitory employment in the social enterprise, while others applying an inclusive model that supplies disadvantaged workers with a permanent job in the organization.

Italy is one of the countries in which this third innovative model has developed. Moreover, Italy distinguishes itself as one of the countries where private alternative work placement initiatives emerged initially and have come to be characterized by some specific traits and practices. Starting in the 1980s, groups of people – volunteers or relatives of disadvantaged people – began establishing initiatives for employing vulnerable people, often taking the legal form of cooperatives. The government recognized these organizations with Law 381 promulgated in 1991, which institutionalizes these 'social cooperatives' and explicitly distinguishes them into two types: one type, denominated 'A-type' social cooperatives, are devoted to the production of general interest services (i.e. education, healthcare services, social services etc.), while another type, 'B-type' social cooperatives, provide work integration services for disadvantaged workers.

Law 381 provides some overarching rules that 'B-type' social cooperatives (WISCs) must abide by. First, they are required to have 30 per cent of the entire workforce composed of disadvantaged persons as defined by the law. The definition of disadvantaged workers is quite broad in comparison to previous (but also to other international) definitions, since it also includes people with physical and sensorial disadvantages, people with mental disorders and psychiatric problems, drug-addicts, people suffering with alcoholism, convicts and ex-convicts who qualify for alternative solutions to prison, and young people with family problems. Second, disadvantaged workers must be ensured a wage and also a contractual relationship that follows the normal rules in force for ordinary workers. Third, the law requires that disadvantaged workers be made members of the cooperative (barring a few exceptions). At the same time, the law ensures WISCs some flexibility and support, since it allows them to conduct any activity in any industry, with the exception of services provided by A-type social cooperatives. It also ensures WISCs some financial benefits and specifically exonerates them from the payment of some corporate taxes, payroll taxes and social security costs for each disadvantaged employee.[4] Moreover, it leaves WISCs the freedom to choose their objectives, and specifically to decide how they aim to re-integrate disadvantaged workers back into the open labour market rather than keeping them perpetually in the social cooperative. Finally, Law 381 ensures easier access to public tenders, although this channel has not been pursued much to date.

Italian national legislation also gives some space to the autonomous action of the regions, which can individually provide for specific regulations and policies. In this regard, an interesting case is that of the province of Trento, where the Local Employment Agency has for twenty years now been promoting specific measures for the work integration needs of vulnerable people. The province of Trento, in particular, provides for additional economic support to WISCs, which is ensured thanks to two tools: the availability of individual additional subsidies for the first two years of employment of disadvantaged workers in the cooperative, and a general subsidy to social cooperatives for the training of their tutors and for their investments in new products and procedures.

The question remains: are these new strategies of work integration a good solution *per se* and how do they compare to the public solutions tried in the past? Up till now very few studies have thoroughly investigated this topic and evaluated the efficiency and effectiveness of the activities conducted by WISCs. A summary of these investigations is presented next.

The social cooperative model: dimensions of the phenomena and winning traits

The evaluation of the potential of social cooperatives can be firstly assessed by looking to the general characteristics of the phenomena and of the organizations themselves. With regard to the former, the evaluation must quantify the relevance of the institution by describing its dimensions and the typologies of workers to whom the activity is devoted. With regard to the identification of the winning traits and the fallacies of organizations, the evaluation must propose indexes of the quality of the work integration process, its effects, technologies adopted, and the stability of organizations.

In this phase, diverse statistical sources can provide data for evaluation: national data collected by the National Institutes of Statistics, surveys carried out on representative samples at national level by collecting data directly from the social cooperatives, and interviews and data collected on subsamples of areas where the phenomena is particularly relevant. Taken together, these investigations help to provide an evaluation of the phenomena involved and have therefore also been used in order to depict the Italian WISC model.[5] It therefore can be firstly claimed that the phenomenon of WISCs is well developed in Italy and continues to increase both in number and people involved. According to the census conducted by the National Institute of Statistics (ISTAT) in 2005, there were 2,419 active WISCs in Italy and their growth has been quite regular from their beginnings in the 1980s, and especially after the approval of Law 381 in 1991.

Cooperation in the field of work integration is also relevant for its impact on employment: in 2005, there were around 85,000 employees in WISCs, 54,000 of whom were ordinary employees and over 30,000 of whom were disadvantaged workers. The average number of disadvantaged workers in these WISCs was thirteen and has gone well above the 30 per cent ratio of disadvantaged to ordinary employees

required by the law, although it has not become so high that WISCs can be likened to sheltered workshops. WISCs are mostly small- to medium-sized firms: 43 per cent of them employ between 15 and 50 ordinary employees, and 26.7 per cent have fewer than 15 workers; however, 30.2 per cent have more than 50 ordinary employees involved in their activity. Volunteerism is also a very important resource available to more than 60 per cent of WISCs.

As provided by the law, WISCs can develop in diverse sectors of activity, but competition with other organizational forms (especially for-profit firms) and the type of disadvantages of their workers tends to find them specializing in sectors that are characterized by relatively simple production processes, rather than those sectors that specialize in the development of high-skill and more competitive areas. The main activity for 50 per cent of the operating cooperatives was related to landscaping, 37.8 per cent were involved in maintenance and cleaning services, and 33.3 per cent were environmental services and garbage collection businesses.

While the presented data help in understanding the dimension of the phenomenon, other important traits and levers of efficiency and effectiveness of WISCs emerge by looking to diverse surveys and can be sketched in the following inventories.

Indexes of evaluation of the WISCs themselves

1. A first index for evaluating WISCs is their level of autonomy. In turn, this index can be firstly approximated by the characteristics of the actors promoting the organization. Italian WISCs are clearly a 'bottom-up' phenomenon; for the most part they are created by groups of people with shared ideals and values (60 per cent), and it is also quite common for cooperatives to 'spawn' new organizations, whereas the cooperatives that are promoted by the public authorities are a minority of the total, as are organizations created by persons seeking employment.
2. As a second lever of autonomy, WISCs demonstrate that they are quite open to the market, since revenues from private sales represent more than 50 per cent of the total while the majority of contracts with public authorities and public funding are awarded as a result of RFPs[6] or other bidding processes where often WISCs are competing with private businesses, thereby requiring the same levels of efficiency and quality assurance of conventional enterprises.
3. WISCs can be also evaluated for their economic health; a majority (over 70 per cent) of them have active balance sheets and the average values of production tend to increase over the course of the years (the average value of production increased from 515,200 Euro in 2003 to 559,600 Euro in 2005).

Indexes of evaluation of the WISCs' social dimension

1. The first question when looking at the social dimension of WISCs is the type of disadvantaged people they employ. The data show the presence of both

workers certified as disadvantaged by public services and supported by the social security costs exemption, and other classes of disadvantaged workers, whose disadvantages are not recognized by law and for whom cooperatives are not subsidized. Specifically, WISCs help primarily those with psychological and physical disabilities (46.3 per cent in total), but the percentage of substance abuse victims is also high (16 per cent) as are other forms of disabilities (15 per cent). The presence of disadvantaged workers who do not fit within the definition of disadvantage given by the law and do not qualify for public subsidies to their host is not marginal: long-term unemployed workers (3.8 per cent) or persons with disabilities not recognized by law (5.2 per cent), young people with disadvantages on the labour market (11.7 per cent), immigrants (6.1 per cent), women who had previously exited the workforce, and persons with low levels of education are involved.

2. WISCs also show a quite balanced distribution along gender lines within the disadvantaged persons population employed in cooperatives (56.4 per cent male versus 43.6 per cent female), although the presence of males is higher in some regions and with regard to some disadvantaged groups.

3. The quality of the job provided to disadvantaged workers can be firstly tested in terms of contractual relationships. The surveys demonstrate that a majority of disadvantaged workers (74 per cent) have open-ended contracts, regardless of the fact that part of the cooperatives' mission is to eventually place their disadvantaged workers on the open labour market. The use of flexible work hours, however, is very common, since half of the population of disadvantaged workers (and mostly people with severe mental disorders) is employed on part-time contracts.

4. The quality of training programmes is verified by the formal and structured path towards employment placement that social cooperatives have progressively created by developing a range of methodologies and skills. The most widely used are individual programmes assessing the evolution of the disadvantaged workers' abilities,[7] which entails the definition of *ad personam* paths to employment for each person in a disadvantaged situation and which are implemented in 81 per cent of WISCs interviewed.

5. The determining factor in the cooperative's success is, however, the presence of ordinary employees with the specific task of supporting the training and education of disadvantaged workers and shadowing and working together with them. Tutors, who concern themselves with supporting the employees in their working routines, are present in the majority of social cooperatives (78 per cent) and the social coordinator, who plans the individual placement of disadvantaged workers, in a high percentage of WISCs (56 per cent).

The data discussed herein therefore confirm that the strategies of continuing training put into practice by these social cooperatives are well structured, specialized and formalized. They can be considered an innovative tool for work integration, developed from the bottom-up.

Indexes of evaluation of the WISCs' ability in creating job opportunities

1. The first index to evaluate the WISCs' efficacy in job placement is their sensibility to the creation of real job opportunities for their disadvantaged workers, as stated by their mission. The national surveys show that the majority of WISCs (52.2 per cent) are open to placement possibilities both inside and outside the organization after the training period and after a concrete evaluation of the worker's skill and disabilities. Additionally, 30 per cent of the organizations declare that their principle objective is to employ their disadvantaged workers indefinitely, while only 17.8 per cent hire them only temporarily in order to find them suitable employment on the open labour market.

2. From theory to fact, the second index to be estimated is the outcomes achieved by WISCs in terms of success of training and work integration. The local surveys show that of the individuals who engaged with the WISCs in 2006, a large majority had concluded their individual training programmes, whereas one out of every four workers had interrupted their training prior to its completion. Data also confirm the ability of WISCs to find opportunities for their disadvantaged workers on the open labour market: among those who completed their programme in 2007, a stunning 64.5 per cent found work outside of the cooperative, for the most part employed by ordinary firms operating in a broad variety of businesses, and only occasionally by other cooperatives or public agencies (in 14 out of 252 cases). Nonetheless, 25.6 per cent of the total (i.e. 139 disadvantaged persons) were still unemployed.

Although positive, the data show that WISCs have still not reached their full potential: the definition of tools for outside placement is still in its initial stages, not least because public policies regarding the matter are still unclear, confusing and generally weak.

Indexes of evaluation of the WISCs in terms of wellbeing and personal growth

1. The effectiveness of the work integration process must also be evaluated by investigating the wellbeing achieved by vulnerable people after their experience in the social cooperatives.[8] The research carried out in the province of Trento collected data on the psychological perceptions of 54 people with diverse types of disadvantages integrated into social cooperatives. The first dimension of wellbeing is that related to the psychological dimensions. The analysis depicts an overall positive picture. People display a high level of self-reliance, they have the necessary resources to manage unforeseen situations and issues at work, and they are able to find solutions to the problems that might arise from time to time. The psychological wellbeing of people interviewed is positive, they perceive themselves to be succeeding; they trust in their abilities and feel happy with their life.

2. The specific dimension of skills development can be investigated in the same way and also reveals positive results. The persons interviewed perceive that the training programme within the social cooperatives has helped them to improve their abilities, especially relationship abilities. They have confidence in their training and preparedness, and in their ability to achieve their goals; they are satisfied with their performance at work since they consider it to be up to the expectations of their cooperative, and declare that they are able to focus on the tasks assigned to them. Their engagement within the workplace is also positive overall, especially in terms of enthusiasm and commitment to their work. Moreover, they found that the social cooperative was characterized by fair procedures and high sensibility to the problems of disadvantaged workers and they felt a high level of support within the workplace. Finally, one of the key objectives of work integration is to foster motivation to continue working. By this metric, these initiatives have been very successful: 87 per cent of those polled declared that they are highly motivated to continue working and they are willing to make the sacrifices necessary to keep their position, and indicated this as one of their most important objectives.

The evaluation of the social cooperative model: efficiency

While the previous section of this chapter has allowed an evaluation of the traits, advantages and some general indexes of the performance of WISCs, the most interesting and maybe difficult level of the evaluation analysis is in modelling the economic efficiency of these organizations. A first and very simple attempt to evaluate the socio-economic performance of work integration social enterprises was conducted by the already-mentioned PERSE project. However, the project had the limitation of indexing economic performance only in terms of monetary and non-monetary resources mobilized by the organizations. By looking mainly at the proportion of income driven by private donations and revenues, the analysis could only make claims as to the level of market-orientation or the dependency of work integration social enterprises on public programmes in different countries (see Vidal and Claver 2004 for Spain; O'Hara and O'Shaughnessy 2004 for Ireland; Spear 2002 for the United Kingdom; Davister et al. 2004 for a general description of the European Union).

A different and interesting approach to the evaluation of the economic dimension of the activity of social enterprises was developed by calculating the Social Return of Investments (SROI index; see Emerson et al. 2000). It represents a measure of the socio-economic impact of a social activity, and has the advantage of accounting for the positive economic consequences generated by the externalization of services from public sector programmes to social enterprises. It therefore represents a valid index for assessing the net returns of government investment in public service programmes. The application of SROI has been particularly interesting in the pilot programme undertaken through Social Economy in Scotland. The programme demonstrates that each investment by the government made to support work integration social enterprises produces cost savings in mental health and support services and welfare benefits, in addition to reductions in employment benefit payments and increases in income tax revenue (Durie and Wilson 2007; NEF 2010). In Italy the model has, to date, only been applied to social enterprises supplying social services (Manetti 2010).

A similar method for estimating the net economic impact of Italian work integration social enterprises was sketched out by Marocchi (1999), with the model being significantly improved by Chiaf (2012). The model assumes that the efficiency of work integration in social cooperatives must be estimated by comparing the costs and revenues produced for the public administration by WISCs, with costs and revenues of alternative public policies supporting vulnerable people, if unemployed, both economically and with social services. The analysis thus monitors the net benefit or costs (i.e. when costs override revenues) of the decision of governments to support work integration activity by social cooperatives instead of supporting the same people otherwise.[9] In other words, since the evaluation takes into exclusive consideration the cost and revenues of engaging in work integration activity, the results can be said to represent the efficiency of the policy. The model has been applied with success in a northern Italian province (Chiaf 2012).

The current chapter introduces the results of an investigation carried out by Euricse (European Research Institute on Cooperative and Social Enterprises) in 2011 by amending the abovementioned evaluation model (Depedri 2013). The model has been implemented on a sample of ten social cooperatives and 194 disadvantaged workers in the province of Trento in Italy. The province is characterized by attentive labour policies towards vulnerable people. Specifically, the local public Employment Agency (Agenzia del lavoro) supports the employment of vulnerable people in social cooperatives by providing them with subsidies in addition to the tax exemptions and other benefits provided by the national law. It therefore becomes of particular interest to understanding whether the policy accomplished by the local employment agency is only a source of net, although socially relevant, public expenditures, or whether it allows public organizations to save money thanks to the decrease in other public spending (e.g. lower services provision to vulnerable people, lower monetary transfers for ensuring them a minimum income). In order to collect the data, some questionnaires were administered to the social cooperatives and to the public programmes supplying services to vulnerable people, by collecting economic information on all the individual incomings and outgoings of WISCs, on their budgets, and on the expenses of all the alternative or additional public programmes.

The economic efficiency of work integration is calculated here as the difference between the revenues that it ensures to public-sector coffers and the costs it implies.[10] Therefore, the estimation of the net benefit must consider the different sources of increasing and decreasing costs that public sector programmes incur when supporting WISCs.[11] These sources of revenues and costs must be split in two dimensions. By looking to the *exchange dimension* we can distinguish between transfers, costs and revenues generated at the organizational level and at the level of the individual worker. By looking to *the type of transfer*, we must distinguish between real monetary transfers from public programmes to the cooperative and from the cooperative to the public coffers, and the implicit costs to and savings for the public sector related to lower usage of public social services and lower monetary transfers to vulnerable people for their socio-economic protection. We now look more closely at this model.

Following Table 6.1 Part I, one must consider that some financial transfers from public service programmes to social cooperatives, and from social cooperatives to the state, emerge at the firm level. As regards to monetary transfers, the social cooperative pays taxes on the added value of its production to government (which is only calculated for the quota produced by disadvantaged workers employed in the cooperative). We register this amount with a positive sign – or in accounting terms, as a 'credit' in the government's ledger – since it is revenue for the public sector. On the other hand, WISCs are granted subsidies by both the local employment agency and the government, and these represent costs for the public sector, which are represented by a negative sign in the calculation (or as a 'debit' in the government's ledger books). At the same time, due to national legislation, as we have already pointed out, social cooperatives enjoy some tax exemptions and tax benefits, which represent lost revenues for the public sector (again, entered as a negative sign).

TABLE 6.1 Evaluation of costs (−) and benefits (+) for public services (values in Euros)

PART I – benefits and costs at organizational level

	Average per year per cooperative (Euros)
+ VAT created from disadvantaged workers	+ 51,077
− Tax free, tax benefits, and fiscal advantages	− 21,718
− Subsidies received from the local agency	− 85,400
− Subsidies received from government	− 3,655

PART II – benefits and costs at individual level

	Average per year per worker (Euros)
+ Taxes paid to the cost of labour	+ 308
+ Lower disability pension (where only 18 per cent of people received it before and only three workers lost it after)	+ 38 (8,320 per person per year)
+ No minimum income/unemployment subsidies (where about 60 per cent of people received them before)	+ 2,149 (max. 6,720 per person per year)
+ Less social and healthcare services	+ 33,200
− Tax free, tax benefits, other fiscal advantages	− 538
− Subsidies per worker by the agency	− 2,392
− Subsidies per worker by government	0

Source: Survey for the Public Agency of Employment, Trento.

Following Table 6.1 Part II, at the individual level (i.e. for each disadvantaged worker employed by the social cooperative through the programme of the local employment agency), the model firstly registers monetary transfers: the payment by the social cooperative of some taxes on the disadvantaged workers' wage (which represents a positive revenue for the public sector); and the subsidies granted by the state and the local Employment Agency to the cooperative for each worker employed (with a negative sign for the public sector). Furthermore, the model registers the state's non-payment of disability pensions, minimum-wage incomes, and unemployment subsidies with a positive sign (these represent state expenditures that would have otherwise been provided to the worker if he or she had not been working). Finally, the public sector registers a decrease in the cost of social, health-care and educational services provided to vulnerable people thanks to the improvement of their health and autonomy (which is, again, a positive sign for the public sector); at the same time, Law 381 provides tax exemptions on individual payments by social cooperatives that can be seen as constituting lost revenue for the public sector (entered with a negative sign in the model).

Data for the application of this model have been collected from three different sources: (1) at the firm level, data on annual accounts, revenues and all monetary exchanges with the public sector; (2) at the individual level, data related to the contractual relationship with the social cooperative and to the public subsidies received for each disadvantaged worker (from information supplied by the WISCs); and (3) again at the individual level, data related to disadvantaged workers' changing recourse to public social and healthcare services, collected by asking each provider of the various public programmes.

The model distinguishes the net benefit at the organizational level and at the individual level as previously described (Table 6.1 Part I and Part II). At the organizational level, the subsidies received by the ten WISCs we surveyed, both from the government and the local employment agency,[12] were quite high, especially in comparison to the taxes paid by each WISC.[13] By summing up all costs and benefits at the firm level, we find that, on average, each year WISCs receive a net monetary transfer from the public sector. However, this was not the case for all WISCs in our sample, since some of them provide – also at the first step of the analysis – higher benefits to the public sector in the form of cost savings when compared to what they received in terms of subsidies and tax exemptions.

When moving to the individual level, we calculate average revenues and costs for each of the 194 disadvantaged workers employed by the cooperatives interviewed. The analysis shows that the money saved by the public sector thanks to the lower money transfers to these vulnerable people employed by WISCs is only partially balanced by subsidies granted to the cooperatives per worker employed. Moreover, we calculated the decreasing costs for the public sector of providing social and healthcare services guaranteed by the better health and the higher social inclusion of disadvantaged workers. By summing up all costs and benefits at the individual level, then, the public sector achieves quite a high net benefit. By dividing the net benefit at the firm level by the number of disadvantaged workers employed in each year and summing it up to the individual net saving, we obtain the total net savings for the public sector. We have found this amount to be a savings of 6,000 Euros per disadvantaged worker per year. This means that in a period of three years, which represents the medium-run for the training process in the social cooperative, the total WISCs considered have produced a net benefit for the public sector of 4 million Euros. Although this result is significantly influenced by the high costs savings generated by the work integration of prisoners (which decreases costs to the public sector by around 35,000 Euros per year), the data shows that the work integration programmes by social cooperatives are highly efficient.

Furthermore, it is possible to calculate the long-term efficiency of the policy by assuming that: (1) people who are still employed (in the cooperative or in another firm) after three years at the end of the training programme have a high probability of holding onto their jobs in the future years, even up to their retirement; (2) people with mental disorders tend to retire at an estimated age of 52 (instead of 65) mainly due to health problems; (3) the evolution of recourse to social and healthcare services will follow different trends, with the probability of seeing a decrease in requests for assistance from people with addiction problems, as well a stability for people with mental and physical disadvantages. By adapting the model to these assumptions, we can also calculate the long-term effects of work integration practices in social cooperatives. For instance, according to our calculations, since at the end of the three years (nine years for the mentally disadvantaged) the number of vulnerable people who were still employed was 111 of the 194 initially integrated in the cooperatives, the net total gain for the public sector can be estimated to be more than 15 million Euros, which means 118,000 Euros on average for each person subsequently employed in the open labour market, and 97,000 Euros for each person maintaining his or her job in the social cooperative.

In order to verify if the positive results achieved by our investigation in the province of Trento are confirmed in other provinces and regions, we replicated the investigation by adopting the same methodology in the province of Venice. Since in this case subsidies from local authorities to these WISCs are significantly lower (or non-existent in some cases), the net benefits for public service programmes is even higher, equalling 7,500 Euros per year per disadvantaged worker on average. Our results offer a lower cost savings for the state than in the case of the province of Trento due to lower taxes on the value added paid by the cooperatives in the province of Venice. On a related note, it is interesting to point out that while, as in the case of Trento province, public programmes tend to grant WISCs higher subsidies, the cooperatives can invest more in training to increase the workers' productivity; in the provinces in which social cooperatives receive lower subsidies their organizational investments tend also to be lower, their added value generated tends to be lower, and thus they pay less tax.

Conclusions

Over the past twenty years, work integration social enterprises have increasingly become a solution to the issues of work placement of vulnerable persons. In this scenario, Italy is characterized as a country in which the phenomenon of WISCs can be considered – we can assert after this investigation – as a model of best practice. The peculiarities that make this model successful derive from both the way in which they are regulated and the work integration tools they have developed. First, WISCs are clearly distinguished from sheltered employment shops, given that these social cooperatives are mandated to hire a significant percentage of disadvantaged workers, but not so high as to compromise their viability as a business. Moreover, WISCs are required to remunerate disadvantaged workers fairly and must meet regular Italian contractual employment standards. Second, they are free to refine their business and job strategies by taking into account the characteristics of each worker, since the law neither encourages the permanent integration of these workers within the cooperative structure nor obliges only temporary employment. Moreover, the business model has been improved over the years by social cooperatives themselves, who have progressively developed specific tools and professional work profiles with the effect of creating what is truly a holistic 'work integration technology'.

This chapter has empirically demonstrated how the phenomenon of WISCs has evolved not only in term of the number of people it touches, but also in terms of the economic stability of these firms, the efficacy of the tools used to make their work integration processes more effective, and of the categories of vulnerable people employed. The chapter has also investigated the efficiency of Italian WISCs through a comprehensive cost-benefit analysis, which also included the cost savings guaranteed to the public sector from the fact that disadvantaged workers employed by WISCs are much less likely to seek out the assistance of healthcare and social public services. The data we have collected and analyzed have come to demonstrate that WISCs indeed represent an efficient solution for work integration public policies since public programmes and institutions gain a net cost savings from the employment of vulnerable people in these organizations. These positive results even hold, we have found, when taking into account the provisioning of specific subsides to WISCs on the part of the public sector and local public agencies.

Based on these findings, we can state conclusively that work integration for vulnerable people cannot be solely, or even mainly, the purview of public service programmes and policies. On the contrary, social enterprises with clear objectives and well organized integration programmes can obtain better results, be more efficient and, more importantly, more effective than most government programmes. Establishing the work integration of vulnerable people is not necessarily a cost, as it is frequently considered, but a net advantage for society, although this result does depends on the way in which the activity is organized.

Notes

1 Informational asymmetries on the labour market mainly concern the incapacity of organizations to evaluate the real skills and the potential productivity of candidates during the selection process of new employees. However, informational asymmetries can also affect potential employees since they are not able to collect all information about the job proposed and the employer/organization during the selection process.

2 Over the course of time, the definition of 'disadvantage' has changed, mostly as a result of the progressive rise of the minimum qualifications required to be employed, and also because of the cultural bias towards persons who have trouble accessing the labour market. Specifically, the notion of disadvantage has evolved from being considered complete and definitive (as well described by the terms 'invalid' or 'disabled') to emphasizing different abilities, or different levels of ability (the concept of 'otherwise able') thereby allowing for the possibility that, by fulfilling each person's individual abilities, most, if not all, will have a chance at being employed. Therefore policies towards the disadvantaged have changed, and have progressively started to focus on developing the individuals' skills to their fullest potential.

3 The law establishes two types of social cooperatives, which are distinguished by their activity and thus are quite specialized. A-type social cooperatives can only provide for social interest services, included education, healthcare services, and other general services for vulnerable people (disabled people, the elderly, young people, immigrants, etc.). B-type social cooperatives can produce in any sector of activity, while training and employing disadvantaged workers. Hereafter, B-type social cooperatives will be defined by their services and thus will be called *work integration social cooperatives* (WISCs).

4 It is important to consider that social security costs amount in Italy to more than 33 per cent of the gross wage.

5 First, the following data will evaluate the dimension of the phenomena by presenting the results of the national census on social cooperatives conducted by the National Institute of Statistics (ISTAT) in 2001 and 2005. Second, some data will refer to a survey (given the name 'ICSI2007 – Investigation on Italian Social Cooperatives') carried out by the Universities of Trento, Bergamo, Brescia, Milano Bicocca, Federico II di Napoli and Reggio Calabria, within the context of a broader Ministerial Research Project (Prin2004) and with additional funding supplied by the Cariplo Foundation. The research was carried out in 2006 on a sample statistically representative at national level and collected data on 99 WISCs; also 900 'ordinary' employees took part in the survey. As a third source of data, a local survey (given the name 'Euricse2009') was conducted by Euricse – thanks to funding and support from Confcooperative–Federsocietà – involving a sample of 127 WISCs operating in the northern provinces of Trento and Brescia, and in the region of Veneto.

6 Request For Proposals.

7 This is carried out via a document where the individual's characteristics are precisely evaluated. The aims of these assessments are to use them to find the best employment match for the worker in terms of the worker's professional role (i.e. in terms of maximizing his or her social, work and professional skills).

8 Few investigations have been conducted on this topic to date, although a huge literature exists on the psychological evolution, on self-perception, on relational abilities, and on the social status of people with mental disorders and disabilities (Boardman *et al.* 2003). One study on the psychological effects of work integration in social cooperatives in Canada and Italy (results on the Italian case published in Zaniboni *et al.* 2011) investigated people with mental disorders and psychiatric problems – the hardest to employ. The authors concluded that most of the workers interviewed displayed high levels of occupational self-efficacy, work productivity and work engagement; they perceived a high level of social support by the members of the cooperative and their symptoms typically decreased over time.

9 It is not the aim of the research to compare WISCs to the integration of vulnerable people in for-profit organizations, since in this case we cannot assume similar training programmes and outcomes for the disadvantaged person.

10 It is exactly the same as estimating the net benefit or the decrease in the waste of public resources ensured by the policy.

11 In this model we do not totally consider the social advantages generated by the work integration of vulnerable people, like for example the decreasing risks of criminal activities and the benefits and decreasing costs for the vulnerable person's family. Therefore, while

complete in the evaluation of economic efficiency, the model is still limited in the real calculation of total advantages.

12 These subsidies provided at the firm level are ensured for the training programmes and the employment of some tutors and professionals.

13 The total amount of taxes that the social cooperative must pay to the government, proportional to its added value, is calculated on the number of hours worked by each individual disadvantaged worker in comparison to all worked hours in the cooperative. This methodology ensures that the part of the taxes calculated only concerns the disadvantaged workers and is not related to the significant presence of ordinary workers employed in the organization and influencing the productivity level.

References

Boardman J., Grove B., Perkins R. and Shepherd G. (2003) 'Work and employment for people with psychiatric disabilities', *The British Journal of Psychiatry*, 182: 467–8.

Borzaga C., Gui, B. and Povinelli, F. (1998) 'Le role des enterprises d'insertion sur le marché du travail: L'éclairage d'une analyse économique', in Defourny, J. and Favreau, L. (a cura di), *Insertion et nouvelle économie sociale. Un bilan international.* Paris: Desclée de Brouwer, pp. 309–16.

Chiaf, E. (2012) 'The evaluation of Work Integration Social Enterprises (WISEs) as social innovation', in Nicholls, A. and Murdock, A. (a cura di), *Social Innovation: Blurring Sector Boundaries and Challenging Institutional Arrangements.* Oxford: Palgrave Macmillan.

Davister, C., Defourny, J. and Gregoire, O. (2004) 'Work integration social enterprises in the European Union: an overview for existing models', EMES Working Papers, no. 04/04.

Depedri, S. (ed.) (2013) *L'inclusione efficiente: L'esperienza delle cooperative sociali di inserimento lavorativo.* Milan: Franco Angeli.

Durie, S. and Wilson, L. (2007) *Six Mary's Place, Social Return on Investment Report*, no. 1, commissioned by Social Economy Scotland – the Equal Development Partnership, Edinburgh.

Emerson, J., Wachowicz, J. and Chun, S. (2000) *Social Return on Investment: Exploring Aspects of Value Creation in the Nonprofit Sector.* San Francisco: REDF.

Manetti, G. (2010) 'La misurazione dell'impatto socio-economico delle imprese sociali beneficiarie di esternalizzazione di servizi da parte della pubblica amministrazioni: il modello della Social Return on Investment (SROI) Analysis', *Azienda Pubblica*, 4: 529–51.

Marocchi, G. (1999) *Integrazione lavorativa, impresa sociale, sviluppo locale.* Milan: Franco Angeli.

Mincer, J. (1991) 'Job training: costs, returns and wage profiles', in Stern, D. and Ritzen, J. M. M. (eds), *Market Failure in Training? New Economic Analysis and Evidence on Training of Adult Employees.* Berlin: Springler-Verlag, pp. 61–98.

NEF (new economics foundation) (2010) *Grounded – A New Approach to Evaluating Runway 3.* London: new economics foundation publishing.

Nyssens, M. (2006) *Social Enterprise at the Crossroads of Market, Public Policies and Civil Society.* New York and London: Routledge.

O'Hara, P. and O'Shaughnessy, M. (2004) 'Work integration social enterprises in Ireland', EMES Working Papers, no. 04/05.

Ritzen, J. M. M. (1991) 'Market failure for general training, and remedies', in Stern, D. and Ritzen, J. M. M. (eds), *Market Failure in Training? New Economic Analysis and Evidence on Training of Adult Employees.* Berlin: Springler-Verlag, pp. 185–213.

Spear, R. (2002) 'National profiles of work integration social enterprises: United Kingdom', EMES, Open Research Online, The Open University.

Spence, A. M. (1974) *Market Signaling: Informational Transfer in Hiring and Related Screening Process*. Cambridge, MA: Harvard University Press.

Vidal, I. and Claver, N. (2004) 'Work integration social enterprises in Spain', EMES Working Papers, no. 04/05.

Zaniboni, S., Fraccaroli, F., Villotti, P. and Corbiére, M. (2011) 'Working plans of people with mental disorders employed in Italian Social Enterprises', *Psychiatric Rehabilitation Journal*, 35(1): 55–8.

7

FOSTERING THE WELLBEING OF IMMIGRANTS AND REFUGEES?

Evaluating the outcomes of work integration social enterprise

Jo Barraket

Chapter overview

Work integration social enterprises (WISE) seek to create employment and pathways to employment for those highly disadvantaged in the labour market. This chapter examines the effects of WISE on the wellbeing of immigrants and refugees experiencing multiple barriers to economic and social participation. Drawing on an evaluation of a programme that supports seven such enterprises in the Australian state of Victoria, the effects of involvement for individual participants and their communities are examined. The study finds that this social enterprise model affords unique local opportunities for economic and social participation for groups experiencing significant barriers to meaningful employment. These opportunities have a positive impact on individual and community-level wellbeing. However, the financial costs of the model are high relative to other employment programmes, which is consistent with international findings on intermediate labour market programmes. The productivity costs of WISE are also disproportionately high compared to private sector competitors in some industries. This raises considerable dilemmas for social enterprise operators seeking to produce social value and achieve business sustainability while bearing high productivity costs to fulfil their mission. Further, the evaluation illuminates an ongoing need to address the systemic and structural drivers of health and labour market inequalities that characterize socio-economic participation for immigrants and refugees.

Introduction

The current era is characterized by increasing mobility – both voluntary and forced – of world populations, and changing demands for human capital in the knowledge economy. Developed countries have unmet needs for skilled and unskilled labour in a range of industries. At the same time, migration can be desirable or necessary for people seeking new economic opportunities, relief from regional conflicts and improved quality of life. At face value, these conditions suggest a certain complementarity of need for people resettling in developed nations and their new countries of residence.

Despite this apparent complementarity, immigrants in many developed countries fare relatively poorly in general terms, experiencing protracted social exclusion, long-term unemployment and the intergenerational effects of disadvantage (Marston 2004; OECD 2006). Recent research suggests that, in many cases, national policies designed to manage immigration are not supported by integration policies that are adaptive to the labour market and educational needs of immigrants (Colic-Peisker and Tilbury 2006; OECD 2006).

In the face of this policy vacuum, a range of niche programmes and services has emerged, driven by civil society organizations, local governments and regional employment service networks. Social enterprise models form part of a suite of 'active labour market' interventions that seek to facilitate employment for those highly disadvantaged in the labour market through tailored skills development and employment creation (see Spear and Bidet 2005). In this chapter, I consider the impacts of work integration social enterprise (WISE) – which provides an alternative training and employment model – on the wellbeing of immigrants and refugees experiencing multiple barriers to economic and social participation. Drawing on an evaluation of a programme that supports seven such enterprises in the Australian state of Victoria, I examine the effects of involvement on individual participants and their communities. I then go on to consider the limitations and possibilities of WISE models for responding to inequities in economic participation and wellbeing for immigrant and refugee populations facing multiple obstacles to participation.

Economic participation and wellbeing for refugees and newly arrived migrants

Poor health and wellbeing is both a predictor and an outcome of limited economic participation. The link between employment and health has been well established. Various studies have identified correlations between unemployment and poor health (see Broom et al. 2006; Outram et al. 2004; Harris and Morrow 2001; McClelland 2000), and between low quality employment and poor health (see Hewitt et al. 2006; Broom et al. 2006).[1] In her work on the relationship between employment and psychological wellbeing, Jahoda (1982) theorized that paid employment provides both manifest benefits, in the form of income, and latent benefits that respond to psychological needs. These latent benefits include: time structure; social contact beyond the realm of family; being part of a collective purpose; being engaged in meaningful activities; and having social status (Jahoda 1982). Social capital research has further identified that individuals and communities experiencing systemic disadvantage are likely to have relatively low levels of bridging social capital – or diverse social, professional and organizational networks – which can limit their access to employment opportunities (see, for example, Onyx and Bullen 2000; Outram *et al.* 2004; Bidet 2009).

With the exception of immigrants sponsored to enter the country by employers, immigrants and refugees to Australia are significantly over-represented in unemployment. This is particularly the case for refugees, with longitudinal data identifying that 43 per cent of working-age people entering the country on humanitarian grounds are unemployed eighteen months after arrival in Australia (Department of Immigration and Citizenship 2006). Where new migrants do gain access to employment, the positions they hold in Australia tend to be less skilled than those they held in their countries of origin (Department of Immigration and Citizenship 2006). This can lead to deskilling, which reduces individuals' capacity to gain more skilled employment over time, and a loss of socio-economic status that can impact negatively on mental health and wellbeing (Colic-Peisker and Tilbury 2006; Papadopoulos *et al.* 2004) and contribute to isolation (Bidet 2009).

Immigrants and refugees face a range of individual and societal barriers to participating in meaningful employment. These include: limited proficiency in the language of the resident country (Murray and Skull 2005; Marston 2004); limited networks that provide access to informal opportunities to gain employment (Colic-Peisker and Tilbury 2006); and relatively poor physical and/or psychological health at the point of resettlement (Schweitzer *et al.* 2006; Brough *et al.* 2003; Bidet 2009).

While individual experiences of health, language acquisition and access to networks impact upon new arrivals' opportunities for economic participation, systemic and structural barriers also play a determining role. These include non-recognition of qualifications gained outside the new country of residence and direct discrimination in hiring practices by employers and in workplace behaviour (Colic-Peisker and Tilbury 2006; Schweitzer *et al.* 2006; Marston 2004; Papadopoulos *et al.* 2004; OECD 2006).

Barriers to employment are also disproportionately experienced by immigrants sharing particular social or experiential characteristics. The existence of established ethnic communities, or communities with shared language, can provide employment opportunities for some new arrivals, which are not available to so-called 'new' ethnic communities. Women face particular barriers to participation. These can include: limited educational opportunities in their countries of origin; limited access to language services while managing home duties; limited access to childcare and/or flexible work opportunities that accommodate childcare responsibilities.

Responding to diverse needs: employment services and social enterprise approaches

Employment services in Australia are dominated by a 'work first' logic, which focuses on moving unemployed people into the open labour market as quickly as possible, and are based on a market model of provision. Federal government is the sole purchaser of services from a 'network' of more than 1,000 for-profit and not-for-profit service providers. State governments provide some niche employment programmes to supplement federal government provision, particularly for citizens defined as 'highly disadvantaged' in seeking employment.

The limitations of current Australian labour market programmes in responding to the needs of highly disadvantaged jobseekers have been comprehensively reported (see Considine 2001; Burgess 2003; Nevile and Nevile 2003; Eardley 2002). The 'work first' approach is limited in its ability to respond to the needs of those facing multiple personal and systemic barriers to employment. The purchaser-provider model for employment service delivery encourages a focus on short-term payable outcomes, which has led to practices by some providers of 'parking' the most difficult to place jobseekers (Burgess 2003). As Burgess also points out, the federal government employment services model is a supply-side reform, which does nothing to stimulate employment creation or guarantee jobs across regionally diverse labour markets (2003: 238).

In light of these inadequacies, some state and local government initiatives seek to stimulate employment creation in local labour markets, particularly for communities of place and communities of characteristic experiencing systemic disadvantage. With regard to the specific employment and training needs of refugees and migrants, a small but growing number of nonprofit agencies are developing WISE and other models as alternative ways of providing these groups with opportunities for economic and social participation.

WISE typically combine training and skills development of marginalized groups in an enterprise that trades in the market and is led by a social purpose (Cooney 2011; Spear and Bidet 2005). This purpose typically combines the work integration objective with the delivery of specific goods and services that serve the unmet needs of the beneficiary group (O'Shaughnessy 2008; Aiken 2007). Training and educative processes – through work-based training, and learning, experiential learning, situated learning, supervision and mentoring – are central to all WISE models (Cooney 2011; Marhuenda 2009). WISE are engaged in the creation of permanent jobs and the development of pathways to employment in the open labour market through intermediate or transitional labour market opportunities.

WISE generate employment, skills development and social participation opportunities for individuals. In this sense, they can simultaneously be sites of economic participation, social connectedness and civic engagement (Marhuenda 2009; Bode et al. 2004). Spear and Bidet (2005) suggest that, unlike other community development activities that emphasize voluntarism as a means of participation, the logic of social enterprise is driven by participation through employment.

Relatively little systematic research has been conducted on the effectiveness of WISE in general and those WISE that target immigrants and refugees, in particular. In terms of outcomes for individuals, it is notable that very little investigation of the long-term employment outcomes of WISE has been undertaken. With regard to wider benefits to individuals, studies in Hong Kong and Australia suggest that WISE facilitate social inclusion both by creating employment and mediating clients' integration into the broader community (Ho and Chan 2010; Mission Australia 2008). In relation to immigrants in particular, Ho and Chan (2010) find that WISE help build the social capital necessary to access meaningful employment in their new countries of residence.

At the systemic level, two studies have raised concerns about the potential effectiveness of WISE. In an examination of WISE in the US, Cooney (2011) notes that the vast majority of WISE operate in low-skilled industries and occupations, which potentially limits the ability of these organizations to mediate client transitions into more stable and meaningful employment in the open labour market. She suggests that WISE and their parent organizations require robust approaches – including well developed partnerships with mainstream employers and education providers, as well as integrated business models – to ensure that they do not reinforce their clients' access to limited, low-skilled work opportunities. In the Irish context, O'Shaughnessy (2008) notes that the statutory requirements of those WISE that are predominately funded by government programmes limits their potential for sustainability, particularly when they are required to work with the most disadvantaged job seekers while simultaneously providing services in the context of market failure. Each of these studies, and an evaluation undertaken by the author on behalf of a large Australian charity, note the productivity limitations on businesses that are staffed by trainees who experience complex barriers to employment, challenge the business sustainability of WISE (Cooney 2011; O'Shaughnessy 2008; Mission Australia 2008).

The WISE programme evaluated

The WISE programme evaluated is operated by a large statutory organization that is a major provider of specialist multicultural education, employment and settlement services in Australia. At the time of conducting the evaluation, this organization had established seven enterprises across four industries (see Table 7.1 for details). All of the enterprises established are work integration social enterprises, combining permanent employment creation and intermediate labour market opportunities. Several of the enterprises also provide goods and services – such as traditional food items, and culturally relevant media services – that serve local communities, consistent with the service model of social enterprise. Each of these enterprises was established by the parent organization with interested clients who wanted to participate in and ultimately operate the business. Most of the enterprises are also supported by partner organizations, including local government authorities, local schools and not-for-profit agencies, which provide practical support. Examples of this support include provision of free or low-cost commercial premises, and marketing of enterprise goods and services through partner organizations' networks.

The industries in which enterprises were established were determined by the enterprise operators, based on some business planning and analysis of the feasibility of proposed enterprises. Factors taken into account in planning the enterprises included: the existing skills and employment needs of enterprise operators; the presence of a viable market for enterprise goods and services; and the presence of industry skills shortages to which enterprises would respond through the training

TABLE 7.1 Description of social enterprises

Enterprise type	Social purpose of enterprise	No. of enterprise operators	Ethnicity and gender of operators
African Catering Service and Bakery	• Employment and training • Provision of traditional food items to local African communities • Provision of healthy lunches to local school	3	Ethiopian, Eritrean women
African Community Newspaper	• Employment and training • Provision of news media services in a range of African community languages	4	Sudanese, Ethiopian, Somali men
Commercial Cleaning Service	• Training and employment • Environmentally sustainable cleaning services	3	Sudanese men
Middle Eastern Catering Service	• Training and employment	7	Lebanese, Syrian, Iraqi, South American women
Russian Catering Service	• Training and employment	3	Russian women
Woodwork Cooperative	• Training and employment • Social support for older community members • Environmentally sustainable small furniture production through timber recycling	7	Iraqi, Eritrean, Ethiopian men
Canteen and Catering Service	• Training and employment • Provision of healthy school canteen services	4	Indian, Eritrean, Bangladeshi, Cook Islander women

of clients. It was an objective of the programme to use established enterprises as ongoing training sites for future groups of clients. In this regard, the enterprises would be active businesses managed by qualified staff and staffed primarily by trainees.

The auspicing organization's[2] aim in establishing social enterprises was to provide their most highly disadvantaged clients with work and training environments within an active business/industry context. The majority of enterprise participants – referred to as enterprise operators – are women, and over one-third of enterprise operators are from so-called 'emerging' ethnic communities (in particular, from a number of Horn of Africa countries). The client group involved with the enterprises reflects the disproportionately high barriers to employment experienced by these groups.

The auspicing organization's experience in working with participants and clients with similar characteristics suggested that three elements were critical in developing successful employment and training outcomes:

1. highly contextualized training and support environments
2. sustained social support
3. training and skills acquisition programmes that can operate at a number of levels including fully accredited courses, targeted short course training and long-term training support programmes.

The programme was initiated and developed on the basis that social enterprise has the potential to offer these features. In addition to the enterprise operators, it was projected that up to 30 clients per enterprise would undertake a range of accredited and unaccredited training activities each year. At the time of conducting the evaluation, twenty people had completed such training.

Evaluation methodology

The purpose of the evaluation was to assess the instrumental employment and training outcomes of the programme, as well as the impacts of enterprise participation on the wellbeing of enterprise operators and their communities.

The evaluation was based on a 'programme logic' model, which considers the diversity of inputs, processes, outputs and outcomes generated by the programme.

A review of hardcopy information about the programme – including original funding proposals, progress reports, promotional material and media documentation – was conducted to identify the core features of the programme model, and intended and actual targets. Descriptive statistical and economic data on programme cost, retention rates and training and employment outcomes were collated to assess programme value and effectiveness.

Semi-structured interviews were conducted with enterprise participants, programme staff, enterprise trainers and representatives from partner organizations to elicit qualitative feedback on the individual, programme and community level impacts of the programme. In total, a purposive sample of 33 people was interviewed about their experience of the programme. Interviewees included: thirteen enterprise operators; eleven staff; two programme volunteers; one contractor; four representatives from partner organizations; and two representatives from the main funding body. Twenty-seven of these interviews were conducted face to face, with seven conducted via telephone. Where the evaluator did not speak the language(s) of enterprise participants, translation was provided by programme staff. Interview data were thematically analyzed to identify the self-reported health and wellbeing outcomes of participation in the programme, drawing on the Victorian Health Promotion Foundation's (2006) framework for evaluating mental health and wellbeing. This framework is grounded in a population health perspective, which incorporates the social dimensions of wellbeing for individuals, communities and societies.

The focus of the evaluation was on individual and community-level effects. Although both quantitative and qualitative data were collected, the focus here is on qualitative findings; in particular, the self-reported effects of the programme from the perspectives of enterprise operators, programme staff and representatives from partner organizations.

The primary limitation of the evaluation was the language barrier between the evaluator and enterprise participants. The role of programme staff in interpreting may have affected participants' responses where they did not feel comfortable to provide critical reflections in front of programme staff with whom they worked on a daily basis. This was overcome as far as possible by seeking perspectives from a diversity of stakeholders in the programme and, where possible, conducting private interviews with those participants fluent in English.

Findings

Employment and training outcomes

At the time of the evaluation, the programme had generated employment opportunities for 31 individuals, all of whom were refugees or immigrants to Australia. Enterprise operators were very positive about the quality and reliability of their employment experiences within the programme. Several women from the catering services indicated that being involved in the design and establishment of the enterprises had allowed them to incorporate issues such as parenting responsibilities and travel concerns into the nature and structure of their work; they reported that these were important factors in allowing them to undertake sustained employment.

In addition to being employers themselves, the enterprises act as intermediaries between the auspicing agency's clients and other local employers. There was some evidence that the industry networks of individual enterprises had been leveraged to secure employment for individuals who had participated in training programmes within the enterprises. For example, programme staff working with the woodworking enterprise reported that, through their contacts with clients purchasing goods, employment opportunities had been generated for two of a cohort of twelve trainees. This may suggest that a unique feature of this social enterprise model is its potential for building industry networks to facilitate positive employment outcomes for highly disadvantaged jobseekers. This is consistent with the OECD's findings that social enterprise is able to develop flexible responses to training and employment that respond to the demands of both individual clients and local employers (OECD 2006: 13). However, this represented the minority experience within the social enterprise programme evaluated, which was still working with its first cohort at the time of evaluation. Other evaluative studies conducted at more mature stages of the Intermediate Labour Market (ILM) initiative have suggested that balancing supply side responses to the needs of participants with demand-side needs of local employers is challenging and requires different programmatic approaches (Bickerstaffe and Devins 2004; Mission Australia 2008). Specifically, Bickerstaffe and Devins (2004) suggest that supply-side interventions require deep engagement with a smaller number of clients, while a demand-side focus requires broad inclusion of a large scale of participants to meet employer needs. An independent evaluation of an intermediate labour market social enterprise run by a large welfare agency, Mission Australia (2008), also found that strong outcomes for participants often resulted in them moving out of the industry and/or the local area in which the ILM operated, thus reducing the potential outcomes for local employers.

While the establishment of the enterprises had created employment opportunities, these were in most cases being underwritten by government-funded training subsidies provided to enterprise operators as they achieved the training qualifications required to run the businesses. The potential for ongoing income generation to sustain employment depended on the overall business sustainability of each enterprise. The evaluation found that individual enterprises were at varying stages of consolidation. However, overall the programme was not financially self-sustainable and required ongoing investment from the auspicing organization and funding bodies, at least in the medium term. This is reflective of an ongoing tension between social purpose and financial viability for social enterprise. Within the social enterprise literature, there is some debate about whether sustainability equates with financial self-sufficiency from earned income. Some argue that financial self-sufficiency is important for social enterprises to maintain their autonomy and entrepreneurial capacity (see Thomas 2004), while others argue that financial self-reliance is neither possible nor an appropriate measure of success where social enterprises are absorbing the social costs of responding to the needs of highly disadvantaged individuals and communities, and producing positive social and environmental outcomes (Pearce 2003). The research reported on here, however, suggested that industry orientation and contextual factors affected the potential for both self-sufficiency and sustainability. These included factors common to all forms of business – for example, the size of profit margins within particular businesses and the relative health or decline of certain industries. They also included factors particular to WISE. For example, several of the food retail businesses in the sample faced constraints on the number of participants they could involve due to occupational health and safety limitations on staff numbers in commercial kitchens, while some sought narrower profit margins relative to commercial counterparts when making their products accessible to socio-economically disadvantaged groups was part of their mission.

The primary objective of the social enterprise model for the auspicing organization was that the enterprises provide active training contexts for their clients on an ongoing basis. Enterprise owners and staff interviewed were unanimous in their perceptions of the benefits of conducting traineeships within the enterprises. Many respondents pointed out that these allowed operators and other trainees to develop important business and industry skills and accreditation in a 'real-world' business context, while receiving a living wage for doing so. The programme had generated vocational and accredited training outcomes for 51 people at the time of evaluation. Several enterprise operators observed that involvement in the enterprises had also improved their knowledge and personal skills in a number of areas.

One of the most significant areas of skills development was linguistic skills. Many programme staff and trainers observed that enterprise operators' English language proficiency improved dramatically as a result of them participating in 'real-world' professional activities on a regular basis. All programme staff who had previous experience of working with similar client groups in other labour market programmes reported that language acquisition was considerably faster and broader for participants of the social enterprise programme. One staff member observed:

> [Participants are] learning English in the real world here. They have regular contact with different people – clients, suppliers as well as [programme] staff and they're getting a feel for language and interaction in the workplace that they can't get in the classroom. We don't focus just on conversational English; we have to talk the language of a workplace. That's what they'll need to do well in future jobs.
>
> *(Programme staff member, woodworking enterprise)*

While language acquisition was a commonly reported benefit of this work integration social enterprise model, a small number of respondents observed that the potential to develop English language skills depended on the nature of the business. 'Front end' retail activities, including customer and supplier interactions, were more likely to create opportunities for language skills development than 'back end' production or tasks done in isolation from others. The ethno-linguistic composition of enterprise participants also affected the extent to which English language was used. That is, the more multicultural enterprises were more likely to encourage the use of English than those comprised of participants from common language groups.

While training in an active industry context appears to have had powerful outcomes for enterprise operators, this type of training requires considerable investment, with staff reporting that some traineeships required more than double the standard hours attributed to classroom-based training models. This is consistent with the findings of other evaluative studies of WISE and similar intermediate labour market programmes, which find that they are relatively higher cost (and, arguably, higher value) than other programmes (Finn and Simmonds 2003; Mestan and Scutella 2007; Mission Australia 2008). The investment requirements of the social enterprise programme has cost implications for the auspicing organization, in terms of the resources required to sustain this approach to training, and for participants, in terms of the time commitments required to fully realize the benefits of this training approach.

While this social enterprise programme seeks to provide empowering alternatives to current training and labour market programmes for highly disadvantaged members of culturally and linguistically diverse communities, it is notable that five of the seven established were within tertiary industries; particularly cleaning and catering. As discussed in the introduction to this chapter, labour market inequities for immigrants and refugees are both reflected in and reinforced by concentration in secondary and tertiary industries. In all cases, the original enterprise operators were themselves involved in deciding in what industry their enterprise would be positioned. Nevertheless, the preference for tertiary industry positioning reflects a tension between the business model and the social objectives of social enterprise. That is, the complexities of establishing sustainable business activities and maintaining the productivity levels necessary to be competitive in the open market where the enterprise's workforce is predominately trainees, can limit the kinds of employment types and industry orientations available to social enterprises and their participants (see Cooney 2011). This is particularly the case where social enterprise is primarily concerned with responding to demands for work integration, as there is a real need to generate business models that can be scaled-up to ensure high quality training opportunities for a relatively large number of participants. This raises questions about the capacity of social enterprise models to respond to the problems of occupational downgrading, as well as unemployment, for immigrants and refugees.

Two programme staff expressed concerns about the limitations in skills and experience placed upon enterprise operators based on the industry in which their enterprise was operating, with one commenting, 'I mean, I wonder what we're setting them up for … the job opportunities aren't great [in this industry]' (programme staff member).

However, each of these staff suggested that the improved self-confidence and language acquisition developed by enterprise operators as a result of being involved in the enterprise provided a sound basis for entry into higher-level employment over time. In this sense, they saw social enterprise as providing a pathway into employment, rather than an employment end in itself. This appears to be consistent with other evaluative evidence, which finds that WISE participants typically move on to other industries and educational opportunities after developing foundational skills and relationships within the social enterprise (Mission Australia 2008).

It is notable that all of the women participants in this social enterprise programme were located within tertiary industry businesses. Gender disparity in favour of men in WISE has been noted elsewhere, either due to purposeful selection of male participants (Ho and Chan 2010) or through business concentration in masculinized industries, such as construction (Mission Australia 2008). The programme discussed here provided more opportunities for participation for women than men at the time of evaluation. Nevertheless, indirect gender inequity is present in the types of industries in which women participants were concentrated compared with male participants.

Health and wellbeing outcomes

The evaluation drew on the Victorian Health Promotion Foundation's (2006) framework for evaluating the mental health and wellbeing outcomes of the programme. It found that, in addition to the employment and training outcomes outlined above, the programme has had considerable positive effects on individual and community-level wellbeing. Enterprise operators reported a range of benefits they had experienced as a result of their participation in the programme, which were reinforced by programme staff observations. These included:

Improved social connections and relationships

All enterprise participants interviewed said they had developed new friendships with other participants and within their broader communities as a result of the programme. Enterprise operators were also very positive about the relationships they had with programme staff and trainers, and staff of partner organizations. This made participants feel more connected. As one enterprise operator commented, 'I now have more people to turn to, and I know who to talk to about certain things' (female enterprise operator, catering enterprise).

The impacts of these relationships extended beyond the enterprise activities. Four enterprise operators described concrete examples where new relationships formed through this activity had helped them: access a social support or health service; get involved in a local community event; or find out something about their civic rights. Two enterprise operators reported that they had taken on new leadership roles in their communities based on the self-confidence they had developed in their social enterprise work.

Improved self-esteem and self-efficacy

Operators reported that the programme had powerful impacts on their self-confidence and sense of self-worth. A number of operators reported that being trained within a 'real business' setting and taking on some of the responsibilities of business management had helped them develop new skills and new confidence about their capacity to succeed in employment. All programme staff interviewed reported the positive changes in operators' self-confidence they had observed within the enterprises, including confidence to talk with suppliers, clients, their broader communities, the media and politicians, and confidence to work with and challenge the auspicing organization and partner organizations. All enterprise operators interviewed indicated that being involved in the enterprise gave them new purpose to participate socially and economically. One participant described his involvement in the enterprise as 'medicine for my mind and my body' (male enterprise operator, woodworking enterprise). Another participant stated that the greatest benefit of the programme for her and fellow owners was, 'We have jobs. We used to sit at home. Now we have a place to go, work to do. It is the best thing' (female enterprise operator, catering enterprise).

Positive intergenerational and intercultural effects

Within each of the enterprises, operators themselves were from diverse ethnocultural backgrounds; in some cases, as they pointed out, from countries or ethnic groups that have long histories of conflict with each other. Several of the enterprise operators indicated that the act of working together improved their cross-cultural understanding and knowledge. Two operators explicitly stated that this understanding had improved their relationships with neighbours in the high-density housing estates where they lived. Experiences such as this suggest that social enterprise activities contribute in a modest way to social transformation through the day-to-day contact involved in operating a business.

Several of the enterprises provided opportunities for interaction between older and younger people from diverse communities. In the case of the woodworking enterprise, younger people from a range of ethno-cultural backgrounds interacted regularly with the older enterprise operators, while participating in various training programmes. One enterprise operator from the woodworking enterprise described the benefits of involvement in the enterprise to an at-risk young person from the same ethnic background as himself. He indicated that he was able to act as a mentor to this young person, stating, 'I showed him what it is to be a proud and honourable man' (male enterprise operator, woodworking enterprise). In this case, the respondent felt that it was important that the young person concerned had the opportunity to experience being involved with a group of men from traditionally warring ethno-cultural backgrounds working constructively together.

In the case of two of the catering enterprises, the businesses were physically located within (and providing services to) local schools at which enterprise operators' children were students. Both enterprise operators and respondents from the schools reported that the day-to-day interactions generated by the presence of the enterprises had positive benefits for students, parents and the school. These included: an increased sense of pride and self-worth among students from ethno-cultural groups represented by the enterprise operators; on-site healthy food choices that were improving students' diets; and considerably higher levels of parent-staff interactions as parents from various backgrounds felt more comfortable participating in the school community as a result of their personal links with the enterprise operators. In these cases, it appears that the enterprises functioned not just as transitional labour market models but as important hubs that linked ethno-cultural communities and school communities in a number of new ways.

Discussion and conclusion

As an alternative to mainstream labour market programmes, the social enterprise model reported on here provides a range of specific features that improve wellbeing for immigrants and refugees facing significant disadvantage in relation to economic participation. The programme has stimulated employment and training opportunities with which participants consistently report a high degree of satisfaction. This qualitative experience is supported by the retention rates of enterprise operators, with only 2 out of an original 33 leaving the programme, both due to personal circumstances unrelated to programme activities. Participants in the programme experienced the manifest benefits of employment; that is, earned income. More significantly for the participants interviewed, the programme generated several latent benefits of economic participation, including new skills, language acquisition, new personal relationships, a sense of common purpose and new social and professional networks. Enterprise participants were unanimously positive in their perception of the benefits of the programme to them as individuals, and to their broader communities. This was supported by the observations of programme staff and a number of partner organization representatives.

While social enterprise models present possibilities for improving highly disadvantaged immigrants' and refugees' opportunities to participate in the mainstream labour market, they are principally focused on stimulating local opportunities for economic and social participation, rather than the broader social and political conditions that inform labour market segmentation. As discussed in the introduction to this chapter, many recent studies of economic participation and its relationship to wellbeing for refugees and new migrants identify systemic and socially constructed barriers to participation as major obstacles (see Colic-Peisker and Tilbury 2006; Schweitzer *et al.* 2006; Marston 2004).

On a micro-level, enterprise operators reported that the act of running their business helped improve cross-cultural understanding and generate positive experiences and representations of diverse cultures in the broader community. This was particularly the case for some of the catering enterprises, with one operator commenting:

> We bring the food and they ask us about it. We explain how it is made, a little bit of our culture. They like it. They come back. I am proud that they know more about me, where I come from.
>
> *(Female enterprise operator, catering enterprise)*

This is consistent with Ho and Chan's (2010) finding that work integration social enterprises facilitate social recognition between marginalized participants and the wider community through the day-to-day activities of doing business.

At a broader level, the social enterprise programme has generated significant interest from the mainstream media, and from other organizations – including local government and not-for-profit agencies – in partnering or establishing new enterprises based on this enterprise model. At the time of conducting the evaluation, seven new partnerships to support the existing enterprises had been established with local government, state government and not-for-profit agencies, including specific ethno-cultural community organizations. The auspicing organization was also receiving regular approaches from other organizations interested in establishing similar programmes. Programme staff reported that a considerable benefit of these new connections is the opportunities for broader education and dialogue about the resettlement issues faced by different immigrant and refugee communities. As discussed above, all of the enterprises facilitated new relationships between people from diverse backgrounds and positions, while some of the enterprises were also evolving as important community hubs. These outcomes suggest that, beyond the instrumental benefits of individual employment, the programme was stimulating a 'network effect', which generated some new knowledge and attitudes about and within particular ethnic communities. It is notable, however, that this network effect is essentially limited to those groups, not-for-profit organizations and government agencies that are predisposed to, or have a statutory responsibility for, assisting immigrants and refugees to resettle in Australia. While the day-to-day business transactions of social enterprise may have transformative social effects at the local level, it is unlikely that these transformations will have a profound influence on macro-level discourses of othering (Grove and Zwi 2005) that are both an effect and constitutive of systemic inequality in labour market and social participation for immigrants and refugees.

A considerable limitation to the transformative potential of the programme is the broader employment services environment in which it is necessarily located. WISE constitute active labour market programmes (Vidal 2005), which are relatively marginal within Australia's 'work first' employment services landscape. At the time of conducting the research, the auspicing organization had to contend with considerable difficulties created by Australian Federal Government price-setting for labour market programmes and state government regulations that prevent access to particular training sources. Some proponents of social enterprise would argue that a major transformative benefit of these initiatives is their independence from government funding and their capacity to generate revenue through commercial means. In Italy, for example, it has been observed that one of the benefits of social cooperatives is their innovation; that is, they do not simply fulfil a policy agenda, but define 'their own sphere of action … [by] deciding which services to start up, how to shape them, and what organizational structure to adopt' (Thomas 2004: 247).

However, where enterprises are heavily reliant on training and employment services income from government sources, as the ones evaluated here are, they are subject to the same tyrannies of government price-setting of employment services as other agencies and programmes not operating on an enterprise model. As Spear and Bidet (2005) have observed of WISE involved in contractual relations with governments in Europe, they are particularly vulnerable to variations in demand. They suggest that this vulnerability is then individualized when enterprise participants face renewed threats of unemployment or other forms of exclusion if an enterprise fails or has to reduce its operations (Spear and Bidet 2005: 223–4). While the programme evaluated was not facing any such immediate danger, its reliance on income streams from national- and state-level employment programmes does illuminate the tensions of employment models that embrace innovative approaches to facilitating economic and social inclusion, while operating in a policy environment that limits adaptability and responsiveness to the training and education needs of particular client groups. O'Shaughnessy (2008) has noted similar constraining effects of statutory requirements on WISE in Ireland. In the Australian context, these problems are exacerbated by at worst, contradiction, and at best, limited coordination, between policy logics that underpin federal and state government employment programmes. In such an environment, it is unlikely that social enterprise and other alternative employment service models can achieve the kinds of scale needed to transform opportunities for economic and social participation available to immigrants and refugees facing multiple barriers to employment. As Giguère (2006: 21) has observed, 'There is a clear mismatch between immigration and integration policies in many countries, with policies to manage immigration rarely being accompanied by strong policies to support integration'.

The social enterprise programme examined in this chapter generates a range of outcomes that support wellbeing for individual participants and their communities. The enterprises are responsive to the needs and availabilities of participants, and thus support the development of a range of skills, networks and relationships. They are sites of social inclusion, which improve self-esteem, self-efficacy and confidence. Some of the enterprises are also important community hubs, which offer opportunities for intergenerational and intercultural learning. A number of the enterprises provide niche services that connect particular ethno-cultural groups with their cultures of origin in ways that support physical and mental health. Individual enterprises also act as intermediaries between enterprise participants and local employers, thus providing bridges into mainstream employment for some participants. More broadly, the enterprises raise awareness among government agencies, employers and the broader community about the strengths, diversity and contributions of migrants and refugees.

While there are many individual and community-level benefits generated by the programme, it operates in an environment where government policies and societal norms perpetuate systemic disadvantage for the clients it serves. While social enterprise provides one useful model for doing things differently, there is an ongoing need to address the systemic drivers of inequality that inform the relationship between wellbeing and economic participation for diverse refugee and immigrant groups. This should include developing a policy environment that enables social enterprise and other innovative models to support locally responsive approaches to supporting resettlement outcomes for individual clients and their communities.

Acknowledgements

This chapter is based on an evaluation of work carried out by Adult Multicultural Education Services (AMES). Nina Yousefpour assisted with updating the literature review. All views expressed are the author's own.

Notes

1 At the other end of the spectrum, sociological research has identified the correlation between over-work and poor health (see Hewitt *et al.* 2006).
2 Where 'auspicing organization' refers to the host or 'parent organization' that supports the start-up of a new social enterprise.

Recommended further reading

Cooney, K. (2011) 'The business of job creation: an examination of the social enterprise approach to workforce development', *Journal of Poverty*, 15(1): 88–107.

Spear, R. and Bidet, E. (2005) 'Social enterprise for work integration in European countries: a descriptive analysis', *Annals of Public and Cooperative Economics*, 76(2): 195–231.

References

Aiken, M. (2007) *What is the Role of Social Enterprise in Finding, Creating and Maintaining Employment for Disadvantaged Groups?* London: Cabinet Office; Office of the Third Sector.

Bickerstaffe, T. and Devins, D. (2004) *Intermediate Labour Markets: Final Report, New Deal for Communities: The National Evaluation*. Sheffield: Centre for Regional Economic and Social Research.

Bidet, E. (2009) 'Social capital and work integration of migrants: the case of North Korean defectors in South Korea', *Asian Perspective*, 33(2): 151–79.

Bode, I., Evers A. and Schulz, A. (2004) 'Facing new challenges: Work Integration Social Enterprises in Germany', Sixth International Conference of the International Society for Third-Sector Research, Ryerson University and York University, Toronto.

Broom, D. H., D'Souza, R. M., Strazdins, L., Butterworth, P., Parslow, R. and Rodgers, B. (2006) 'The lesser evil: bad jobs or unemployment? A survey of mid-aged Australians', *Social Science and Medicine*, 36(3): 575–86.

Brough, M., Gorman, D., Ramirez, E. and Westoby, P. (2003) 'Young refugees talk about well-being: a qualitative analysis of refugee mental health from three states', *Australian Journal of Social Issues*, 38(2): 193–208.

Burgess, J. (2003) 'Reviewing the model behind the job network', *Australian Journal of Labour Economics*, 6(2): 227–40.

Colic-Peisker, V. and Tilbury, F. (2006) 'Employment niches for recent refugees: segmented labour market in twenty-first century Australia', *Journal of Refugee Studies*, 19(2): 203–29.

Considine, M. (2001) *Enterprising States: The Public Management of Welfare-to-Work*. Cambridge: Cambridge University Press.

Cooney, K. (2011) 'The business of job creation: an examination of the social enterprise approach to workforce development', *Journal of Poverty*, 15(1): 88–107.

Department of Immigration and Citizenship (2006) 'Longitudinal Survey of Immigrants to Australia', (accessed 10 December 2006) Available at http://www.immi.gov.au/media/research/lsia/index.htm.

Eardley, T. (2002) 'Mutual obligation and the job network: the effect of competition on the role of non-profit employment services', *Australian Journal of Social Issues*, 37(3): 301–13.

Finn, D. and Simmonds, D. (2003) *Intermediate Labour Markets in Britain and an International Review of Transitional Employment Programmes*. London: Department for Work and Pensions. Available at http://research.dwp.gov.uk/asd/asd5/working_age/wa2003/173rep.pdf (accessed 31 July 2012).

Giguère, S. (2006) 'Integrating immigrants: finding the right policy mix to tackle a governance problem', in OECD (ed.), *From Immigration to Integration: Local Solutions to a Global Challenge*. Paris: OECD, pp. 21–30.

Grove, N. and Zwi, A. B. (2005) 'Our health and theirs: forced migration, othering, and public health', *Social Science and Medicine*, 62: 1931–42.

Harris, E. and Morrow, M. (2001) 'Unemployment is a health hazard: the health costs of unemployment', *Economic and Labour Relations Review*, 12(1): 18–31.

Hewitt, B., Baxter, J. and Western, M. (2006) 'Family, work and health – the impact of marriage, parenthood and employment on self-reported health of Australian men and women', *Journal of Sociology*, 42(1): 61–78.

Ho, P. A. and Chan, K. (2010) 'The social impact of work-integration social enterprise in Hong Kong', *International Social Work*, 53(1): 33–45.

Jahoda, M. (1982) *Employment and Unemployment*. Cambridge: Cambridge University Press.

McClelland, A. (2000) 'Effects of unemployment on the family', *Economic and Labour Relations Review*, 11(2): 198–212.

Marhuenda, F. (2009) 'Work integration in social enterprises: employment for the sake of learning', in Stenström, M. L. and Tynjälä, P., *Towards Integration of Work and Learning: Strategies for Connectivity and Transformation*, Netherlands: Springer, pp. 77–91.

Marston, G. (2004) 'A punitive policy: labour force participation of refugees on temporary protection visas (TPV)', *Labour and Industry*, 15(1): 65–79.

Mestan, K. and Scutella, R. with Allens Consulting Group (2007) *Investing in People: Intermediate Labour Markets as Pathways to Employment*. Fitzroy: Brotherhood of St Laurence.

Mission Australia (2008) Working for Renewal: An Evaluation of Mission Australia's UREEP, a Social Enterprise and Transitional Labour Market Programme. Available at: http://www.missionaustralia.com.au/document-downloads/category/47-social-policy-reports# (accessed May 2010).

Murray, S. B. and Skull, S. A. (2005) 'Hurdles to health: immigrant and refugee health care in Australia', *Australian Health Review*, 29(1): 25–9.

Nevile, J. W. and Nevile, A. (2003) 'Evaluating the structure and performance of the job network', *Australian Journal of Labour Market Economics*, 6(2): 241–51.

OECD (2006) *From Immigration to Integration: Local Solutions to a Global Challenge*. Paris: OECD.

Onyx, J. and Bullen, P. (2000) 'Measuring social capital in five communities', *Journal of Applied Behavioral Science*, 36(1): 23–42.

O'Shaughnessy, M. (2008) 'Statutory support and the implications for the employee profile of rural based Irish work integration social enterprises (WISEs)', *Social Enterprise Journal*, 4(2): 126–35.

Outram, S., Mishra, G. D. and Schofield, M. J. (2004) 'Sociodemographic and health related factors associated with poor mental health in midlife Australian women', *Women and Health*, 39(4): 97–115.

Papadopoulos, I., Lees, S., Lay, M. and Gebrehiwot, A. (2004) 'Ethiopian refugees in the UK: migration, adaptation and settlement experiences and their relevance to health', *Ethnicity and Health*, 9(1): 55–73.

Pearce, J. (2003) *Social Enterprise in Anytown* (with a chapter by Alan Kay). London: Calouste Gulbenkian Foundation.

Schweitzer, R., Melville, F., Steel, Z. and Lacherez, P. (2006) 'Trauma, post-migration living difficulties, and social support as predictors of psychological adjustment in resettled Sudanese refugees', *Australian and New Zealand Journal of Psychiatry*, 40(2): 179–87.

Spear, R. and Bidet, E. (2005) 'Social enterprise for work integration in European countries: a descriptive analysis', *Annals of Public and Cooperative Economics*, 76(2): 195–231.

Thomas, A. (2004) 'The rise of social cooperatives in Italy', *Voluntas: International Journal of Voluntary and Nonprofit Organizations*, 15(3): 243–63.

Victorian Health Promotion Foundation (2006) *Planning Monitoring and Evaluation Mental Health Promotion*. Available at: http://www.vichealth.vic.gov.au/assets/contentFiles/Mental_Health_Mapping_Tool.pdf (accessed 10 May 2006).

Vidal, I. (2005) 'Social enterprise and social inclusion: social enterprises in the sphere of work integration', *International Journal of Public Administration*, 28(9): 807–25.

8

DOES SOCIAL ENTERPRISE OFFER ANY ADDED VALUE?

A comparative evaluation of the outcome benefits of work-integration programmes in the third and private sectors

Richard Hazenberg

Chapter overview

In recent years the UK government has increasingly utilized work-integration social enterprises (WISEs) in the delivery of employment enhancement programmes (EEPs) to young people not in education, employment or training (NEET). This is partly due to the perceived 'added value' that WISEs are seen to offer; however, this 'added value' has not been evidenced through rigorous academic research. This chapter reports the results of research that took a comparative, intervention approach to study the 'outcome' performance of two such work-integration organizations. One of these organizations was a WISE and the other was a 'for-profit' private company utilized in this study as a 'comparison group' (CG). The NEET participants at both organizations completed general self-efficacy (GSE) questionnaires before and after engagement in their respective programmes (T1 and T2). In addition a mixed-methods approach was undertaken, with semi-structured interviews held with the NEET individuals in order to elicit their perspectives of change having completed the intervention programme. In order to explore the organizational factors behind the intervention programmes offered by the WISE and the CG, semi-structured interviews and focus groups were held with the owners and staff at both organizations. This provided the research with an organizational perspective of how the aims, values and structures impacted upon the delivery of the EEPs at both organizations. Results revealed no significant difference between the outcome benefits experienced by the NEETs at the WISE and those at the for-profit organization. However, analysis of the organizational aims, values and structures, suggests that the 'added value' offered by the WISE came from the different induction policy that it operated, which allowed it to work with more 'socially excluded' individuals. The findings presented in this chapter have interesting implications in answering the question, 'Is social enterprise working?'

Social enterprise and WISEs

Prior research has focused upon the differing organizational structures, aims and values that are inherent to social enterprises when compared to other third-sector or private-sector organizations (Borzaga and Defourny 2001; Dart 2004). Indeed, social enterprise has been viewed as a new organizational form, distinct from other third-sector organizations (Laville and Nyssens 2001) and operating within the economy on the boundary of the third and private sectors (Pearce 2003). What unites the founders of social enterprises is a belief that a social ill exists, which the traditional mechanisms of state and market are unable to deal with (Defourny *et al.* 1998). In defining what constituted a social enterprise, the 'Emergence de L'Economie Sociale' (EMES) identified five social dimensions that must be present. The EMES definition stated that a social enterprise must have an 'explicit aim to benefit the community', be an 'initiative launched by private citizens', have a 'decision-making process not based upon ownership', have a 'participatory nature for all stakeholders' and operate a 'limited profit-distribution model' (Borzaga and Defourny 2001). Campi *et al.* (2006) identified that in relation to this, social enterprises had aims that were economic, environmental and socio-political and it was this 'triple bottom line' of aims that distinguished social enterprise from other forms of business. Work-integration social enterprises (WISEs) are one of the more common types of social enterprise to be found in Europe and focus upon reintegrating the disadvantaged unemployed back into employment. There are numerous types of WISE, ranging from 'commercial integration organizations' (CIOs) and 'intermediate labour-market organizations (ILMOs) that offer temporary employment or training to the unemployed, through to 'social firms' (SFs) and 'worker cooperatives' (WC) that offer permanent employment to disadvantaged and disabled individuals (Aiken 2007).

Research conducted by Gui (1991) and Reid and Griffith (2006) explored the unique 'dual ownership' structure operated by social enterprises that gave both the owners, beneficiaries and other stakeholders ownership over the company through access to its decision-making functions in a form of 'associative democracy'. This dual-ownership structure allowed a social enterprise to draw upon the 'social capital' available in the community and to utilize this 'social capital' in order to deliver its social mission (Coleman 1990; Putnam 1993). Additionally, Campi *et al.* (2006) also highlighted how the multi-stakeholder approach adopted by many social enterprises allowed them to source income from the private, public and third sectors. This flexibility in income generation allows the social enterprise to bring 'added value' to its operations through flexible income generation such as private trade or public sector contracts, as well as through the utilization of 'social capital' from the community such as volunteering (Haugh and Kitson 2007; Reid and Griffith 2006). However, other research has identified the pressures that such diversity of income can bring to social enterprises, with the 'mission drift' that can occur due to pressures from funders (mainly in the public sector) being particularly acute (Aiken 2006; Seddon *et al.* 2012).

Despite this focus upon the unique organizational aims, values and structures of social enterprises, there has been little attempt to evaluate the impact that such structures have upon social enterprise performance. In relation to work-integration social enterprise (WISE), whilst some prior research has been conducted into the performance of WISEs across Europe that demonstrated that they had a positive effect on their beneficiaries (Borzaga and Loss 2006) this research has been limited by sub-optimal methodological approaches that have reduced the academic rigour of such evaluations (Denny et al. 2011). Additionally, there has been no comparative research that has sought to compare WISE performance with that of comparable for-profit organizations (Peattie and Morley 2008) and to do so within an organizational analysis centred upon the aims, values and structures of differing organizational forms, although Mason (2010) identified the impact that governance and employment structures had upon the abilities of social firms to achieve their social aims.

Securing robust, valid and reliable tools for the evaluation of EEPs delivered by WISEs or for-profit organizations presents a range of problems. The evaluation of EEPs can be both simple and complex depending upon whether the focus of the evaluation is on *output, outcome* or *impact* (McLoughlin et al. 2009). 'Output' can be defined as the relationship between the number of unemployed individuals accessing the programme and the number who subsequently gain employment. An 'outcome' represents psychological benefits experienced by participants that will enhance their future employability. 'Impact' is an even longer-term benefit and is the 'impact' on society resulting from the reduction of unemployment (i.e. reduced unemployment benefits). This research study focused upon comparing the 'outcome' performance of a WISE and a for-profit comparison group that delivered EEPs to young people not in education or training (NEET). In conducting this comparison the study built upon prior research by Denny et al. (2011) that established a research method for the evaluation of the 'outcome' benefits experienced by NEET individuals who engaged with employment enhancement programmes (EEPs). This prior research tested the suitability of employing a mixed-methods, longitudinal, intervention methodology within a qualitative framework that utilized both a general self-efficacy scale (GSE) and semi-structured interviews at both T1 and T2 in order to measure 'outcome' performance at a WISE delivering an EEP to NEETs (Denny et al. 2011).

NEETs and general self-efficacy

Young people in the United Kingdom aged 16–24 years who are not in employment, education or training are classified as NEET. The term NEET originated in the 1990s following a study by Instance et al. (1994) that had labelled unemployed young people as 'Status Zero'. This was then changed by researchers to NEET partly due to a lack of clarity as to what 'Status Zero' meant and partly for political reasons as the term was not considered politically neutral (Furlong 2006). Yates and Payne (2006) interviewed 855 young people through the Connexions agency and from these interviews concluded that NEETs are a more heterogeneous than homogeneous entity. Yates and Payne defined three potential NEET subgroups: (1) 'transitional', i.e. those who are temporarily NEET due to individual circumstances but who quickly re-engage with employment, education or training; (2) 'young parents', i.e. those who are young parents and make a conscious decision to disengage with employment, education or training in order to look after their children; and (3) 'complicated', i.e. those young people who are NEET and who also exhibit a number of 'risks' in their lives (i.e. being homeless, engaging in criminal behaviour, and/or having emotional/behavioural problems). Prior research also provides strong evidence of a close relationship between 'social exclusion' and NEET status (Yates and Payne 2006). 'Social exclusion' can be viewed as the way in which people are excluded from society due to political, economic or cultural differences (Concannon 2008). Social exclusion can be predicated on poor academic achievement, low levels of school attendance, chaotic living arrangements, low socio-economic status and exclusion from school (Furlong 2006). This 'social exclusion' leads to what Ball *et al.* (1999) termed the 'hazy-future' NEETs who have no definitive aspirations and are generally associated with the 'complicated' NEET sub-group (Yates and Payne 2006).

General self-efficacy (GSE) can be defined as 'belief in one's overall competence to effect requisite performance across a wide-range of achievement situations' (Chen *et al.* 2001: 63). Prior research into general self-efficacy reports that success in life, persistent positive vicarious experiences, verbal persuasion and psychological states can augment general self-efficacy (Bandura 1997; Chen *et al.* 2001). Judge *et al.* (1997) stated that GSE is a psychological construct that refers to an individual's confidence, motivation and self-belief. Denny *et al.* (2011) proposed that the negative influences of social exclusion reported above could similarly have a negative effect on NEET GSE. Furthermore, their research validated the use of GSE as a measure of 'outcome' performance for organizations that deliver EEPs to NEET individuals.

The research study

The primary aim of the research was to reveal and compare the 'outcome' performance of both the case-study organization's EEPs and to explore any differences in such performance in relation to organizational aims, values and structures. The research sought to evaluate two EEPs for NEETs, one delivered by a WISE and the other by a for-profit comparison group (CG). The research involved two separate and distinct phases. The first phase utilized a mixed-methods, longitudinal intervention methodology. The quantitative element of Phase 1 involved the use of a GSE scale that has been extensively validated in prior research (Schwarzer and Jerusalem 1995) in order to test for changes in NEET GSE scores between commencing the EEP (T1) and completing the EEP (T2). In total 79 NEET individuals participated in the quantitative element of this phase (32 at the WISE and 47 at the CG), of which 40 completed the intervention programmes and hence GSE scales at T2 (16 at the WISE and 24 at the CG). From these 79 individuals a random sample of 39 NEETs was selected to take part in semi-structured interviews at T1 (19 at the WISE and 20 at the CG), of whom 17 were still present at the end of the intervention to participate in T2 interviews (10 at the WISE and 7 at the CG). All quantitative data was inputted into and analyzed using SPSS 17.0. The data was tested for normality utilizing box-plots and was found to be normally distributed. In addition, Cronbach's α tests revealed that the GSE scale used performed reliably at both case studies with a Cronbach's α value above the recommended minimum of .70 (Kline 1999). The qualitative interview data was analyzed utilizing 'Constant Comparative Method', a method of analysis based in 'Grounded Theory' (Glaser and Strauss 1967; Lincoln and Guba 1985), which has been validated in prior social enterprise research (Haugh 2007; Denny *et al.* 2011). The quantitative and qualitative data is then used to support the research conclusions together through a process of triangulation (McLeod 1994). This first phase of the research aimed to test the following two hypotheses and one research aim:

Hypothesis 1: The participants taking part in the training programme delivered by the WISE will display a statistically significant greater increase in their levels of GSE from T1 to T2 than their counterparts at the for-profit comparison group (CG).

Hypothesis 2: There will *not* be a statistically significant difference between the T1 GSE scores of the NEETs at both work-integration organizations.

Research Aim 1: To elicit participant perspectives of their engagement with the EEP through an inductive analysis of semi-structured interview data gathered at both T1 and T2.

The second phase of the research involved the researchers conducting semi-structured interviews and focus groups with the owners and staff at both of the case-study organizations in order to understand how their organizational aims, values and structures impacted upon 'outcome' performance. A total of 19 individuals participated in this phase of the research (12 at the WISE and 7 at the CG). Specifically, it aimed to explore the following research question.

Research Aim 2: To critically assess each case-study organization's aims, objectives and structure with reference to how these factors impact upon the provision offered to NEET participants.

Changes in General Self-Efficacy (Phase 1)

Paired-sample t-tests were employed to explore the change in GSE scores between T1 and T2 for NEET individuals at both the WISE and CG case-study organizations (see Table 8.1). Results of the paired sample t-tests revealed a statistically significant increase in GSE ($p < .05$) between T1 and T2 for individuals who completed the WISE intervention programme and a statistically significant increase in GSE ($p < .01$) for those NEETs that completed the CG intervention programme

TABLE 8.1 Phase 1 results

Paired-sample t-tests for GSE scale at T1 and T2

Descriptive statistics for T1 to T2 changes

Organization	N	Intervention phase	Mean (%)	+/− (%)	SD (%)
WISE	16	Time 1	67.81	+ 4.53★	8.46
		Time 2	72.34		5.81
CG	24	Time 1	77.81	+ 3.75★★	4.85
		Time 2	81.56		6.20

Change in GSE between T1 and T2 with organization as the factor

Organization	N	Change between T1 and T2	SD	F
WISE	16	+ 4.53%	7.43	.13 (NS)
CG	24	+ 3.75%	6.03	

Differences in participant GSE at T1 with organization as the factor

Organization	N	T1 GSE score (%)	SD	F
WISE	32	68.36	8.67	10.14★★
CG	47	75.16	9.73	

Note: ★ = $p<.05$, ★★ = $p < .01$, ★★★ = $p < .001$ and NS = non-significant.

(see Table 8.1). A one-way ANOVA was then conducted to compare the difference between the T1–T2 change in GSE at the WISE and the T1–T2 change in GSE at the CG (see Table 8.1). The overall results revealed no statistically significant difference between the increases in GSE experienced by the NEETs at the WISE and the CG organizations. *Hypotheses 1 not confirmed.* A one-way ANOVA was conducted in order to explore the difference in GSE scores at T1 for the NEETs at the WISE and the NEETs at the CG. The results revealed that there was a statistically significant difference between the T1 GSE scores of the NEETs at the WISE and the T1 GSE scores of the NEETs at the CG, with the NEETs at the WISE having an average T1 GSE score that was 6.80 per cent lower that the NEETs at the CG. *Hypothesis 2 not confirmed.* Additionally, when highest educational achievement was analyzed utilizing Chi-squared tests for each case-study organization separately (see Table 8.1), the results showed that the WISE was inducting NEETs with fewer educational qualifications onto their programmes than the CG. At the WISE a larger proportion of the NEETs enrolled had no qualifications at all (31.3 per cent), compared with the CG (17.00 per cent). Additionally, only 21.9 per cent of the NEETs at the WISE had 5+ GCSEs compared to 42.6 per cent of the NEETs inducted at the CG.

Work-integration programmes – the NEET experience (Phase 1)

The analysis and results of the qualitative NEET interview data gathered at T1 and T2 is presented below for each individual case-study organization.

NEET interviews at T1 (WISE)

Analysis of the T1 interview transcripts involved the researcher engaging with the five stages of CCM. During 'immersion', the researcher identified 43 discernibly different units of analysis from the data (e.g. 'negative employment experience' and 'family breakdown'). During 'categorization', these 'units of analysis' were grouped into 12 'categories' and from these 12 categories four 'themes' emerged through a process of 'phenomenological reduction'. These four emergent 'themes' were subsequently interpreted by the researcher as: 'environmental influence', 'prior experience', 'self' and 'future'. A diagrammatic illustration of this qualitative analysis process is provided for further clarification (see Figure 8.1) and the same process was then undertaken for all subsequent analyses.

Note that the numbers displayed in Figure 8.1 in the 'categories' boxes correspond to the relevant units of analysis contained in that category. The numbers in the 'themes' boxes correspond to the relevant category contained in that theme.

NEET interviews at T2 (WISE)

During immersion, the researcher identified 37 discernibly different 'units of analysis' (e.g. 'achievement' and 'further education'). 'Categorization' resulted in 12 'categories' emerging from the 37 'units of analysis'. During 'phenomenological reduction', four 'themes' emerged from the 12 'categories'. These four emergent 'themes' were subsequently interpreted by the researcher as 'supportive environment', 'the programme', 'self' and 'future'.

NEET interviews at T1 (CG)

Analysis of the Time 1 interview transcripts involved the researcher engaging with the five stages of CCM. During 'immersion', the researcher identified 35 discernibly different units of analysis from the data (e.g. 'educational experience', 'exam results' and 'previous programmes'). During 'categorization', these 'units of analysis' were grouped into ten 'categories' and from these ten categories four 'themes' emerged through a process of 'phenomenological reduction'. These four emergent 'themes' were subsequently interpreted by the researcher as 'environmental influence', 'prior experience', 'self' and 'future'. These four themes were identical to the four themes that had emerged at T1 at the WISE.

NEET interviews at T2 (CG)

During immersion, the researcher identified 35 discernibly different 'units of analysis' (e.g. 'teamwork' 'creativity' and 'maturity'). 'Categorization' resulted in ten 'categories' emerging from the 35 'units of analysis'. During 'phenomenological reduction', four 'themes' emerged from the ten 'categories'. These four emergent 'themes' were subsequently interpreted by the researcher as 'supportive environment', 'the

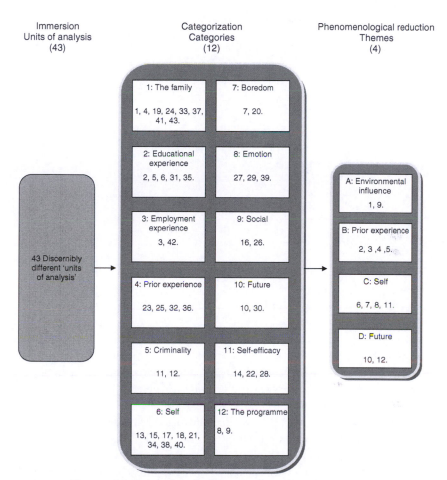

FIGURE 8.1   Phases of CCM analysis for NEET interviews at T1 (WISE)

programme', 'self' and 'future'. These four themes were identical to the themes that had emerged at T2 at the WISE.

The perspectives of the WISE owners, managers and staff

Analysis of the interview and focus group transcripts from the WISE case study involved engaging with the five stages of CCM. During 'immersion', 61 discernibly different units of analysis were identified from the data (e.g. 'funding pressures' and 'foundation learning'). During 'categorization', these 'units of analysis' were grouped into 14 'categories' and from these 14 categories five 'themes' emerged through a process of 'phenomenological reduction'. These five emergent 'themes' were subsequently interpreted as 'state contracting', 'stakeholders', 'NEETs', 'organization' and 'the programme'.

A non-social enterprise perspective (CG owners, managers and staff)

Analysis of the transcripts from the interviews and focus groups gathered at the CG involved engaging with the five stages of CCM. During 'immersion', the researcher identified 53 discernibly different units of analysis from the data (e.g. 'profits' and 'mentor'). During 'categorization', these 'units of analysis' were grouped into 16 'categories' and from these 16 categories five 'themes' emerged through a process of 'phenomenological reduction'. These five emergent 'themes' were subsequently interpreted by the researcher a: 'state contracting', 'stakeholders', 'NEETs', 'organization' and 'the programme'.

Discussion

Phase 1

Changes in GSE

The overall results of the current research support the findings of Denny *et al.* (2011), which reported that an intervention methodology utilizing a scale designed to measure GSE provides an appropriate measure of *outcome* in assessing an EEP. Analysis of the quantitative data from the current research revealed some surprising results with the null hypothesis being confirmed for both research hypotheses. In relation to the first hypothesis, for the NEETs who completed the EEP programmes at both organizations there were statistically significant increases in GSE of +4.53 per cent at the WISE ($p < .05$) and +3.75 per cent at the CG ($p < .01$). When the changes in GSE scores for the NEET participants at both organizations were compared, no statistically significant difference was found. This suggests that there was no discernible difference in 'outcome' performance between the WISE and the CG in the area of GSE. This offers support to prior research that suggested that WISEs have a beneficial effect upon the unemployed individuals that engage with them in relation to 'outcomes' (Borzaga and Loss 2006; Denny *et al.* 2011). However, it also suggests that such an effect is not confined to WISEs, but that it may also occur at for-profit organizations. This is interesting as it demonstrates that at least in relation to GSE the WISE case study offered no 'added value' in the area of 'outcome' performance.

When testing the second hypothesis a very interesting result was also obtained from the data. Results revealed a statistically significant difference between the T1 GSE scores of the NEETs at the WISE and the CG ($p < .01$). The NEETs at the CG organization had higher (+ 6.80%) GSE scores at T1 than those at the WISE. This, combined with the differences in highest educational achievement outlined by the Chi-squared analysis, suggests that the CG inducted less 'socially excluded' NEET individuals than the WISE. This implies that the induction process may be less open and more selective, hence leading to an induction of NEETs that are closer to and easier to reintegrate into employment. Whilst the NEETs at both case-study organizations can be categorized as 'complicated' NEETs with a 'here and now' mentality (Ball *et al.* 1999), who were all at NVQ Level 2 or below, this result also offers support to prior research that suggests that the NEET cohort is heterogeneous, even at sub-group level (Yates and Payne 2006). This difference in the NEETs inducted at both organizations also requires a re-evaluation of the results outlined for hypothesis one, as whilst the WISE was achieving similar 'outcome' performances to the CG it was doing so with a more 'socially excluded' NEET population. It could therefore be suggested that the added value offered by WISEs arises not through the more easily measured 'output' and 'outcome' performance, but through their willingness to induct NEET individuals who are less employable, less academically able and more 'socially excluded' (Furlong 2006).

The NEET experience at T1

The qualitative element of the research during Phase 1 offered support to the quantitative data through a process of triangulation (McLeod 1994) and this analysis will now be discussed. Supportive quotes from the interviews will be included in the discussion in order to illustrate some of the points made. The emergent themes from the NEET interviews at T1 at both case studies revealed that the majority of the participants had suffered from 'social exclusion' and could therefore be viewed as 'complicated' NEETs (Yates and Payne 2006). The current research also supported prior research reporting that NEETs are a heterogeneous entity (Yates and Payne 2006) but suggested that within the subgroup 'complicated' NEETs there was some homogeneity of experience. This was characterized in the current research sample through the emergent themes of 'environmental influence' and 'prior experience'. These two themes revealed links and provided a common story amongst the NEETs of family breakdown, problems and occasionally withdrawal from school, and ultimately failure in the workplace or further education.

> No, my Mum and Dad split up when I was young. I still see him sometimes and err … Mostly he is in and out of prison though.
>
> *(P3, WISE)*

> It was all right until my Mum went away and then I went a bit off-track, like not going in [to school] and playing up. Then the teacher started not liking me and I didn't get any help.
>
> *(P23, CG)*

This finding supports prior research that suggested that familial problems and educational failure were highly likely to lead to NEET status and 'social exclusion' (Furlong 2006; Yates and Payne 2006). These negative 'environmental influences' and 'prior experiences' impacted upon the theme of 'self' in which the NEETs articulated a largely negative view of themselves that was centred upon low self-confidence, motivation and self-belief. This negative self-image was based in the participants' negative 'prior experience' and the negative 'environmental influences' in their lives. This lack of confidence, motivation and self-belief was interpreted by the researcher as indicating low self-efficacy, as prior research has shown these constructs to be key components of self-efficacy (Judge *et al.* 1997). Self-efficacy beliefs are based upon past experiences (Gist and Mitchell 1992), as positive mastery experiences reinforce efficacy beliefs and negative experiences reduce perceived efficaciousness (Bandura 1997). Additionally, environmental influences can also affect efficacy beliefs as individuals also develop self-efficacy through the 'vicarious experience' of watching others close to them succeed (Bandura 1977).

> I get quite knocked if I don't do it first time around, it was like at school. I remember being the only one that couldn't answer a certain maths question and the teacher had gone over every single way possible about getting it and I still couldn't get it. So I thought you know what I'm not doing it, and I didn't even acknowledge she was there I just blanked her completely. If I can't do something first time around I probably won't do it again.
>
> *(P6, WISE)*

> My main confidence issue is when I have a group of people staring at me, like when you do talks, that is when I get less confident ... I just feel shy because everyone is staring at me and half the people I don't know and I have to sit there and talk about what I'm doing, it's again mainly pressure on me.
>
> *(P26, CG)*

Interestingly, whilst the themes of 'environmental influence' and 'prior experience' emerged from the T1 data at both case studies, these were more negative for the NEETs at the WISE case study when compared to the CG. Whilst the participants at the CG had also suffered 'social exclusion' in the form of family breakdown and bereavement as well as negative peer relationships, the participants had not experienced some of the more acute problems reported by the NEETs at the WISE, such as parental abuse or criminality. Additionally, instances of criminal behaviour and alcohol and drug abuse were found to be fewer for the NEETs at the CG than those at the WISE.

> I don't know I think it was the people I was hanging around with. That's when I started drinking and all that stuff like that and taking drugs ... I don't really want to do it most of the time but I just do it.
>
> *(P5, WISE)*

These differences impacted upon NEET individual's self-perceptions leading the NEET individuals at the CG to be more realistic in their self-assessments, and whilst confidence was still an issue it was restricted to social situations rather than being a general lack of confidence as was the case with the participants at the WISE. It is suggested that this reduced anxiety and higher self-efficacy is based upon the more positive 'prior experience' of the NEETs at the CG, which enabled higher self-efficacy through mastery experiences (e.g. higher educational qualifications). This led the participants at the CG to articulate aspirations that were less vague and unrealistic than the NEETs at the WISE, who seemed to be drifting without any real goals.

> Well, [friend] just said about joining it and it was something to do instead of just being at home doing nothing whilst I wait for somebody to ring back about a job in whatever, so I thought I would do it.
>
> *(P10, WISE)*

> My aim now is to get into Retail and Customer Service because you just get new things every day, you know, new things to deal with.
>
> *(P28, CG)*

This suggests that the participants enrolled at the CG had generally suffered from less 'social exclusion' than those enrolled at the WISE. It also supports the notion of the heterogeneous nature of NEETs (Ball *et al.* 1999; Yates and Payne 2006), even when the focus is on a particular sub-group (i.e. 'complicated NEETs') (Yates and Payne 2006). The findings also provide support for the interpretation of the quantitative data gathered at T1 through a process of triangulation (McLeod 1994), which suggested that the CG was inducting less 'socially excluded' individuals on to its work-integration programme who had higher initial GSE scores and higher educational attainments.

Qualitative results T2

The findings from the analysis of the NEET interviews at T2 revealed that the participants at both case studies perceived positive 'outcome' benefits related to their time spent on the work-integration programme. The participants talked about the 'supportive environment' that they experienced on 'the programme', which alleviated the impact of the negative themes of 'environmental influence' and 'prior experience' that had emerged at T1. They also talked positively about the enhanced employability skills that the work-integration programmes had given them and how this had led to more structured job-search activity. This led to the emergence of a more positive theme of 'self' at T2 in which the participants talked about increased confidence, motivation and creativity that was interpreted as increased GSE (Judge *et al.* 1997). The fourth emergent theme of 'future' was thus also more positive with participants articulating realistic career aspirations, which importantly were grounded in actual 'career plans' detailing how they would achieve their goals. Researcher interpretations of the emergent themes at T1 and T2 indicate the positive effect that both the case studies had upon the NEET participants in terms of *outcome* benefits. Triangulation (McLeod 1994) of the results of the qualitative analysis with the quantitative results outlined above confirms that there were no significant differences in the 'outcome' benefits experienced by the NEETs at either case-study organization.

The T2 theme of 'supportive environment' that emerged from the interviews at the WISE and CG, replaced the negative theme of 'environmental influence' that emerged at T1. The participants talked about the support that they had received and how they had been treated 'like an adult' and given 'trust' and 'responsibility'. Participants positively contrasted this support with their negative 'prior experiences' and talked about how the 'supportive environment' offered to them had allowed them to positively develop their confidence, motivation and self-belief. This was interpreted as increases in participant self-efficacy, through verbal persuasion (Judge *et al.* 1997; Chen *et al.* 2001). The theme of 'prior experience' that emerged from the data at T1 at both the WISE and the CG was not present at T2, which may be symptomatic of how the 'supportive environment' at the WISE and CG diminished the effect of these negative experiences and so reduced 'social exclusion' (Yates and Payne 2006).

> Because like with all the other places I haven't had a lot of respect for them because they didn't to me. But then the minute I came here I felt welcome and stuff like that, like [previous school] and [previous course] just didn't speak to you. But like here I've had loads of people speaking to me and stuff like that, so I felt welcome straight away.
>
> *(P2, WISE)*

> The teachers back in my old college, they wouldn't really help you, it is just basically they will go through it once and then that's it you have to do it. The ones that come here you have got more support from these people than the last place.
>
> *(P24, CG)*

The theme 'the programme' emerged from the T2 interview data at both case-study organizations and was predicated upon participant evaluations of the programme that they had just experienced. The participants discussed the educational qualifications that they had gained (i.e. BTECs), as well as other 'outputs' that they had achieved such as CV enhancement and employability skills. These educational 'mastery experiences' were one of the main factors behind improvements in participant self-perceptions and the participants linked their ability to succeed to the 'supportive environment' offered by both the programmes. The researcher proposes that this 'supportive environment' allowed for 'mastery experiences' via 'verbal persuasion', both of which augmented self-efficacy beliefs (Bandura 1997; Chen *et al.* 2001).

> I would sometimes say something bad about myself instead of saying something positive, whereas now I would always say something positive. Recently I just had an interview and the person said after the interview I did a really good interview so I can see straightaway it has helped me a lot.
>
> *(P26, CG)*

There was also an acknowledgement that they had been able to develop their social skills and overcome fear of new situations. Again, the researcher interpreted this as an increase in self-efficacy as the participants were more open to new and challenging environments (Lindley and Borgen 2002). Finally, the NEETs at both case studies talked about the importance of meeting other young people in similar situations, which allowed them to mitigate feelings of isolation.

> Well, it's like when I first started I was like shy at first, because obviously I didn't know anybody … I got put in their group and after about three days I was just like a team leader if you know what I mean.
>
> *(P2, WISE)*

This social experience coupled with the 'supportive environment' provided a 'substitute family' for some of the participants, which allowed them to reduce the effect of the negative 'environmental influences' and 'prior experiences' talked about at T1 and hence contributed to reducing the effects of 'social exclusion' (Furlong 2006; Yates and Payne 2006).

The theme of 'self' also re-emerged at T2 from the interview data at both case-study organizations and was much more positive due to the positive effects of 'the programme' and the 'supportive environment' outlined above. The NEETs at both case-study organizations expressed increases in confidence, increases in motivation and improved self-belief. The participants stated that these changes in confidence, motivation and self-belief were due to the work-integration programmes that they had completed, and in particular the process of undertaking and completing tasks on the programme. This finding has been interpreted as representing increases in general self-efficacy augmented through 'mastery experiences', 'vicarious experience' and 'verbal persuasion' (Bandura 1997; Chen *et al.* 2001; Judge *et al.* 1997).

> Well, it feels better because I know now I can actually achieve something if I try. So I didn't really believe in myself last time like when I was at school, I just felt stupid, but now I know if I try I can.
>
> *(P5, WISE)*

> It's like my confidence is … well, towards work I can work better in a team now than I did before. I can work a lot more and be a lot more confident with people that I don't know.
>
> *(P27, CG)*

Such an evaluation is also supported by the quantitative results outlined earlier through a process of triangulation (McLeod 1994), which detailed statistically significant increases in GSE between T1 and T2 at both case studies. However, participants had still retained some negative self-perceptions in the form of recognizing that they still had emotional problems (i.e. anger management issues). This is quite understandable and it would be unrealistic to state that the 'social exclusion' discussed by the NEETs could be fully overcome by a work-integration programme. Nevertheless, the overall effects upon the NEET participants' self-image at both case studies were positive and offer support to prior research that suggests that work-integration programmes have a beneficial effect upon the 'human and social capital' of participants who engage with them (Borzaga and Loss 2006). The 'supportive environment' and mastery experiences offered by 'the programme' not only had a positive effect upon the theme of 'self', but also caused a much more positive and optimistic theme of 'future' to re-emerge at T2. The participants had moved away from what Ball *et al.* (1999) termed the 'here and now' and 'hazy futures' groups towards the 'definitive group' in which the NEETs had 'clearer' aspirations. This provided a buffer for and limited the other constraints on a young person's career choices caused by their negative 'prior experiences' and 'environmental influences'.

> Well, after I finished at [WISE] I'm going to go and get my forestry qualifications, because I'm going to do this because it is a lot better for me.
>
> *(P7, WISE)*

> No, I didn't really have a clue before. Nothing was planned out. Ever since I've come here they have helped me in my career choice.
>
> *(P24, CG)*

Finally, throughout the qualitative analysis of the interview data at T2, no significant differences in the experience of the NEETs at both case-study organizations was found, with both organizations seeming to have a positive effect upon the young people who completed the programmes in relation to the 'output' and 'outcome' benefits received. This supports the quantitative data through a process of 'triangulation' (McLeod 1994), which also found no statistically significant difference in GSE-related 'outcome' performance for the WISE and CG organizations.

Phase 2

The perspectives of the owners, managers and staff at both organizations

In relation to the qualitative data gathered from the owners, managers and staff at the WISE and the CG, the data revealed the importance of stakeholder relationships. Stakeholder relationships were found to be crucial to programme provision. Staff, clients and trustees were viewed as the most important stakeholders at the WISE, as securing their 'buy-in' to the social mission and developing their potential had the biggest impact upon programme delivery and this underlined the dual ownership structure operated by the WISE (Gui 1991; Reid and Griffith 2006). The use and development of this 'social capital' (Coleman 1990; Putnam 1993) was viewed as key to securing successful 'outcome' benefits (McLoughlin *et al.* 2009).

> [The new member of staff] would come thinking he was only going to be a [job title] and we would have to say well actually we are looking for

something deeper. We are looking for somebody who is totally committed to the social enterprise and everything that we are.

(P18, WISE)

However, external stakeholders (i.e. local authorities or employers) were also seen to affect programme delivery and performance and in particular a lack of 'trust' or 'engagement' from external stakeholders was viewed as a limiting factor in allowing optimal programme delivery. This caused problems in the decision-making process as the social entrepreneurs, managers and staff had to spend valuable time negotiating with these external stakeholders rather than focusing upon the social mission. The CG organization also adopted a multi-stakeholder approach, although this was more limited than the relationships forged by the WISE, with the main external stakeholder being the local authority.

[W]e have worked very closely with Connexions and we do believe in working with people and networking.

(P30, CG)

This can be seen as representing more limited 'social capital' as the CG did not utilize the same breadth of stakeholders in pursuing its mission (Coleman 1990; Putnam 1993). As with the WISE, staff training was seen as important, although the CG owner was the first to admit that this was an area that they could improve upon.

The owners/managers and staff at the WISE were extremely positive about the impact of the organizational structure on the delivery of the work-integration programme. The dual ownership structure operated by the WISE (Gui 1991; Reid and Griffith 2006) in which the staff had input into the decision-making processes at a strategic and operational level allowed the staff to be more flexible in programme delivery.

It has a massive impact and that is where the trust and the support that you get from your overarching body … When you go to a meeting and say we could lose [money] this year … And they said right okay let's have a look, who have we saved, who is a better person … they are prepared to just look at that and say we will not just turn into a sausage factory.

(P21, WISE)

This allowed the staff to focus upon the 'triple bottom line' (Campi *et al.* 2006), which freed them to pursue social goals even at the expense of economic considerations. This allowed the WISE to resist the pressures placed upon it by state contracts more robustly than the CG, although the pressure to morph from a client-focused to funder-focused organization was sometimes irresistible (Aiken 2006). The CG case-study staff and owner talked about how the organizational structure that was in place was there to allow the fulfilment of the CG's economic *and* social goals. Indeed, the company ethos was centred to a degree upon a social mission of 'helping people', although this was often tempered by economic considerations.

> When you join the company and the ethos was the learner and the journey and things like that, and progressively it has become more about finances and figures and achievements and all that kind of thing and I'm not that kind of person really.
> *(P34, CG)*

There was an important difference between the CG and the WISE in how they responded to pressure from state contracting, with performance evaluation and strict delivery guidelines viewed by the CG staff and owner to be a hindrance upon performance. The need to meet targets in order to secure funding and remain financially viable meant that 'mission drift' occurred in relation to the social goals of the organization (Aiken 2006; Seddon *et al.* 2012).

> The senior management think that they [NEETs] have got to come here every day, because ultimately if they are here every day then they will achieve earlier and we are a business so then you can get the next one in. But then there are learners who can't do that, so when you suggest that they are only going to do an hour and a half per day for six weeks … then that learner is going to be on the program as far as the books are concerned for three times the length of time and yet we only get the same amount of money [as normal].
> *(P33, CG)*

Finally, whilst the WISE reinvested *all* its profits into either the 'social mission' or infrastructure, the CG neither withdrew profits from the business nor invested in anything other than infrastructure, preferring to instead leave the money in reserve in order to secure the company's long-term future. This raises an interesting point as to whether the non-distribution of profits in social enterprises is indeed unique, or whether many small- and medium-sized businesses also do the same? This is an important question that future research should seek to answer.

In relation to the work-integration programmes that were delivered, the owners, managers and staff at the WISE saw the supportive environment provided as key to the success that they had in assisting NEET individuals. This support was offered mainly through the use of mentors who acted as role models to the young people, and also via small class sizes that allowed more one-to-one interaction. The staff members stated that it was important in developing the NEETs to set the young people goals that they could achieve and that they often offered encouragement to the young people as they progressed. This was interpreted as being the mastery experiences and verbal persuasion that are crucial in the development of self-efficacy (Bandura 1997; Chen *et al.* 2001).

> I think all of us here make an effort that if any of the guys do something even reasonably well or even just give them a go, we make sure that we praise them

and I think that that actually helps to develop their confidence because they realize 'I'm not useless and I actually do have ability'. So then they take pride in themselves.

(P17, WISE)

Additionally, the staff talked about the increases in individuals' confidence, motivation and self-belief that they witnessed as the young people progressed through the course, which again was interpreted as increases in GSE (Judge *et al.* 1997). The WISE staff viewed such 'outcome' benefits as being more important than the 'output' benefits (i.e. qualifications gained). They felt that the pressures inherent in state contracts to meet these 'output' criteria meant that their ability to deliver 'outcome' benefits to the NEETs was compromised, leading to inevitable 'mission drift' (Aiken 2006).

The staff and the owner at the CG case study also discussed the importance of providing a supportive environment within their programme. As with the staff, owners and managers at the WISE they saw this as being key to obtaining 'outcome' benefits such as increases in confidence, motivation and self-belief (GSE) (Judge *et al.* 1997). The allocation to each individual of a life-coach was seen as important in developing trust with the NEETs, as was offering them a structured programme that had to be adhered to.

Here it is part of the programme [having a life-coach] and I think that some of them they don't like talking about it but actually they are the ones that benefit more. It is tailored so that if somebody needs more support then they see somebody more often.

(P35, CG)

This structure consisted of giving the young people clearer and more structured career aspirations and plans and helped give the young people a definitive and positive perception of their future (Ball *et al.* 1999). The key difference between the programmes delivered by the WISE and the CG however, was in relation to the induction policy. The induction policy at the CG was not open and instead relied on the young people attending an interview during which it was decided whether they were suitable for the programme. The decisions at these interviews were made based upon the young person's past experience and their attitude at the interview.

Sometimes alarm bells would ring [at the induction interview] and so we would just say we will ring you up. You know we have had learners come in and they have been to ten other training providers. Well, what is going on then if you're coming here to do the same program? So we ring up some of the other providers and find out why.

(P31, CG)

Whilst there was no rigid entry criteria set this process did allow the CG to perhaps filter out the NEETs that were not suitable for the programme or the organization, and this offers a possible explanation for the higher levels of GSE at T1 of the NEETs at the CG and the greater 'social exclusion' that the WISE NEETs reported at T1.

In relation to the NEET individuals, the owners, managers and staff at the WISE and the CG articulated similar perceptions of the origins of NEET status. The role of the young person's home environment and their familial background were seen as particularly important, as was educational experience, with low academic achievement being seen as a barrier to employment or further education. The owners, managers and staff at both organizations also acknowledged the heterogeneous nature of the NEET cohort (Yates and Payne 2006) and talked about how the recent recession had increased this heterogeneity with less 'socially excluded' individuals now becoming NEET. The negative impact of 'social exclusion' upon NEET confidence, motivation and self-belief was also discussed and this was interpreted as being a negative impact upon GSE (Judge *et al.* 1997) due to negative past experiences (Gist and Mitchell 1992). Finally, the staff at the WISE also acknowledged that the organization's open-access induction policy meant that they had to achieve the same results as other work-integration organizations but with a more 'socially excluded' NEET cohort.

> I have always felt as an organization we are almost morally obligated to take on some of the learners the other sites won't take, which has within itself great challenges but it also has greater rewards from a social point of view … That is the beauty of social enterprise and where we sort of step into the equation.
>
> *(P15, WISE)*

Summary

The quantitative analysis of 'outcome' performance at the two organizations showed that both the WISE and the CG had a positive impact on the GSE levels of their NEET participants. Crucially, the GSE data revealed no significant differences in the 'outcome' performance of the WISE and for-profit CG. However, the quantitative data did reveal that the NEETs at the WISE had significantly lower GSE levels at T1 than their counterparts at the CG. The interview data gathered from the NEETs at both organizations at T1 and T2 supported the quantitative results through a process of triangulation (McLeod 1994). The interviews with the owners, managers and staff at both organizations revealed that the differences in levels of 'social exclusion' and GSE scores at T1 was due to the differing induction policies operated by both organizations, with the WISE operating an open-access induction process. Additionally, whilst the social missions at both organizations were restricted by the pressures of state contracting, the WISE was able to resist such 'mission drift' (Aiken 2006) more robustly than the CG. The results of this research therefore suggest that the 'added value' offered by WISEs that deliver EEPs to NEETs may not be measurable in 'outcome' data, but rather may be related to their willingness to take on more 'socially excluded' individuals (Yates and Payne 2006) and to their ability to better resist the 'mission drift' pressures inherent in state contracting (Aiken 2006). Such research that undertakes a comparative, longitudinal analysis of WISE 'outcome' performance utilizing mixed methods offers interesting insights into the potential 'added value' offered by WISEs, as well as providing valid and reliable methods for evaluating work-integration programme performance in both the private and third sectors.

References

Aiken, M. (2006) 'Towards market or state? Tensions and opportunities in the evolutionary path of three UK social enterprises', in Nyssens, M. (ed.) (2006) *Social Enterprise*. Oxon: Routledge.

Aiken, M. (2007) *What is the Role of Social Enterprise in Funding, Creating and Maintaining Employment for Disadvantaged Groups?* London: Office for the Third Sector.

Ball, S. J., Macrae, S. and Maguire, M. (1999) 'Young lives, diverse choices and imagined futures in an education and training market', *International Journal of Inclusive Education*, 1999, 3(3): 195–224.

Bandura, A. (1977) 'Self-efficacy: toward a unifying theory of behavioural change', *Psychological Review*, 84(2): 191–215.

Bandura, A. (1997) *Self-Efficacy: The Exercise of Control*. New York: W. H. Freeman and Company.

Borzaga, C. and Defourny, J. (eds) (2001) *The Emergence of Social Enterprise*. London: Routledge.

Borzaga, C. and Loss, M. (2006) 'Profiles and trajectories of participants in European WISEs', in Nyssens, M. (ed.) *Social Enterprise*. Oxon: Routledge, pp. 169–94.

Campi, S., Defourny, J. and Grégoire, O. (2006) 'Work-Integration Social Enterprises: are they multiple goal and multi-stakeholder organisations?', in Nyssens, M. (ed.) (2006) *Social Enterprise*. Oxon: Routledge, pp. 29–49.

Chen, G., Gully, S. M. and Eden, D. (2001) 'Validation of a new general self-efficacy scale', *Organisational Research Methods*, January 2001, 4(1): 62–83.

Coleman, J. S. (1990) *Foundations of Social Theory*. Cambridge, MA: Harvard University Press.

Concannon, L. (2008) 'Citizenship, sexual identity and social exclusion: exploring issues in British and American social policy', *International Journal of Sociology and Social Policy*, 28(9–10): 326–39.

Dart, R. (2004) 'The legitimacy of social enterprise', *Non-Profit Management and Leadership*, 14(4): 411–24.

Defourny, J., Favreau, L. and Laville, J. L. (eds) (1998) *Insertion et Nouvelle Économie Sociale*. Paris: Un Bilan International, Desclée de Brouwer.

Denny, S., Hazenberg, R., Irwin, W. and Seddon, F. (2011) 'Social enterprise: evaluation of an enterprise skills programme', *Social Enterprise Journal*, 7(2): 150–72.

Furlong, A. (2006) 'Not a very NEET solution: representing problematic labour market transitions among early school leavers', *Journal of Work, Employment and Society*, 20(3): 553.

Gist, M. E. and Mitchell, T. R. (1992) 'Self-efficacy: a theoretical analysis of its determinants and malleability', *Academy of Management Review*, 17(2): 183–211.

Glaser, B. G. and Strauss, A. L. (1967) *The Discovery of Grounded Theory*. Chicago, IL: Aldine.

Gui, B. (1991) 'The economic rationale for the third sector', *Annals of Public and Cooperative Economics*, 62(4): 551–72.

Haugh, H. (2007) 'Community-led social venture creation', *Entrepreneurship Theory and Practice*, 31(2): 161–82.

Haugh, H. and Kitson, M. (2007) 'The third way and the third sector: New Labour's economic policy and the social economy', *Cambridge Journal of Economics*, 31: 973–94.

Instance, D., Rees, G. and Williamson, H. (1994) *Young People Not in Education, Employment or Training in South Glamorgan*. South Glamorgan: South Glamorgan Training and Enterprise Council.

Judge, T. A., Locke, E. A. and Durham, C. C. (1997) 'The dispositional causes of job satisfaction: a core evaluation approach', *Research in Organisational Behaviour*, 19: 151–88.

Kline, P. (1999) *The Handbook of Psychological Testing*, Second Edition. London: Routledge.

Laville, J. L. and Nyssens, M. (2001) 'The social enterprise: towards a theoretical socio-economic approach', in Borzaga, C. and Defourny, J. (eds) (2001) *The Emergence of Social Enterprise*. London: Routledge, pp. 312–32.

Lincoln, Y. and Guba, E. (1985) *Naturalistic Inquiry*. Beverly Hills, CA: Sage.

Lindley, L. D. and Borgen, F. H. (2002) 'Generalised self-efficacy, Holland theme self-efficacy and academic performance', *Journal of Career Assessment*, 10(3): 301–14.

McLeod, J. (1994) *Doing Counselling Research*. London: Sage.

McLoughlin, J., Kaminski, J., Sodagar, B., Khan, S., Harris, R., Arnaudo, G. and McBrearty, S. (2009) 'A strategic approach to social impact measurement of social enterprises: the SIMPLE methodology', *Social Enterprise Journal*, 2(2): 154–78.

Mason, C. (2010) 'Choosing sides: contrasting attitudes to governance issues in social firms in the UK', *Social Enterprise Journal*, 6(1): 6–22.

Pearce, J. (2003) *Social Enterprise in Anytown*. London: Calouste Gulbenkian Foundation.

Peattie, K. and Morley, A. (June 2008) *Social Enterprise: Diversity and Dynamics, Contexts and Contributions*, Conference paper presented at Fifth Annual Social Enterprise Research Conference, 26–27 June 2008, London Southbank University, ESRC Publication.

Putnam, R. D. (1993) 'The prosperous community: social capital and public life', *The American Prospect*, 13: 35–42.

Reid, K. and Griffith, J. (2006) 'Social enterprise mythology: critiquing some assumptions', *Social Enterprise Journal*, 2(1): 1–10.

Schwarzer, R. and Jerusalem, M. (1995) 'Generalized self-efficacy scale' in Weinman, J., Wright, S. and Johnston, M. (1995) *Measures in Health Psychology: A User's Portfolio*, Windsor: NFER-Nelson, pp. 35–37.

Seddon, F., Hazenberg, R. and Denny, S. (2012) 'Evaluating the partnership between a university and a social enterprise development agency engaged in the set-up and development of a social enterprise', Conference paper presented at the Twenty-sixth Annual United States Association for Small Business and Entrepreneurship, 15 January 2012, New Orleans, USA.

Yates, S. and Payne, M. (2006) 'Not so NEET? A critique of the use of 'NEET' in setting targets for interventions with young people', *Journal of Youth Studies*, 9(3): 329–44.

9

HOW DO WE KNOW IF SOCIAL ENTERPRISE WORKS?

Tools for assessing social enterprise performance

Kelly Hall and Malin Arvidson

Introduction

Being able to demonstrate achievements and success has become an essential preoccupation for social enterprise organizations of today. How can such organizations know what they achieve? And how can they communicate this? These are challenging questions when applied to interventions aimed at delivering social and environmental impacts, and for organizations dealing with an array of stakeholders that may have very different views on how these impacts should be defined and evidenced. This chapter contributes to current debates about these and related questions held in the social enterprise community and among commissioners, grant-making bodies and social investors.

In the first part of the chapter we provide a background to the use of evaluations and performance measurement in social enterprises and charities. Here, we point out how recent events related to policy and funding arrangements have created considerable interest in impact evaluation. We also identify the confusion and concern that has been voiced around the vast array of evaluation tools available and the different ways in which social impact and achievement is communicated. In doing so, we pose questions such as: How should an organization select an appropriate evaluation tool?; How can we make sense of evaluation results and use them to understand the impact of an organization?; Can we use results of evaluations to compare across different organizations? In the second part of the chapter, we address these questions by examining three impact evaluation frameworks, namely Social Return on Investment, the Outcomes Star, and randomized controlled trials. By investigating the three frameworks together we can highlight and better understand both their similarities and their considerable differences. In providing this analysis we illustrate how evaluations are not just instrumental tools to assess achievements but also frameworks that encompass value systems that often remain unrecognized in current debates.

Evaluation and measurement in social enterprise

The use of measurements and evaluations in social enterprises and charities is nothing new, but the rationale for and means of measuring social value has changed over time. In the UK in the early twentieth century, charities used quantifiable measurements to demonstrate the need for interventions and to legitimate their role as welfare providers (Barman 2007). Since then a range of developments related to the measurement of achievements in private and public sectors has influenced the way social enterprises measure and evaluate their activities. The concept and practice of 'performance management' has migrated from the private to public and non-profit sectors (Paton 2003). This has often been related to a move towards general rationalization and professionalization of third-sector organizations, resulting in an increased pressure for such organizations to monitor, evaluate and manage performance (Hwang and Powell 2009). In recent decades public funding to the third sector has risen (NCVO 2011) and with partnership and contracts come requirements for formal accountability: what has been achieved with the support of taxpayers' money? We can also notice methodological advances that allow us to capture and communicate organizational achievements, including those that are intangible. In sum, institutional culture, funding arrangements, and the availability of evaluation tools have all come to present social enterprises with expectations and opportunities to measure their performance.

Financial, political and normative contexts matter greatly in how evaluations are conceptualized and what motivates their use. Since the late 1990s UK government policy has promoted an outcomes-focused basis for assessing the delivery of public services, which is different from a previous focus on output targets (Ellis 2009). As the third sector has become increasingly involved in delivering public services and thus being a government partner, this outcomes agenda has come to influence the way in which the work of third-sector organizations is assessed and managed. More recent policies place emphasis on how evidence of what works will drive the allocation of funds (Cabinet Office 2011; Department of Health 2011). The open public service reform, introduced in 2011 (Department of Health 2011) emphasizes 'evidence of what works' and the so-called Social Value Act of 2012 (Public Services (Social Value) Act 2012) is aimed, among other things, at ascertaining that social value, in addition to financial value, is considered by commissioners in procurement procedures. With the recession and increasing financial cuts to the welfare state that affect private, public and third sectors alike, funders in general are becoming concerned with finding ways of ascertaining that money is allocated in a wise way, making best use of scarce resources. We also notice new funding opportunities opening up, such as social impact bonds and contracts based on payment-by-results that can only be accessed based on demonstrable outcomes. Concepts such as 'investment ready' and 'returns on investment' reveal a new basis for relations being formed between funders and organizations (Barclays Wealth and New Philanthropy Capital 2011; Kane and Allen 2011). The impetus to assess achievements does, of course, also come from within organizations. Evaluations can serve a variety of functions including as political tools, an important means for competition, to enhance legitimacy, as the basis for accountability and to fulfil moral obligations towards different stakeholder groups. They can also act as an important basis for learning and for furthering our understanding of complex social problems (Lyon and Arvidson 2011; Nicholls 2009).

Today, there is a plethora of impact evaluation frameworks to choose from; the evaluation arena is characterized by methodological pluralism and there is no short-age of options. The context in one sense presents organizations with a coherent call for evidence and evaluations. Nevertheless, social enterprise organizations looking to embark on comprehensive impact assessment face some challenges. The decision regarding how and what to measure is not easy, since 'the voluntary sector is com-plicated by the absence of a single and shared criterion for success' (Barman 2007: 104). Furthermore, a whole host of outside stakeholders presents organizations with competing ideas about the role the sector should play in society (Kendall 2009; Kendall and Knapp 2000), resulting in conflicting ideas about what to measure and how to measure it.

In the following section we look into three specific evaluation frameworks. Two of them (SROI and the Outcomes Star) have been developed with social purpose organizations specifically in mind, and a third example (randomized controlled trials) has an established tradition as an impact evaluation tool in various settings. An impor-tant common denominator for the frameworks is that they go beyond registering inputs/outputs and aim at capturing more comprehensive achievements by interven-tions aimed at solving complex social problems. While *inputs* and *outputs* are often tangible and relatively straightforward to monitor and report, *outcomes* and *impacts* are soft, intangible achievements that are more difficult to capture and value. Outcomes are achieved as the result of a chain of activities and they are usually set out in the objectives of an organization or intervention. Impact refers to a wider range of effects that reaches beyond the immediate beneficiaries such as families and communities, and can include intended as well as unintended outcomes (see Wainwright 2002).

Research into evaluations covers a wide range of topics, including methodol-ogy, validity and utilization of evaluations, as well as performance management, accountancy and accountability. Our intention here is to introduce the reader to some important features that have particular relevance to the examples we raise, and that also have a general bearing for the implementation and use of impact evaluation in the social enterprise setting. In brief, these features refer to the values underlying the frameworks, the way impact is defined, and the language used when presenting evaluation results. We will return to these issues in a concluding discus-sion, and also comment on the question, 'On what basis do we make a choice between these three frameworks?'

Social Return on Investment (SROI)

SROI was developed by the Roberts Enterprise Development Fund in the United States in the 1990s in an attempt to develop a measure that would reflect the overall value (economic, social and environmental) of an organization. The tool was then adapted for use in the UK in the late 1990s by the New Economics Foundation, and more recently has been adapted by the Office of the Third Sector (Nicholls *et al.* 2012). It has been used across a variety of different social enterprise sectors in the UK, most notably within employment programmes and the health and social care sector. It is based upon the principles of accountancy and cost–benefit analysis as it uses money as a unit of analysis to quantify and express social value creation. It measures the social benefits generated by an organization (or intervention) in relation to the economic cost of achieving those benefits. The result is a ratio of monetized social value. For example, a ratio of 4:1 indicates that an investment of £1 into a project generates the equivalent of £4 in social value.

The purpose of SROI is to 'tell the story of how change is being created' (Nicholls *et al.* 2012: 8) and although it does produce a quantitative monetary ratio of value, an SROI evaluation also includes qualitative data. Outcomes data including the amount and type of value created is collected from different groups of stakeholders (people who benefit from the service or intervention). By including multiple stakeholders in the initial stage of impact-mapping, several benefits (and any drawbacks) of the intervention can be recognized and included, rather than just those that the organization itself has identified as goals. SROI is therefore flexible and designed to measure multiple effects of a social enterprise and may include the social value generated by an entire organization, or focus on just one specific aspect of the organization's work.

Box 9.1 Using SROI in an alcohol and drug rehabilitation service

SROI has been used in a social enterprise project that provides housing and rehabilitative care for families recovering from alcohol/drug dependency. The project is built on the premise that by rehabilitating parents, children become happier and more settled. To undertake a forecast SROI, five key stakeholder groups were identified: adults who use the service, their children, other family members, state agencies (e.g. NHS, social services, police) and commissioners. Discussion with stakeholders was undertaken to create an 'impact map' which detailed the inputs (e.g. volunteer time), outputs (e.g. number of people housed) and outcomes (e.g. keeping children out of care, reduced hospital admissions) created by the service. The outcomes were then valued or monetized using financial proxies, e.g. the cost of a hospital admission. The SROI analysis produced a ratio of 3.42:1 so for every £1 invested in the service, there was a potential social return of £3.42.

(Adapted from Department of Health 2010)

A major challenge in all impact evaluations is to deal with the counterfactual, i.e. what would have happened anyway. SROI presents a framework for how to work out the extent to which the benefits derived are directly attributable to the activities of that organization, as well as the extent to which the benefits would have been achieved without the intervention (also referred to as 'deadweight'). The degree to which the benefits of an intervention are at the expense of other groups (displacement) should also be considered within the analysis, e.g. a group helped into work by an intervention may deny those jobs to other people outside of the intervention. Finally, SROI also considers 'drop off', that is if the benefits of an intervention can be maintained in the long term.

An SROI can be either *evaluative,* which assesses the actual social return on investment of past activity, or *forecast,* which is an estimate of future returns if the activities meet their intended outcomes. Although much focus is on the SROI ratio, it is also a framework that aims to communicate an organization's 'story of change' through case studies and qualitative data (Nicholls *et al.* 2012). It can therefore show why and how outcomes are created. This information can be used externally to attract funding, but also internally as an instrument for organizational learning and improvement by enabling staff to recognize the strengths and weaknesses of a service through the eyes of stakeholders and service users (New Philanthropy Capital 2010).

The benefits and drawbacks of SROI

SROI is an internationally recognized tool that can be used in any organization that creates social and/or environmental value. It has been promoted in the UK by the Office of the Third Sector (Nicholls *et al.* 2012) and the Department of Health (Department of Health 2010) and is considered especially useful as a framework to provide evidence of savings to the public purse, e.g. savings through reduced hospital admissions or getting people into work. By presenting outcomes in a monetary way, SROI provides a unique tool that communicates cost savings to existing and potential funders, and to the general taxpayer. This can give organizations a competitive advantage in tenders for public-sector contracts (Ryan and Lyne 2008), which is especially important in the current context where competition and the ability to demonstrate value for money are driving public-sector funding decisions.

There are, however, a number of difficulties associated with SROI (Millar and Hall 2012; Arvidson *et al.* 2012). This includes the limitations around the extent to which social value can actually be monetized. The outcomes created by social enterprises are often intangible and not immediately evident, e.g. increased confidence or self-esteem, and so are difficult to attribute financial value. However, in practice, evaluations may focus on outcomes that are more monetized and for which financial proxies are available, for example getting someone into work, which can be measured through reduced benefit payments and increased tax revenue. By focusing on these tangible outcomes, SROI may fail to capture the true social benefits produced by an organization, especially those that enhance a person's overall quality of life. Nonetheless, financial proxies are continually being developed, as noted in an addition dated 2011 to the government's so-called Green Book (a guidance on economic assessment) which presents guidelines as to how non-market impacts can be valued (HM Treasury 2011). The SROI UK network also provides guidelines on proxies and indicators, which gives an important incentive for transparency in how evaluations and ratios are calculated. Such developments are likely to enhance consistency of SROI calculations across different organizations.

Other difficulties associated with SROI, and indeed other impact evaluations as we will discuss further, regard attribution (the extent to which the outcomes are caused by other organizations or interventions) and counterfactuals (the extent to which the outcomes would have occurred anyway, without intervention). SROI refers to established ways of coping with these issues, and some of these problems can be resolved by using multiple groups of stakeholders who are well placed to assess the value of the intervention, especially in comparison to other interventions in the area. Nevertheless, it leaves considerable room for individual judgement by organizations, and this combined with limitations on the availability of financial proxies can cause problems with inconsistencies in how SROI evaluations have been conducted and ratios calculated (New Philanthropy Capital 2010). Furthermore, SROI is subject to considerations on the time period by which the intervention is measured. Differences in indicators, proxies and time periods over which an intervention is measured mean that SROI ratios are often specific to an organization so cannot be used to compare across different organizations.

Outcomes Star

The Outcomes Star (OS) is a measurement tool that was designed to both support and measure change in vulnerable service users. The first prototype version of the Star was developed by Triangle Consulting in 2003 on behalf of St Mungo's, a homelessness charity in London. It was then tested and improved in a range of other homelessness agencies, and the first publicly available version was published by the London Housing Foundation in 2006. It has since been adapted to a variety of different settings and user groups, including young people (Teen Star), mental health (Recovery Star) and parenting (Family Star). The tool is visual in design and was developed using a 'bottom-up' approach, by engaging with staff and service users to ascertain what the main outcomes of a service should be and how those outcomes can be achieved. OS is therefore not rigid in its design and so new versions can be created according to the needs of a specific service or user group. By being adaptable, the tool can appeal to a wide range of users, for example the Teen Star uses a relatively short, simple quiz format designed to hold the attention of teenagers.

As it is a relatively new evaluation tool, OS has not yet been academically evaluated in a robust way as for example SROI has (except see Burns *et al.* 2008; Dickens *et al.* 2012). However, the tool is underpinned by ideas from existential phenomenology (De Castro 2003) and is based on the principles of participatory action research (Carr and Kemmis 1986), which have strong traditions within the evaluation field (Brisolara 1998). OS was designed based around three key ideas: the empowerment of service users; collaboration between users and workers; and the integration of the tool into the everyday working practices of a service (MacKeith 2011a). OS is therefore a measurement tool that intends to closely reflect the reality of those receiving services as well as those delivering them by being an integral part of the treatment process. The tool is now used widely and supported by key national bodies, including the Department of Health (Department of Health 2009) and NESTA (NESTA 2010).

All versions of the OS consist of a number of scales arranged in the shape of a star (see Figure 9.1) onto which expected behaviour and attitudes are displayed. These outcomes differ in each version of the star according to the needs of service user groups. The scales are constructed around a model of change that defines a series of end goals and the steps required to achieve those goals (MacKeith 2011a). The scales represent different areas of the service user's life and the purpose of the star is to plot the extent to which each has been achieved to give an overview of the person's current situation, and then the process is repeated some time later to provide a picture of change. This is an interactive process developed around user-defined goals and can be used to self-assess recovery journeys, to look at the interplay

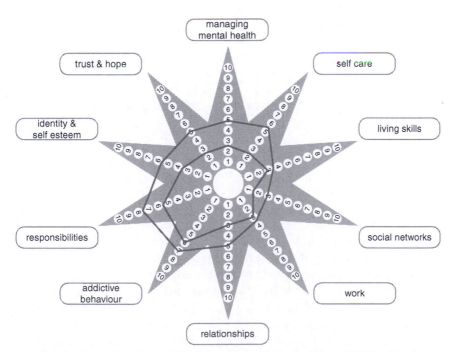

FIGURE 9.1 Example of a completed Outcomes (Recovery) Star (© Triangle Consulting Social Enterprise, reproduced with permission, see www.outcomesstar. org.uk)

between different areas of the recovery journey and to identify areas for further support.

The benefits and drawbacks of Outcomes Star

The flexibility of OS means that different versions can be developed for a very wide range of client groups and therefore could potentially be used in most organizations (social enterprise, as well as public, private and third sector) that work with vulnerable groups. It does however require an ongoing relationship between service users and key workers so could not be used for example in advice or drop-in centres where a client is only seen once.

The tool is designed to be integrated into the everyday working practices of an organization. Crucially, it not only measures outcomes, but is instrumental in helping those outcomes to be achieved. This bottom-up process means that the different versions of the tool are rooted in a real understanding of the nature of recovery and change of individuals of different backgrounds, in different contexts.

Whilst some measurement tools, including SROI, are criticized as being a burden and something done in addition to the 'real work' of an organization (Millar and Hall 2012), this staff-implemented tool is intended to be an integral part of delivering (and running) a service rather than a separate exercise. It is rooted in participatory evaluation principles that move away from the notion of the expert evaluator to one that empowers service users and promotes localized learning (Brisolara 1998). In such evaluations stakeholders should be actively involved in evaluation processes as 'facilitators' or 'agents of change' as they 'hold critical,

---

Box 9.2 Using the Star in a mental health service

The 'Recovery Star' is a version of the OS tool that is used to support and measure change when working with adults who are accessing mental health support services. The tool is used as an integral part of the key work process by enabling front-line staff and service users to reflexively assess ten domains of the user's life (see Figure 9.1 above for the ten domains). For each of the ten areas, the user (supported by the worker) plots where they are on their journey to recovery using a scale of 1 to 10. This is used to draw up an action plan based on areas in which they are achieving well and those in which they need additional support. This process is then repeated over time, e.g. six months later, to ascertain where and how much change has occurred and to identify new areas to work on (Figure 9.1 shows that most change has occurred in 'self care'). The data can be presented visually and numerically for each user, and numerical data can be collated across a service to ascertain how it is performing as a whole.

(Adapted from MacKeith and Burns 2008)

sometimes elusive, knowledge about the dynamics of the program and the needs that the program is intended to fulfil' (Brisolara 1998: 25).

OS can be useful to support the internal development of an organization (what they are doing well, what needs improving) and in encouraging discussions around consistency in the work of front-line staff. It also aspires to be a tool that can provide robust outcomes data, which is important for organizations and perhaps particularly appealing to commissioners who wish to refer to evaluation data as a basis for decision-making. Indeed, MacKeith (2011b) found that some commissioners have requested its use in 'Payment by Results' contracts. If commissioners appreciate that the tool can measure the progress of users as opposed to the extent to which predefined outcomes are achieved, this may in turn encourage organizations to take on users with more complex needs, which prevents the 'creaming' of clients most likely to help an organization meet its targets.

The tool is intended to be practical, easy to use and engaging for service users for whom it can help visualize their recovery journey (MacKeith 2010). Its simple methodology and use of scale data makes it possible for staff to analyze their individual work as well as to make comparisons across a service or different groups (MacKeith 2010). However, disadvantages also lie in its interactive features. It is reliant on subjective discussion and judgments about how service users feel, and on staff implementing it in a coherent way (i.e. intervention fidelity). There is a risk of respondent or 'courtesy' bias, where respondents tell you what they think you want to hear (White and Phillips 2012). There is also a risk of evaluator bias, where evaluators may interpret results in different ways or staff may exaggerate levels of improvement to exemplify their own performance. An organization may also do this to ensure targets are met or to boost income (such as under Payment by Results). Such evaluator bias does not necessarily come from a conscious favouritism but may simply be a result of lack of understanding of the wider context in which the intervention is taking place.

The risks of different types of biases are by no means exclusive to the OS framework. However, one may argue that the way the evaluation is framed makes it particularly sensitive, since the boundaries between being a counsellor and an evaluator become blurred. It could also be argued that through its participatory approach, the tool prioritizes the empowerment of users and staff over any claims to objective evaluation. Ideals of the evaluator as neutral and removed from the phenomena being studied cannot be upheld here, however OS stems from participatory action research, which challenges the view that in order to be credible, research and evaluation must be objective and value-free (Greene 1997). Instead, it is possible to embrace the notion of knowledge as being socially constructed and embedded within a system of values and human interaction with the purpose of research being able to bring about change (Brydon-Miller et al. 2003).

Randomized controlled trials (RCT)

In medical science the use of randomized controlled trials (RCT) is a well established way of assessing the effects of medical treatments. Although less prevalent in social science, we can note that RCTs are regularly conducted in areas such as mental health, education, parenting and reoffending. It is often referred to as the gold standard of evaluations but also attracts considerable criticism (Cartwright 2007; Donaldson *et al.* 2009). Some of the critical issues around both the implementation (feasibility and fidelity) of RCTs and their underlying understanding of the relationship between cause and effect are of wider value for a general discussion around evaluations and although so far only used relatively sparsely in the context of social enterprises, it helps us to understand the different principles that underpin evaluation frameworks.

RCT is set in the tradition of experimental methods-based approaches to evaluations. It puts causality at the heart of the evaluation, and aims to measure impact through the comparison of two groups – one that has received treatment and another that has not (Rossi *et al.* 2004). By using a control group as the basis from which to measure the impact of an intervention, the RCT approach claims to reduce uncertainties related to counterfactuals, i.e. 'what may have happened anyway' (Scriven 2009). The method is based on a simple model where evaluation is conducted in groups A and B, at times 1 and 2 (see Figure 9.2).

The implementation of an RCT can be illustrated with a study conducted on a small charity in the UK working with a parenting programme (Gardner *et al.* 2006). Conduct problems in children have been identified as a serious and costly problem, and parenting classes have been recognized as one tool that can effectively be used to achieve behavioural change in children. The aim of this RCT was to assess whether a particular approach, the Webster-Stratton method, a collaborative approach focused on parental skills, could be successfully implemented by a small and locally based voluntary organization. A scaling up of this programme would rely on a successful implementation by a small charity, with limited skills and resources relative to pilot projects conducted in larger institutional settings. The 14-week intervention used a combination of videos, training sessions and phone calls to support parents in building confidence and skills in their role as parents. The organization offers this service to around 200 families per year. The program is oversubscribed, which provided an ideal situation for a randomized assignment of families to treatment and control groups. Families on a waiting list were randomly allocated (based on a computer-generated selection) to either the next available parenting group, or to a waiting-list control group. The researchers conducting the trial were unaware of which of the families were in each group.

The families were assessed pre- and post-intervention. Assessments took place at the families' home using standardized instruments based on parents' own reporting

	Pre-intervention		Post-intervention
A: Experimental group	A1		A2
		x	
B: Control group	B1		B2

FIGURE 9.2 Intervention × group

and researchers' direct observations to measure parenting skills, confidence and mood (which were strictly structured). The assessments were identical for both groups. The results of the trial were analyzed using recognized scales to investigate the relationship between variables including observed child behaviour and parental confidence. The intervention proved to have positive effects in some areas but none in others. The report concludes that 'change in positive parenting skills appear to partially and significantly mediate change in observed child problem behaviour, whereas change in parent mood or sense of competence did not contribute to child outcome' (Gardner *et al.* 2006: 1129). The results have implications for the plans to scale up the intervention across the third sector.

The benefits and drawbacks of RCT

While simple in theory, the implementation of the RCT presents us with practical, ethical and conceptual challenges.

Firstly, it is clear from this brief summary that RCTs lean on scientific methods for retrieving, processing and analyzing data. This makes the evaluation procedure transparent, but also highly demanding in terms of the skills required by the evaluator. But there are further, perhaps more serious, challenges associated with creating a control group. We can appreciate this through exploring the meaning and importance of 'randomized sampling'. For the model to produce credible claims of impact of a specific intervention, we need to create two identical groups. The ideal way of doing this is through randomized assignment of treatment in a situation where a programme is oversubscribed. 'Random' in this context is based on a highly controlled and systematic way of allocating treatment. As Rossi *et al.* explain,

---

Box 9.3 Using RCT to trial a new therapy

Since RCTs can be costly and difficult to undertake, the examples of RCTs in social enterprise settings in the UK are so far quite rare. The Brandon Centre provides an exception, and highlights the context within which they can be used and how results can inform policy and enhance collective learning. The Brandon Centre is a small organization in London which addresses the need for confidential and free support for young people with mental and sexual health issues. The organization is pioneering a programme called multisystemic therapy (MST), intended for families of young people with severe conduct problems. With funding support from the Department of Health, the organization is running an RCT to test the effectiveness of the programme in this new context. The results of the RCT are being shared with government, the NHS and other charities, and evidencing change and impact in this way has given the organization national prominence as an example of good practice.

it 'requires considerable care to ensure that every unit in a target population has the same probability as any other to be selected for either group' (2004: 240). There must be no bias, based on for example needs or motivations, between the two groups. Furthermore, there are real challenges in establishing the counterfactual (see Gertler *et al.* 2011). Since the model hinges on an understanding that change is caused by an external and pre-identified intervention, we would need to make sure that no other factors come to influence either of the two groups during the course of the intervention. In sum, in order to establish the causal element and the counterfactual, the implementation of an RCT requires a great deal of precision and control of both the intervention itself, the identification of the groups, and the contexts related to both control and treatment groups.

By creating a control group we are presented with a second challenge, which is around the extent to which it is ethically right to deny one group potentially beneficial treatment, which in the case of the above example is aimed at supporting behavioural change. The implications of denying one group treatment may have negative consequences for individuals and may hence be hard to justify from an ethical point of view. The third challenge relates to the way RCT conceptualizes causality and its underlying interpretation of impact and change. Pawson and Tilly (1997) argue that the way RCT interprets cause and effect leans on dubious and unrealistic assumptions. In an RCT, evaluation focus is put entirely on the external intervention as the cause of change. This means that the motives and unobservable characteristics of the individual taking part in a programme are completely ignored as agents of change. Hence, we can gain no understanding of causality based on RCTs. Others raise similar points (e.g. Donaldson *et al.* 2009) and ongoing debates present arguments about what counts as credible evidence of 'what works' and what methods can best underpin an understanding of causality and impact.

Discussion

The three frameworks we present are all ambitious in that they aim to capture and communicate intangible or soft outcomes achieved as a result of an intervention. Each framework can be used in the evaluation of social enterprise organizations, but they are underpinned by diverse principles and values, resulting in very different evaluation processes, definitions and languages when presenting results. OS is rooted in the principles of participatory evaluation (Brisolara 1998) with its focus being on the empowerment of service users, with the role of the evaluation itself being important in the achievement of change. It is underpinned by ethical principles that emphasize that the evaluation procedure aspires to reverse roles that are underlined by power and knowledge (Chambers 2005). In practice, this means that the evaluator steps back and allows users' experience and knowledge to guide the evaluation process. As a result, outcomes are flexible as they are defined and measured from the 'bottom up' by service users and front-line staff. It places user experience at the heart of how impact is defined and not only measures but supports the achievement of change as an integral part of service delivery. SROI also emphasizes stakeholder involvement, especially in defining outcomes. However, compared to the levels of user participation and empowerment in OS, the stakeholder group is wider (clients, funders and other beneficiaries such as family members) and their involvement in SROI is instrumental as opposed to transformative. These stakeholders are asked to identify what outcomes, including unintended and negative, are important benefits (or drawbacks) from the intervention, but the SROI principles do not specifically prescribe interaction with the intent to empower.

RCT does not engage with user groups or other stakeholders. Instead, it is based on the idea that evaluators should not be involved in the implementation of a project itself; they should remain outside of the change process as an objective observer. The tool is designed and implemented by evaluators at a 'top-down' level. RCT aims to fulfil scientific criteria, and what is defined as credible evidence here comes from methodological integrity based on handling counterfactuals. Involving stakeholders in directing the evaluation process would result in trade-offs in this scientific credibility. The focus on creating a control group that provides the right benchmark for measuring impact is key to assessing impact. However, the unintended effect of this is that one group will be denied treatment, which could be seen as unethical practice. Consider a group of individuals who have all signed up to enrol in a drug-addiction programme. Half of the group will be randomly selected for treatment, while the others will be allocated a position in the control group and thereby denied access to treatment. While the control group is essential for the evaluation, and in a sense a collective effort to define 'what works', the effect of being denied treatment could be highly detrimental to the individual.

The motivation for or against involving clients or other stakeholders in the evaluation procedure leads us to the second point regarding definitions of impact. In RCT, impact is defined as the difference in change between the treatment and the control group. The change refers to predefined goals as set out by a project, such as changes in parental skills, confidence and child behaviour. By restricting focus to predefined outcomes, the tool ignores any unintended outcomes, such as better relations with siblings and relatives that may come as a result of improved parental skills and child behaviour. In the case of RCT, credibility of the evidence is claimed through reference to methodological rigour that prioritizes standardization, tested research tools and scales for analysis. However, its contextual and realistic validity may be questioned: does the evaluation reflect the actual effects of an intervention, according to those affected by it? It can be argued that social interventions seldom have the intended effect, and by recognizing their actual effect we may understand more about both the intervention and the needs of users.

In contrast to RCT, SROI and OS utilize a flexible approach to the definition of impact and invite subjective judgements on what counts as valid impact. They emphasize 'contextual meaningfulness' and the idea that social programmes 'should be evaluated according to the merit and worth of their actual effects, independent of their intended effects' (Greene 1994: 534). Credibility and validity are claimed through making stakeholders a central feature of evaluation; the focus and result of the evaluation should reflect client experiences and the interests of other stakeholders as far as possible (Pawson and Tilly 1997). The implication of this approach is that the evaluation addresses both the effect of an intervention as well as the intervention itself by opening up the question, 'Does this program effectively meet an important need among the designated beneficiaries?' (Greene 1994: 534).

Finally, in terms of the use and usefulness, we can look to the intended audience of each tool and the context within which they may be used. RCT uses technical and academic language, aiming to present scientifically credible evidence on 'what works'. It taps into requests for such evidence to be used by policymakers and commissioners when making decisions about what types of interventions to scale up and invest in. It can, however, also be intended for internal assessment, to try out new approaches and interventions. The monetized language used by SROI can communicate added social value and may appeal to a wide audience of funders and policymakers. The language is derived from the private sector rather than that commonly used by social enterprises and charities, and so is motivated by a previous inability to reach an audience that plays an instrumental role in making funding decisions. It is therefore an attempt to assist social enterprises to become more competitive vis-à-vis the private sector in the process of tendering for public service contracts (Ryan and Lyne 2008). In addition, its stakeholder engagement and bottom-up approach makes it useful for internal development by ascertaining what does and does not work and through identifying areas for further investment. The visual aspect of the OS provides a powerful and simple way of communicating the progress achieved by an individual. Whilst principally used as a tool for internal assessment and also instrumentally to facilitate development, it also seems clear that the creators are very aware of the need to convince commissioners that the tool produces credible and valid evidence of impact and as such attempts have been made to integrate the tool into Payment by Results schemes (MacKeith 2011b).

Concluding remarks

In the context of social enterprise, evidencing outcomes and impact presents us with particular challenges since we deal with effects that are intangible and hard to demonstrate. Furthermore, such organizations often deliver a vast range of services and with them produce a variety of outcomes, which raises the question of what to actually measure. The fact that these organizations speak to an array of stakeholders, of different backgrounds and interests, is also one aspect to be taken into account when understanding the choice and use of evaluations. There are, of course, practical realities of organizational life that will also guide the choice of evaluation framework. These aspects include the cost, time and skills required to implement an evaluation. Other issues also need to be considered, including the implications of introducing a particular evaluation tool on the relations between staff and clients. In relation to the practical constraints of each tool, OS can be made into an integral part of the service delivery and therefore has relatively low time and resource implications. The tool has gone some way in responding to critiques that monitoring and evaluation tools are a burden, interfering with the work staff should in fact be doing (see for example Christensen and Ebrahim 2006). RCT works hard to fulfil scientific criteria and in doing so requires significant cost, capacity and skills (New Philanthropy Capital 2011). SROI also requires considerable inputs of time and resources (Millar and Hall 2012), and relies on existing and trustworthy financial proxies (New Philanthropy Capital 2010). Such tools may therefore be of limited use for small organizations.

So, on what basis would an organization make a choice between these three frameworks? The purpose of this chapter has been to introduce the reader to some important features of three impact evaluation frameworks, and in doing so illustrate that evaluations are not just instrumental tools to assess achievements but also frameworks that encompass complex value systems. Furthermore, it is clear that evaluations are not neutral tools that can provide evidence on what works, as the choice of tool along with the way it is implemented requires at least some level of subjective judgement based around the organizational context. The three examples presented here illustrate an existing diversity in evaluation frameworks that can be used by social enterprises, each feeding into different ideas about definitions of impact, the role of evaluations and what counts as evidence.

References

Arvidson, M., Lyon, F., McKay, S. and Moro, D. (*forthcoming*) 'Valuing the social? The nature and controversies of measuring social return on investment (SROI)', *Voluntary Sector Review* (accepted July 2012).

Barclays Wealth and New Philanthropy Capital (2011) *Wealth Early Interventions: An Economic Approach to Charitable Giving About Barclays Wealth*. Available at: http://www.barclayswealth.com/insights/early-interventions-an-economic-approach-to-charitable-giving.htm (accessed 1 March 2012).

Barman, E. (2007) 'What is the bottom line for nonprofit organizations? A history of measurement in the British voluntary sector', *Voluntas: International Journal of Voluntary and Nonprofit Organizations*, 18(2): 101–15.

Brisolara, S. (1998) 'The history of participatory evaluation and current debates in the field', *New Directions for Evaluation*, 80: 25–41.

Brydon-Miller, M., Greenwood, D. and Maguire, P. (2003) 'Why Action Research?', *Action Research*, 1(1): 9–28.

Burns, S., MacKeith, J. and Graham, K. (2008) *Using the Outcomes Star: Impact and Good Practice*. London: Homeless Link.

Cabinet Office (2011) *Modernising Commissioning: Increasing the Role of Charities, Social Enterprises, Mutuals and Co-operatives in Public Service Delivery (1–27)*. London: Cabinet Office.

Carr, W. and Kemmis, S. (1986) *Becoming Critical: Education, Knowledge and Action Research*. London: Falmer Press.

Cartwright, N. (2007) 'Are RCTs the gold standard?', *BioSocieties*, 2: 11–20.

Chambers, R. (2005) *Ideas for Development*. London: Earthscan.

Christensen, R. and Ebrahim, A. (2006) 'How does accountability affect mission? The case of a nonprofit serving immigrants and refugees', *Nonprofit Management and Leadership*, 17(2): 195–209.

De Castro, A. (2003) 'Introduction to Giorgi's existential phenomenological research method', *Psicologia desde el Caribe, Universidad del Norte*, 11: 45–56.

Department of Health (2009) New Horizons: Towards a Shared Vision for Mental Health: Consultation. London: Department of Health.

Department of Health (2010) Measuring Social Value – How Five Social Enterprises Did It. London: The Stationery Office.

Department of Health (2011) *Open Public Services White Paper*. London: Department of Health.

Dickens, G., Weleminsky, J., Onifade, Y. and Sugarman, P. (2012) 'Recovery Star: validating user recovery', *The Psychiatrist*, 26: 45–50.

Donaldson, S., Christie, C. and Mark, M. (eds) (2009) *What Counts as Credible Evidence in Applied Research and Evaluation Practice?* London: Sage.

Ellis, J. (2009) *The Case for an Outcomes Focus*. London: Charities Evaluation Service.

Gardner, F., Burton, J. and Klimes, I. (2006) 'Randomised controlled trial of a parenting intervention in the voluntary sector for reducing child conduct problems: outcomes and mechanisms for change', *Journal of Child Psychology and Psychiatry*, 47(11): 1123–32.

Gertler, P. J., Martinez, S., Premand, P., Rawlings, L. B. and Vermeersch, C. M. J. (2011) *Impact Evaluation in Practice*. Washington DC: The World Bank.

Greene, J. C. (1994) 'Qualitative program evaluation. Practice and promise', in N. K. Denzin and Y. S. Lincoln (eds), *Handbook of Qualitative Research*. Michigan: Sage Publications, pp. 530–44.

Greene, J. C. (1997) 'Evaluation as advocacy', *Evaluation Practice*, 18(1): 25–35.

HM Treasury (2011) *Green Book Appraisal and Evaluation in Central Government*. Available at: www.hm-treasury.gov.uk/data_greenbook_index.htm (accessed 1 March 2012).

Hwang, H. and Powell, W. W. (2009) 'The rationalization of charities: the influences of professionalism in the nonprofit sector', *Administrative Science Quarterly*, 54: 268–98.

Kane, D. and Allen, J. (2011) Counting the Cuts. The Impact of Spending Cuts on the UK Voluntary and Community Sector. London: NCVO.

Kendall, J. (2009) *Losing Political Innocence? Finding a Place for Ideology in Understanding the Development of Recent English Third Sector Policy*. Third Sector Research Centre, Universities of Birmingham and Southampton.

Kendall, J. and Knapp, M. (2000) 'Measuring the performance of voluntary organizations', *Public Management Review*, 2(1): 105–32.

Lyon, F. and Arvidson, M. (2011) *Social Impact Measurement as an Entrepreneurial Process*, Third Sector Research Centre, Briefing Paper No. 66.

MacKeith, J. (2010) *Review of Outcomes Tools for the Homeless Sector*, Second Edition. London: Homeless Link, Available at: http://www.homelessoutcomes.org.uk/resources/1/ReviewofTools%20second%20editionRebranded.pdf (accessed 1 March 2012).

MacKeith, J. (2011a) 'The development of the Outcomes Star: a participatory approach to assessment and outcome measurement', *Housing, Care and Support*, 14(3): 98–106.

MacKeith. J. (2011b) *Payment by Results and the Outcomes Star*. London: London Housing Foundation.

MacKeith, J. and Burns, S. (2008) *Mental Health Recovery Star: Organisational Guide*, London: Mental Health Providers Forum.

Millar, R. and Hall, K. (2012) 'Social Return on Investment (SROI) and performance measurement: the opportunities and barriers for social enterprises in health and social care', *Public Management Review*, published online 30 July 2012. Available at: http://dx.doi.org/10.1080/14719037.2012.698857

National Council for Voluntary Organisations (NCVO) (2011) *The UK Civil Society Almanac 2011*. London: NCVO.

NESTA (2010) *Whose Story is it Anyway? Evidencing Impact and Value for Better Public Services*. London: NESTA. Available at: http://www.nesta.org.uk/library/documents/Whose_story_is_it_anyway_v6.pdf (accessed 1 March 2012).

New Philanthropy Capital (NPC) (2010) *Social Return on Investment Position Paper, April 2010*, Available at: http://www.thinknpc.org/publications/social-return-on-investment-position-paper/(accessed 1 March 2012).

New Philanthropy Capital (NPC) (2011) *Examples of Charity Analysis. The Brandon Centre*. London: NPC.

Nicholls, A. (2009) '"We do good things, don't we?" Blended value accounting in social entrepreneurship', *Accounting, Organizations and Society*, 34: 755–69.

Nicholls, J., Lawlor, E., Nelzert, E. and Goodspeed, T. (2012) *A Guide to Social Return on Investment*. London: Cabinet Office.

Paton, R. (2003) *Measuring and Managing Social Enterprises*. London: Sage.

Pawson, R. and Tilly, N. (1997) *Realistic Evaluation*. London: Sage.

Public Services (Social Value) Act 2012. Available at: http://www.legislation.gov.uk/ukpga/2012/3/pdfs/ukpga_20120003_en.pdf (accessed 1 March 2012).

Rossi, P. H., Lipsey, M. W. and Freeman, H. E. (2004) *Evaluation: A Systematic Approach*. London: Sage.

Ryan, P. W. and Lyne, I. (2008) 'Social enterprise and the measurement of social value: methodological issues with the calculation and application of the social return on investment', *Education, Knowledge and Economy*, 2(3): 223–37.

Scriven, M. (2009) 'Demythologizing causation and evidence', in Donaldson, S., Christie, C. A. and Mark, M. M. (eds) (2009) *What Counts as Credible Evidence in Applied Research and Evaluation Practice?* London: Sage, pp. 134–52.

Wainwright, S. (2002) *Measuring Impact. A Guide to Resources*. London: NCVO.

White, H. and Phillips, D. (2012) *Addressing Attribution of Cause and Effect in Small Impact Evaluations: Towards an Integrated Framework*, International Initiative for Impact Evaluation (3ie), Working Paper 15, May 2012.

PART IV

Evaluating social enterprise: a critical perspective

10

FILLING THE CAPITAL GAP

Institutionalizing social finance

Alex Nicholls

Case study

Ethical Property Company

The Ethical Property Company (EPC) is a UK- and Belgium-based social enter-prise that has been a pioneer in developing a series of 'alternative' or 'ethical' public offerings of share equity to satisfy its own growth capital needs. Set up in 1998, EPC supports innovative and progressive organizations working for social change by providing affordable office and workspace, and fair and transparent property management. Groups in its centres benefit from flexible tenancy terms and office space, and facilities designed to meet their needs. The centres are also managed to minimize energy use, waste, car travel and harmful materials. In 2012, EPC owned fifteen centres in England and Scotland and a further two in Belgium. Further expansion into Europe may include new centres in Amsterdam, Hamburg and Paris.

With the help of Triodos Bank and Malcolm Lynch Solicitors, EPC launched its first ethical share issue in May 1999. This closed in December 1999, having raised £1.72 million. The company invested these funds in setting up seven new centres in Bristol, London, Leeds and Oxford. Three subsequent alternative public offerings – in 2002, 2006 and 2010 – have raised a total of £12.85 in equity capital for EPC. The 2010 share issue raised £1.79 million from 272 existing shareholders and £1.94 million from 22 new investors. Of this, over £850,000 came from three foundations: the Esmée Fairbairn Foundation, the Joseph Rowntree Charitable Trust and the Friends Provident Foundation. Mainstream corporations were also shareholders with AVIVA investing £603,750, whilst Rathbone Greenbank invested just over £323,800. Two social enterprises – Oasis Relations and the Phone Co-op – also participated whilst individual retail investors took up most of the remainder.

EPC's shareholders come from a wide variety of backgrounds, reflecting the social diversity and core values of the company. Rathbone Greenbank Investments and Morley Fund Management are the largest shareholders and there are also a number of trusts and foundations as investors. There is no majority share-holder and only 42 investors have holdings over 50,000 shares. The smallest investors have only 100 shares. EPC has paid a dividend every year between 3 and 3.25 pence per share. Shareholders are offered the choice to waive their dividend each year. If a shareholder wishes to exit then EPC shares can be traded on a 'swaps' market run by the stockbrokers Brewin Dolphin.[1] In this market all the shares that are up for sale are listed and potential purchasers are matched with sellers. The share price is not free floating – as in a conventional market – or driven by supply and demand issues or estimations of the value of discounted future cash flows, but rather as a function of the market value of EPC's property portfolio. EPC was the first company into which ethical unit trusts have made a substantial investment that puts social and environmental values at its core and is not quoted on the stock exchange.

Introduction

Developing mechanisms to allocate capital for social as well as economic value creation is not new. Indeed, there is a long history of faith-based, charitable, and mutual/cooperative finance organizations and models across many countries. However, over the past twenty years a range of new organizations and financial instruments has emerged that reflect a set of significant institutional changes around the social contexts and objectives of finance (Emerson and Spitzer 2007; Nicholls and Pharoah 2007; Nicholls 2010a, 2010b; Bishop and Green 2010). Partly this has been driven by the needs of social organizations that cannot easily access commercial finance to start-up and grow due to their projected financial returns failing to match their perceived levels of riskiness. But another driver has been a growing body of owners of capital seeking to allocate their resources to generate social value as well as (or, sometimes, instead of) seeking financial returns.

Furthermore, as it has grown, the size and scope of the social finance sector has started to attract a wide range of interest across the public, private and civil society sectors. For example, it is now estimated that the UK submarket of social finance that returns at least the principle to the owner of capital (the so-called social *investment* part of the spectrum – see further below) could grow from £165 million allocated in 2010 to £1 billion by 2016, a 38 per cent per annum growth rate (Brown and Swersky 2012).[2] Moreover, mainstream players are now beginning to enter the market, for example Deutsche Bank became the first commercial bank to raise a social investment fund[3] and the European Investment Fund has also made a direct investment into the UK social finance marketplace. However, despite the maturing of the social finance market over recent years, it is still far from completely institutionalized.[4] It is the purpose of this chapter to present this emerging landscape of social finance and to set out its key elements, major challenges and future trajectories.

This chapter prefers to use the broad term *social finance* rather than the narrower alternative *social investment*. This is for two reasons. First, because an analysis of the capital allocation decisions that fund social purpose organizations demonstrates a complex blend of logics and rationalities driven as much by personal or cultural values as rationalistic calculations of a specified set of returns on investment expectations (Nicholls 2010a). Thus, some of the funding activity in this sector resembles consumption as much as investment – effectively buying outcomes prioritized by the investor rather than building long-term capacity or increasing returns over time. Second, using the term social finance also allows this chapter to capture the full range of instruments, hybrid funding models, and structured deals that blend different types of capital that are evident across this emergent sector. These include: philanthropic donations; government grants; 'soft' return debt and equity; mutual finance; as well as 'finance first' impact investing. In practice social finance includes a wide range of risk and return models from the 100 per cent loss capital allocation of philanthropy to the market – or above market – returns achieved by some social venture capital funds, such as Bridges Community Ventures.[5] The wide variety of types of capital available in social finance – and the complex set of risk and return calculations attendant on each type – offers opportunities for innovative structured deals and funds that do not exist outside of this sector. It is suggested here that only such blends of capital can offer the critical support needed by socially entrepreneurial organizations if they are to tackle the 'wicked problems' currently confronting the world (Rayner 2006).

This chapter accepts that all notions of the *social* are culturally constructed and contingent on a range of institutional logics and legitimacies (Suchman 1995) rather than being institutional absolutes. Nevertheless, the meaning of *social* presented here draws upon the well established analyses that have been used to define civil society and the social sector as distinct from the public and commercial sectors (e.g. Salamon and Anheier 1999; Evers and Laville 2004; Anheier 2004). Of particular significance here are: a public benefit focus (often taking the form of creating public goods or positive externalities); a significant attention to stakeholder voice and accountability; a distributive focus on the beneficiary rather than the owner (this is sometimes legally formalized as in the non-distribution constraint typical of charities). Given the contingent nature of the social, such distinctions can, of course, blur in reality, particularly around issues of intentionality. Thus, the *social* component in social finance is taken here to include the capital that goes to all projects or organizations that give a strategic priority to achieving outcomes that are socially positive in any given normative societal context.[6] This includes organizations whose social impact is exogenous via the production of goods or services and also those whose impact is endogenous via organizational structures and processes (notably work integration social enterprises: see Nyssens 2006). Social finance may also support the positive 'social externalities' (perhaps better described as 'intentionalities') that are the deliberative consequence of socially entrepreneurial action. Finance that supports environmentally positive projects or organizations is also included here.[7]

After the early examples of charitable and mutual, the next sector of social finance to emerge grew out of the mainstream as investors began to recognize that capital allocated through conventional market processes often failed to value the negative externalities consequent from some investments. The result was the development of screened, or selective, equity portfolios under the umbrella heading of *Socially Responsible Investing* (SRI).[8] SRI aims to deselect companies in contentious or potentially problematic sectors (defence, tobacco, alcohol, gambling) from portfolios according to investor 'ethical' preferences, whilst also maintaining (near) market-rate returns. Subsequently, the clean energy or green technology sectors have also grown significantly in terms of investment over the past decade or so. More recently, changes in not-for-profit funding models have seen the emergence of social enterprises that aim to deploy profitable business models to address social and environmental issues. Such organizations can take debt and issue 'social' equity shares. In the foundation sector, innovations in the management of charitable assets have led to a growth in Mission Related or Programme Related Investment (Campanale 2005), in which fund managers deploy a proportion of a charity's core assets towards mission-related objectives rather than in the conventional model of using such capital only to maximize financial returns to support grant-making. Changes in the shape and function of the state have also catalyzed social finance as the public sector has retreated from the provision of some traditional welfare services under conditions of demographic or economic stress. This shift in the role of government from direct deliverer to commissioner or facilitator of welfare services has driven a range of new social finance initiatives from developing new contractual models, such as Social Impact Bonds (UK, USA) or Social Benefit Bonds (Australia), to market building via direct support for new social finance intermediaries, such as Big Society Capital in the UK. Patterns of dramatic economic growth in many developing countries have also opened up new foreign direct investment (FDI) opportunities that increasingly go beyond the traditional 'hot capital' examples of short-term investment lacking significant local value creation. Instead, FDI into agri-funds and sustainable energy projects offers the chance for positive social and environmental impacts as well as attractive returns to investors. The globalization of securitized microfinance debt products on mainstream markets has also driven the growth of a new sector increasing defined as *impact investment* (O'Donohoe *et al.* 2010: see further below). Finally, after the global financial crisis of 2008, a whole raft of new market opportunities for social finance has emerged in many institutional landscapes increasingly characterized by market failures in the provision of social and environmental goods.

However, despite these innovations, the current architectures of mainstream capital allocation and its attendant instruments and metrics have severe limitations in terms of financing organizations and projects focused primarily on social value creation. This chapter suggests that this is the product of two interlinked issues. First, mainstream markets fail to price and, therefore, value other types of value creation (or destruction) beyond the purely financial into their capital allocation decisions. This undermines the *social* efficiency of capital markets in terms of return on investment calculations and their attendant risk and discount rates. Such effects are already well recognized in terms of the historic failure to price the environmental impact of carbon emissions into company share valuations in the energy and heavy industry sectors, for example. Second, the alternative institutions and mechanisms of social finance are currently fragmented and at an early stage of institutionalization.

In social finance, as in mainstream finance, the market is structured by three interlinked elements: supply, demand and intermediation. On the supply side of social finance there is a wide range of owners of capital seeking different 'blended' returns on their capital allocation (Emerson 2003). These include individuals,[9] institutions and governments. Charitable donations and legacies constitute an important source of capital for social finance. In the UK alone there is assumed to be £60–80 billion of endowment assets available for grant-making or investment (Nicholls 2010a). In the USA this figure is estimated at £324 billion (Nicholls 2010a). Individuals also indirectly 'allocate capital' via the taxes they pay. All government spending is to some degree social finance since it capitalizes the production of public goods. But a subset of this capital allocation has been directed towards social finance specifically. For example, the UK government has been a global leader in capitalizing the social finance market investing over £1 billion of public money in the sector from 2001 to 2011 (Nicholls 2010a).

The recipients of social finance on the demand-side of the social finance market include social enterprises, charities, cooperatives, social businesses and hybrid organizations combining elements of the state, the private sector and the civil society sector engaging in social innovation (Nicholls and Murdock 2011). Many social investees have been in existence for a long time, for example faith-based charities and mutual societies that are over a century old.

The intermediaries that link supply and demand in social finance include: dedicated institutions such as Bridges Ventures, Acumen Fund, Nexii or the Impact Investment Exchange Asia; mainstream financial players such as investment banks and asset managers; government funds and wholesale institutions such as Big Society Capital. Associated with these is an emergent ecosystem of specialist professional service organizations that support the social finance market – for example, legal firms, consultancies, market makers and capacity-building organizations. The intermediary segment of the social finance market represents the site in which most innovation can currently be discerned. However, it is also the least fully institutionalized.

Following this introduction, this chapter goes on to make the case for the distinctiveness of social finance from mainstream capital allocation mechanisms in terms of its logics and rationalities. Building on this analysis, it is proposed next that hybridity – conceived at several different levels – is a key defining feature of social finance. This section also outlines key trends and sectors within social finance, such as microfinance, impact investing and venture philanthropy. The chapter also presents an analysis of the current institutionalization of social finance and suggests two areas that are in most pressing need of further development for the sector to go to scale.

Conclusions outline a trio of potential future trajectories for social finance as well as an outline research agenda for future work on the sector and its attendant market structures.

The distinctive logics of social finance

Of particular importance in terms of conceptualizing social finance is a separation of value creation and value appropriation (Nicholls 2010a, 2010b). In conventional finance, the owner of allocated capital expects to benefit from an appropriate, risk-adjusted proportion of the resultant value created. This provides one of the under-pinning logics of pure market theory extrapolated from Adam Smith's original conception of the 'invisible hand' of the rational, utility-maximizing *homo economicus*. However, in social finance, the expectations of the owner of capital are typically more complex with respect to value appropriation. For example, a philanthropist will likely judge a grant by the value created for a beneficiary not for herself; a dedicated social finance fund may be seeking a blend of financial value returned to the owners of capital and social value for another party; finally, an impact investor may be seeking primarily a 'conventional' financial return to himself whilst still creating social value for others, for example by buying equity in a microfinance company.

A defining feature of social finance in practice is innovation in terms of the institutional norms that govern the relationships between its capital allocation logics (focused on the outcomes of placing capital) and 'investor' rationalities (focused on the objectives of placing capital). Whilst these two dimensions are typically aligned in the normative logics of conventional capital allocation – namely to maximize returns (outcome) to the owner of capital (objective) – they have a more complex set of interactions in social finance that challenge the conventions of both main-stream investing and traditional philanthropy. To explore this further, each of these two dimensions will now be considered in turn to demonstrate how different capital allocation logics and investor rationalities are being combined in different models to construct the social finance landscape as a dynamic institutional space.

Capital allocation logics

Social finance encapsulates three capital allocation logics. First, it can focus on generating only social and environmental returns, for example through government spending or support for social movements. Second, it can generate 'pure' financial returns to capital in an analogous way to conventional investing, for example in clean energy stocks. Both of these logics reflects well-established institutional traditions based in civil society and mainstream capital management respectively. However, social finance is unique in including a third logic – blended value creation (see Emerson 2003) – that combines both an attention to financial return and a focus on social outputs and outcomes. Blended value creation aims to challenge the Pareto assumption that achieving greater social impact inevitably reduces financial returns to capital (see Emerson and Spitzer 2007; Emerson *et al.* 2007).

The heterogeneity of capital allocation logics within social investment is demonstrated by the presence of diverse – sometimes bipolar – risk and return models and their attendant financial instruments (see further below). It is also reflected in the range of bespoke organizations that manage such finance across the field. The result is a wide diversity of methods and types of action within the social finance space typical of a developing, pre-paradigmatic field (Kuhn 1962; Nicholls 2010a). This spectrum suggests that, for the owners of capital, there is a variety of capital allocation approaches that offer different blends of financial and social risk and return to fit their own rationality for engaging with social finance. In turn, different institutions in the social finance landscape enact different capital allocation logics along the spectrum from philanthropy to mainstream asset management. At the one extreme, charities and foundations provide grants and debt guarantees to civil society organizations. At the other, mainstream investment banks trade securitized microfinance portfolios and raise clean energy funds. In the middle – blended – space, entirely new organizations are emerging that seek hybrid deals that mix various types of return. The latter includes potentially lucrative social venture capital opportunities that may return market (or above market) Internal Rates of Return whilst also achieving a clear social or environmental objective (this is the investment approach of Bridges Community Ventures, for example) as well as opportunities for many small-scale individual social investors that seek different blended mixes of social and financial return (for example by buying shares in a fairtrade company that pays limited dividends or holding a savings account with Charity Bank that offers zero interest).

Whilst these distinct capital allocation logics determine the financial instruments and deal structures typical in social finance, the full complexity of the field can only be understood by setting this dimension against the diverse rationalities of the owners of capital also present in practice.

Rationalities of owners of capital

Weber (1978) famously identified two ideal types of objective, macro-level rationality within social action termed instrumental and substantive. These were mapped against two forms of subjective/conative, micro-level, decision-making processes: *zweckrational* (means–ends rational orientation) and *wertrational* (values-rational orientation). Reflecting changes in his own contemporary society, Weber presented these two rationalities as – to some degree – in opposition with instrumentalism inevitably moving to dominance in an age driven by science, new technical processes, increasing bureaucracy and mass industrialization. Weber was clearly concerned about these changes in society, suggesting that they may result in a dehumanizing loss of freedom for the individual. However, more recent work has used Weber's rationalities as ahistorical ideal types to analyze sociological phenomena in late modernity centred on issues of constraint and freedom in individual choice-making (Weber 1987, 2002; Cockerham *et al.* 1993; Biggart and Delbridge 2004). Whilst acknowledging that such an approach is not without theoretical hazard, this chapter positions itself within this tradition by suggesting that modern social finance offers a new arena in which means-ends driven and values-driven rationalities – as Weberian ideal types – are clearly important drivers of social action.

The ideal type of *zweckrational* entails social action that rationally takes account of – and weighs up – the ends, means and any secondary effects of a given decision. Whilst Weber clearly acknowledged that *zweckrational* action may include values-driven choice-making, he also stated that instrumentality may be expressed simply in terms of giving preference to action prioritized according to a subjectively created scale of the urgency of individual needs and wants. In this latter case, individual action is determined by utilities that are not situated in social norms or personal value systems. *Wertrational* behaviour, on the other hand, is categorized as driving action that is 'dutiful, obligatory, and sometimes antithetical to self-interest' (Cohen *et al.* 1975: 235) within established normative frames and personal values.

In an initial analysis of the two traditions behind modern social finance, both ideal types are evident at the institutional level: *zweckrational* in the high bureaucracy of instrumentalism typified by atomized modern capital markets; *wertrational* in the values focus of philanthropy, state support and mutuality.

Using Weber's ideal types to analyze the rationalities of owners of capital achieves two outcomes. First, it provides a conceptual framework to distinguish social finance driven by means-ends calculations (*zweckrational*) from social finance for other, values-driven purposes (*wertrational*). Thus, *zweckrational* (means-ends) social finance typically focuses on efficient processes and measurable outcomes corresponding to a rationality aiming to maximize returns to capital (although this may be calculated in subjective terms such as an increased sense of personal wellbeing for the owner of capital): whereas *wertrational* social finance typically maps onto a rationality aiming at returns consistent with personal values and beliefs with less regard for means-ends efficiency or maximizing returns to capital.

Second, this dichotomy suggests that – in practice – a third type of rationality is needed to capture the activity that does not conform to one of the two Weberian ideal types of rational social action. This 'systemic rationality' reflects a deliberate combination of means-ends and values-driven rationalities and is typically demonstrated by a focus on developing the optimal processes to generate mixed – blended – returns. Systemic rationality captures the Weberian insight that *zweckrational* ideal-type behaviour may include values-driven judgements according to the individual actor's personal marginal utilities. Thus, a choice between alternative and conflicting ends and results may well be determined in a values-rational manner (Weber 1978: 26). In this way, capital allocation decision-making can rationally take into account a wider set of risk and return models that include values-driven considerations without, necessarily, becoming classified as 'pure' *wertrational*.

A Weberian analysis of the rationalities of owners of capital in social finance thus provides an explanatory framework for the distinction – evident in practice – between social finance in which returns are primarily directed towards the owners of capital and those where returns are generated for investees/beneficiaries or a mix of both. The distinctiveness of each of these rationalities is demonstrated, for example, by the need for its own set of performance metrics (see Nicholls 2009). Thus, whilst measures of return on investment are well established within financial economics, state expenditure has traditionally relied on welfare economics to provide a cost-benefit analysis of its spending on public goods. Charities have traditionally used simple output measures of grant performance rather than any sophisticated outcomes metrics. Furthermore, blended value performance metrics are still largely under development, although the social return on investment methodology is gaining increasing prominence in this area (Nicholls 2004). The issues around social performance measurement will be considered further below in the context of the under-institutionalization of the social finance market more generally.

In conclusion, social finance offers a distinctive set of markets that mix a range of capital allocation logics with a variety of rationalities that suit different agendas across owners of capital. The result is that social finance is institutionalized in a far more complex range of markets than conventional capital allocation. A second – and related – defining feature of social finance is the institutionalization of hybridity. This is considered next.

Institutionalizing hybridity

It is suggested here that social finance is characterized by hybrid logics and rationalities that reflect a range of blended value objectives (see Billis 2010). At the operational level, these complex logics and rationalities are reflected at a variety of institutional levels, including (from macro- to micro-): market sectors, organizations, deal structures. Each of these is now considered in turn.

Hybrid market sectors

As has already been noted, a wide range of logics and rationalities characterize the social finance market and determine its capital allocation processes. One consequence of this is that social finance is best conceived not as a single unified market, but as a variety of different markets that share a focus on blended value creation, but whilst otherwise being quite distinct. Each of these submarkets demonstrates different approaches to the relationship between social and financial performance that can be conceived as a spectrum from grants and philanthropy that only offer the owner of capital 'pure' social returns to capital that generates market or near market-rate financial returns in tandem with social value. Each of the main hybrid markets of social finance is set out below along this spectrum from engaged 'venture' grant-making to SRI capital that is close to mainstream finance.

Venture Philanthropy

Venture Philanthropy (VP) takes a 'business-like' approach to grant-making that endeavours to maximize 'soft' returns to the donor (namely that their philanthropic capital is effective according to their own set of outcome objectives). Often this engages the philanthropist as an active participant in the management of her grant-making activities. This approach changes the institutional logic of the philanthropic process from hands-off gift-giving to deep engagement around a grant (John 2006). This innovation in philanthropy imported logics from business into grant-making and was developed by a new generation of high net worth entrepreneurs for whom conventional models of giving were seen as inefficient and unreliable (many of the 'new' philanthropists were also closely associated with venture capital in their commercial lives). VP follows private equity methods in particular by offering highly engaged (and demanding) grant-giving linked to clear and agreed outputs and outcomes.

VP has also proved to be controversial, particularly as presented in the neologism 'philanthrocapitalism' (Bishop and Green 2008). Some see it as further evidence of the encroachment of the market into non-marketizable areas of human life – namely gift-giving – as well as undermining or, at least, undervaluing the traditional role of the not-for-profit/civil society sector in opposition (or as a counterbalance) to the state or commercial private sectors (Edwards 2008).

Starting in the USA, VP has now become common in Europe (supported by the European Venture Philanthropy Association – EVPA) and is emerging in Asia (supported by the Asian Venture Philanthropy Network – AVPN: see, for example, Advantage Ventures 2011; Impact Investment Shujog 2011). The size and scale of VP investments is hard to judge accurately as philanthropists are notoriously secretive about their giving, but some estimation can be made from publicly available figures from VP asset management organizations. These suggest that the market is – comparative to mainstream philanthropy – very small. Available data suggests total VP investments of approximately £2 billion over the past decade in Europe and the USA at an annual rate of roughly £350 million.

Mission Related Investment

Mission Related Investment (MRI) has emerged as a new approach to managing the assets of charities and foundations.[10] MRI aims not to maximize the financial returns to the owners of capital but rather to align the returns of capital with the values-driven objectives of the charities and foundations themselves. Currently, the majority of charitable assets is not directed towards social finance opportunities, but rather is invested in standard market-rate products that aim to maximize return and minimize risk. The minority of charity assets that do aim for a positive social as well as financial return are known as Mission Related Investment. Data on the percentage of charitable assets employed in MRI across the entire sector have not been calculated, so here a proxy figure will be derived from a single example – the FB Heron Foundation that directs 22 per cent of its assets towards MRI (FB Heron Foundation 2007), defined as:

• programme-related investments, typically low-interest senior or subordinated loans or equity-like investments to non-profit or for-profit organizations whose work closely corresponds with the Foundation's programmatic interests

- market-rate insured deposits in low-income designated credit unions or community development banks
- other mission-related investments including, but not limited to, targeted fixed-income securities, positively screened public equity, and private equity offering a risk-adjusted market rate of return with substantial social benefits to low-income families and communities.

FB Heron Foundation has been a pioneer in terms of MRI, so an adjusted figure of 15 per cent of MRI across all charitable assets will be used here. Given that total charitable assets in the UK and USA amount to approximately £400 billion this gives a figure of £60 billion for the MRI investment market.

Impact Investing

JP Morgan Chase – supported by the Rockefeller Foundation – pioneered research into the impact investment market. O'Donohoe *et al.* (2010) and Saltuk *et al.* (2011) specifically assessed the potential demand for this form of social finance. In the first report, the authors analyzed potential demand for impact investment in the developing world.[11] This aimed to establish impact investment as a new asset class within portfolios, similar to equities or property. In doing so the authors believed that greater institutional resources would be committed to impact investment.

O'Donohoe *et al.* (2010) calculated that impact investment deals in the USA totalled £1.5 billion in 2010 (1,105 actual deals) spread across a range of sectors dominated by investments in housing of £490 million (31.8 per cent of total) and in microfinance of £410 million (26.6 per cent). Sixty-five per cent of the deals were under £0.6 million. This influential report also estimated the demand for impact investment over the next ten years as between £250 billion and £610 billion representing a profit 'opportunity' of between £113 and £410 billion.[12] This demand was predicted chiefly in housing (£132–£484 billion) and microfinance (£108 billion) with the Bottom of the Pyramid (BoP: Prahalad 2006) market estimated at potentially reaching £5 trillion annually.[13] Such figures are supported by research elsewhere that suggests that the demand for investment by social enterprises working in the clean water and sanitation sector in Asia alone will be £7–£21 billion by 2020 (Advantage Ventures 2011). In 2011, the total figure for impact investment was estimated to have grown to £2.7 billion in over 2,200 deals (Jackson and Harji 2012). In the UK, whilst total social investment in 2010 has been estimated at only between £165 million (Brown and Norman 2011) and £190 million (Cabinet Office 2011a), the market is estimated to have the potential to grow to £1 billion by 2016 (Brown and Swerksy 2012).

A subset of impact investment has emerged that provides funding to organizations that operate in markets for consumers characterized as being at the Bottom of the Pyramid (BoP). According to Hammond *et al.* (2007), there are four billion BoP consumers globally – defined as all those with annual incomes below 2,000 in local purchasing power. Despite being poor, together they have substantial purchasing power, constituting a £3 trillion global consumer market that is growing fast in certain sectors. For example, between 2000 and 2005 the number of mobile subscribers in developing countries grew more than fivefold to nearly 1.4 billion. There are, however, large variations across regions with Asia (including the Middle East) having the largest market of 2.9 billion people compared with Eastern Europe's 254 million people. Sector markets also range widely in size and development including: water (roughly £8 billion); health (£60 billion); transportation (£68 billion); housing (£127 billion); energy (£165 billion); food (£1.2 trillion).

Microfinance

Microfinance is, perhaps, the most celebrated sector of social finance. It includes not only microcredit (its most famous product), but also microsavings and microinsurance. Microcredit attempts to address market failure in the provision of capital to the uncollateralized individual or small organization. In the process it has established microfinance as a new and growing sector within mainstream finance that represents the most significant social finance market globally. Microcredit, which has grown most strongly in developing markets, offers small-scale entrepreneurs the first step towards bank finance and, ultimately, access to capital markets. Stein *et al.* (2010) suggested that of the 365 to 445 million micro-, small- or medium-sized firms in developing countries, 70 per cent need, but do not have access to, external financing. These firms are thought to generate 33 per cent of GDP and 45 per cent of employment in the analyzed developing countries – a figure that is even greater if informal organizations are also included. It is calculated that their unmet demand for debt credit is equal to £1.3 to £1.5 trillion or 14 per cent of total developing country GDP.

Global microcredit volumes have been growing rapidly from £2.5 billion in 2001 to £16 billion in 2006 (Deutsche Bank Research 2007). Key investors in microfinance include: bilateral aid agencies (USAID); multilateral development banks and UN agencies (World Bank, UNDP); development finance institutions (DFIs) – the private sector arms of government-owned bilateral and multilateral development agencies (e.g. the International Finance Corporation); foundations (Gates Foundation); institutional investors (Deutsche Bank); international Non-Governmental Organizations (ACCION); microfinance investment vehicles (Blue Orchard); and individual investors (e.g. via Oikocredit, Kiva). As the sector has grown, mainstream investors, such as Citibank and Morgan Stanley, have become increasingly involved in trading securitized microfinance loan books, significantly increasing the volume of capital available. For example, in 2004–05 Blue Orchard issued £54 million of collateralized debt obligations backed by a portfolio of loans to microfinance institutions.

Furthermore, the successful initial public offering of 30 per cent of Compartamos – a Mexican microfinance institution – in 2007 realized £290 million and demonstrated the potential for highly attractive returns on investment. At the end of the third quarter in 2009, the bank had a loan portfolio of £341 million with a return on average equity of 42.6 per cent (Martin 2009).

Mutual and community finance

In 2008, UK cooperatives and mutual societies had revenues of more than £98 billion and assets of over £572 billion (Mutuo 2009). In continental Europe, over 240,000 cooperatives were economically active in 2005 working in many sectors, particularly agriculture, financial intermediation, retailing and housing, and as workers' cooperatives in the industrial, building and service sectors. These cooperatives provided direct employment to 3.7 million people and had 143 million members (Chavez and Campos 2008; Defourny and Nyssens 2008). At a global level, in 2008, cooperatives were responsible for an aggregate turnover of £700 billion with estimated assets of over £3 trillion. These assets generated financial returns to cooperative members, who in this model are both the beneficiaries from and owners of invested capital. These figures suggest that mutual finance may be the largest single segment of the social finance market despite the fact that it usually operates outside of mainstream secondary markets

Community finance refers to the provision of financial services to under-served communities and includes banks, credit unions and loan funds. It has proved influential in the USA and, more recently, in Europe. In the USA, the Community Reinvestment Act (CRA), originally passed in 1977, provided incentives to increase investment in poor communities such that, in 2007, £16 billion was invested as a result of the CRA. In the UK, the Community Investment Tax Relief scheme (CITR) was introduced in 2002 as a tax incentive to investors in community development finance institutions (CDFIs). The CITR relief is worth up to 25 per cent of the total investment. By 2007, CITR has generated between £53 and £58 million in new investments in CDFIs (CDFA 2007). CDFIs lend and invest in deprived areas that cannot access mainstream finance. In 2009, CDFIs invested a record £113 million in the UK. There is a less well-defined community investment sector in continental Europe, so data are unavailable.

Clean energy investment

Financing clean energy offers the potential for high financial returns to investors whilst also benefiting the environment. Historically, the growth of this sector has been driven largely by the attractiveness of its returns to mainstream investors rather than by its environmental impacts. Despite a dip in 2009, the overall global trend in clean energy investments over the past ten years has demonstrated strongly positive growth. According to New Energy Finance, global clean energy investments (including direct investment asset finance and research and development, technology and equipment) grew from £22 billion in 2004 to £90 billion in 2009 (New Energy Finance 2009). Europe and the USA accounted for around 40 per cent of all the investment, but China and India are also emerging as important markets. Among the many funds focusing on clean energy finance are Generation Investment Management, which integrates sustainability into its equity analysis and which closed a £400 million Climate Solutions Fund in 2008, and Mission Point

Capital Partners, who have a £210 million fund focused on solutions that contribute to a low-carbon economy. Mainstream venture funds Kleiner Perkins Caufield and Byers and Draper Fisher Jurvetson are also important players in this space.

Socially Responsible Investment (SRI)

Socially Responsible Investment (SRI) aims to combine market-level financial returns with an investment management strategy that acknowledges social and environmental variables. The growth of SRI over the last 25 years has been well documented and is now a multi-trillion dollar business. Eurosif (2008) identified two categories of SRI:

- Core SRI: typified by elaborated screening strategies impacting portfolio construction and implying a values-based approach. Investments are characterized by ethical exclusions (more than two negative criteria), as well as by different types of positive screening (e.g. best in class). Increasingly, thematic investment around sustainability screens has also become popular.
- Broad SRI: typified by the mainstreaming of SRI reflecting the growing interest in this area among institutional investors. Investments are characterized by simple exclusions ('sin' stocks), and by active shareholder engagement with company strategy concerning environmental, social and governance issues ('ESG risk'). This has led to the development of enhanced analytics that integrate a wider range of social and environmental factors in conventional financial analysis.

In 2007, the total amount of SRI assets under management in Europe was £2.2 trillion with a compound annual growth of 42 per cent. This figure represented 17.5 per cent of the all assets under management in the region. Of this figure, broad SRI amounted to £1.7 trillion of assets under management (81 per cent) and core SRI amounted to £0.5 trillion (19 per cent). In the same period, the broad SRI market in the USA amounted to £1.5 trillion with core SRI estimated at approximately £300 billion. This represented 11 per cent of the total of all assets under management and a compound growth of 9 per cent annually (compared with only 3 per cent across the market as a whole: Social Investment Forum 2008).

Researchers in the financial services industry have long recognized the gradual emergence of social concerns in the preferences of some investors. How important the investors' social concerns are to them, and the social benefit realized by these investment products are matters of debate, of course – not least because much SRI is based on negative screening alone that uses quite limited criteria. The cluster of roles and practices associated with SRI are increasingly linked through institutional structures of professional networks, conferences and publications (e.g. Eurosif; EIRIS; UKSif).

Hybrid organizations

The second form of hybridity that is characteristic of social finance can be seen in a variety of innovative intermediary organizations that have emerged to connect the supply of, and demand for, capital allocated for blended value creation. Due to the fragmentary nature of this market, such organizations typically act as market makers as well as fund managers – often developing their own performance measurement systems and other institutional structures to remove transaction costs for their clients. To date this has worked against the standardization of data or performance metrics across the field (see further below). The next section provides two illustrative examples of such hybrid organizations.

Impact Investing Exchange Asia (IIX)

IIX aims to provide social enterprises in Asia with greater access to capital, allowing them to expand the impact of their activities more rapidly. Based in Singapore, IIX was founded in 2010 by Durreen Shahnaz, an investment banker-media-executive-turned-social-entrepreneur from Bangladesh. While teaching Social Innovation and Social Finance at the Lee Kuan Yew School at the National University of Singapore, Shahnaz began exploring the notion of creating a 'social' stock exchange that would eliminate many of the barriers to market opportunity that currently exist for social purpose organizations to help them scale to their full potential. While the idea was in its very early stages, the Rockefeller Foundation supported the creation of IIX under their social finance grant programme. Subsequent support has come from the Asian Development Bank (ADB) and the Economic Development Board of Singapore (EDB). IIX comprises three operational units: Impact Investment Shujog; Impact Partners; Impact Capital.

Impact Investment Shujog is an advocacy, research and capacity-building non-profit organization that aims to foster growth, maturity and innovation in social enterprises and across the impact investment sectors of Asia. Shujog's products and services focus on preparing social enterprises with the organizational skills to measure their impact effectively, develop effective governance models and demonstrate sound financial management in order to maximize opportunities to raise funds from the mainstream capital markets or through the two trading platforms within IIX itself.

Impact Partners is an exclusive network and private placement platform where impact investors are given access to social enterprises seeking private investment capital. The online platform is a dedicated matching service for investors interested in making private investments in pre-screened social enterprises that match their investment criteria. Unique to Impact Partners is the fact that the social enterprises on the platform have been assessed on their social impact and financial capacity through a market-readiness assessment framework.

Impact Capital is due to be launched in 2013 and will operate like a traditional stock exchange. The platform will provide liquidity to investors by supporting listings, trading, clearing and settlement of securities issued by social enterprises. Once operational, Impact Capital will allow investors to purchase and trade shares issued by for-profit social enterprises and bonds issued by either for-profit or not-for-profit social enterprises. Impact Capital will establish listing criteria to promote and reward the best social enterprises in an environment that ensures transparency and accountability for investors.

Initially, Impact Capital will focus on social enterprises operating in healthcare, education, affordable housing, clean energy and microfinance. The platform will utilize criteria typical of a traditional exchange (corporate governance, accounting standards, operating track record and financial performance) as well as additional requirements that limit inclusion to companies with core social or environmental missions. Each listed entity will provide investors with both regulated financial reports and bespoke social/environmental reports that will be third-party audited. All reporting will follow the regulations of the issuing country as well as Singapore, where Impact Capital is based. Finally, Impact Capital will offer market data on social enterprises to key news services, as well as to other interested parties and investors. It is intended that this information will be useful to the impact investors, research firms, brokerage firms and others who will stimulate trading on the exchange.

Big Society Capital (BSC)

In 2005, the New Labour government in the UK established an independent Commission on Unclaimed Assets and tasked it with exploring the potential of a Social Investment Bank (later Social Investment Wholesale Bank) funded by the bank account assets held dormant for fifteen years or more in high street banks. The Commission issued a consultation paper in 2006 and reported back to government shortly afterwards (Commission on Unclaimed Assets 2006). The purpose of SIWB was set out as to raise funds and leverage other investors to capitalize social invest-ment intermediaries via debt and equity to grow the supply of finance to the third sector (OTS 2009). The Bank did not aim to have a retail function and would not engage in grant-giving – its overall aim was financial sustainability and long-termism. In addition, the SIWB aimed to develop the provision of advice and support across the social investment sector generally.

As a result of the impending general election in 2010, no further policy work on the SIWB took place under New Labour. However, after the formation of the Coalition Government it became clear that the SIWB policy agenda had not been abandoned. In February 2011, the government issued a joint report from the Cabinet Office and the Office for Civil Society (the renamed Office of the Third Sector), *Growing the Social Investment Market: A Vision and Strategy* (Cabinet Office 2011a). This report included a specific chapter on the Big Society Bank (2011a: 37–44) as the centrepiece of the Coalition's social finance proposals and set out its operational objective and guiding principles.

This was followed by a second report in May 2011 that set out details of the Bank's proposed legal form and structure. This document also refined the strategic objectives of the Bank as follows (Cabinet Office 2011b: 2–3):

- To develop intermediaries to ease the flow of capital into the social sector.
- To connect social entrepreneurs to capital markets to access growth capital.
- To support financial innovation so that social sector organizations can be rewarded by performance.
- To develop the investor market through the creation of social investment vehicles to support high growth ventures and smaller local organizations.
- To support the development of community-led social enterprises to improve opportunities for young people.
- To develop 'robust investment propositions … with clearly articulated social and financial risks and returns'.
- To provide reliable independent research on social investment.
- To create effective financial markets to trade and issue securities in social investment.

The project aimed to build the market for social finance in the UK and, as part of this, supported important research that scoped the potential size and structure of such a market (Joy *et al.* 2011). The Bank was to be set up as a company limited by shares owned by a company limited by guarantee (Big Society Trust) and would have a charitable arm to attract donations. As set out in Project Merlin,[14] the big banks were to contribute £200 million in equity at 'commercial rates' plus £60–£100m dormant bank assets in year one. The Bank aimed for an eventual capitalization of £400m in total. Despite its principle of self-sufficiency, it was acknowledged that the Bank was likely to suffer 'some attrition of the value of its capital' in the first five years (Cabinet Office 2011b: 13). The Bank finally became operational in April 2012 under a new name that avoided toxic associations with the banking industry: Big Society Capital.

Hybrid deal structures

As was noted above, another defining feature of the social finance market is a wide variety of capital allocation logics and rationalities across many different types of owners of capital. Each of these groups has different perceived risk and return profiles for their capital (though, see further below) and each has distinct social impact and financial return objectives. For example, government may have strong social impact objectives, but be far more tolerant of lower returns, higher risk or longer payback periods. Alternatively, an owner of capital focused purely on financial objectives may be very keen to participate in social finance, but be unwilling to tolerate any reduction in return below the market rate irrespective of social impact. A third, very broad constituency is the growing group who might be willing to consider a host of trade-offs between, and combinations of, financial and social value creation and appropriation. One consequence of this diversity is that social finance intermediaries and fund managers have a unique opportunity to balance and combine different (social) risk and return profiles in innovative 'structured' finance products. Such products blend different types of risk and return to allow each distinct investor group to achieve their desired blend of social and financial outcomes without limiting the capital allocation opportunities to the bipolar extremes of either 100 per cent loss grant-making or mainstream market returns. Such transactions will be essential to grow the social finance market and leverage mainstream capital into this space. However, because of their individualized nature, they can be costly and inefficient to arrange. The case study that follows provides a good example of a hybrid, structured deal.

Case study

Hackney Community Transport[15]

Hackney Community Transport (HCT) was established in the UK in 1982 as a company limited by guarantee when 30 community groups in the London Borough of Hackney formed a pool of six vehicles with a grant from Hackney Borough Council. It set out to provide low-cost van and minibus hire for local community groups and a door-to-door alternative to public transport for people with disabilities. In 1993, the company realized that the best way to become sustainable was to compete commercially for contracts. This marked the start of HCT's 100-fold growth from a turnover of £202,000 in 1993 to £23.3m by 2010. In the mid-2000s, the group expanded to merge with Lascot, a Leeds local transport provider and took over CT Plus and CT Plus Yorkshire. It formed a joint venture with Ealing Community Transport to deliver the Olympic Park contract taking construction workers to the Olympic site in the run-up to the UK's hosting of the Olympic Games in 2012. By 2010, it had successfully won the contracts to operate eight London bus routes. Such contracts, secured through open and competitive tendering processes, accounted for 97 per cent of HCT's income. Its fleet of 314 buses were housed in ten depots and financed on a combination of lease and purchase.

In 2009, it changed its name to 'HCT Group' to reflect its reach beyond the community of Hackney. It was this level of growth in operations, combined with its robust track record at winning contracts, which gave rise to ambitious forecasts for future service provision, and to the search for the capital required to realize these plans. Going forward, HCT Group wanted to:

- lower its cost of finance and reduce its dependency on bank loans
- reconfigure the financing of its vehicle fleet, to reduce costly leasing arrangements and increase the proportion of outright ownership of the assets
- finance investigations into other potential mergers or joint ventures

- secure further cash replenishments, in part to meet its commitment to re-invest at least 30 per cent of its profits in community development.

To this end, it sought to create a flexible, innovative and transparent package that fitted with the asset-locked status of its holding charity, HCT Group. It aimed to:

- raise at least £4m with as much of it in the form of fixed rate debt as possible, but without resorting to bank debt again
- increase staff engagement and sense of 'ownership' in the company to extend its social impact
- include commercial as well as social finance in the deal – as proof of HCT's commercial viability
- use financial tools available in a flexible and innovative way
- maintain its operational flexibility and its social mission, whilst securing finance.

HCT explored several ways of raising the capital it required to continue growing.[16] These included: a fixed rate bank loan; a corporate bond; an initial public offer of shares; raising capital through an intermediary firm; mixing a bond with a revenue-participation debt product.

After eighteen months of negotiation, the final deal that was constructed in 2010 took the form of a two-part loan package: one fixed term, fixed rate loan (5 per cent over five years) and one fixed-term 'social loan' on a quasi-equity type arrangement, in which investors received a 1 per cent share of every £1 million increase in revenues generated over an agreed threshold. The quasi-equity loan allowed investors to share in both the risks and the returns of HCT (if HCT did not reach threshold growth targets, there would be no returns to the investors), but it contained a greater upside than the fixed loan could generate. This part of the package was known as the social loan to remove the legal issues around an association of share capital with a charity.

In terms of putting the deal together, HCT saw it as critical to get a well-respected cornerstone investor in first to send out a message of confidence to other potential investors. The company approached Bridges Ventures, a leading social venture capital firm, to play this role and, after some negotiations, they agreed. Bridges effectively 'priced' the whole the deal – that is to say, they agreed the terms of the loan, which would then be presented to other potential investors. Bridges agreed to invest a total of £1.5 million from its Social Entrepreneurship Fund – £1 million of social loan plus £0.5 million of fixed loan at a 5 per cent rate of return over five years. With £1.5 million already committed, the remaining unallocated social loan stood at £1m and the remaining fixed loan at £1.5m.

Having secured Bridges' commitment, HCT sought out other investors interested in the different types of loans on offer. The second investor to commit to the deal was the government-backed fund Futurebuilders, which was managed by Social Investment Business. Futurebuilders invested £0.5 million towards the social loan and £1 million towards the fixed-rate loan. The next player to come into the deal was Big Issue Invest (BII). BII had a longstanding relationship with HCT, having provided loan finance for its asset base since 2006. In total, BII invested £417,000 in the social loan and £208,000 in the fixed loan (sticking to the 2:1 ratio of loans originally set by Bridges). The last piece of the financial jigsaw was to secure the involvement of a private-sector investor to take up the remaining fixed loan. It was important to HCT to demonstrate the credibility of the deal beyond the social finance sector alone. Rathbone Greenbank, a private-sector investment house with an interest in social and environmental investments, was considered the ideal investor to approach. All announcements regarding the capital raised through the three confirmed investors were delayed until a private-sector investor's engagement was confirmed. For Rathbone Greenbank to be able to offer an investment in HCT to its clients was interesting and gave it a competitive advantage over its rivals who may not have access to such a deal. Rathbone Greenbank invested £500,000 in the five-year fixed-rate loan.[17] This commitment completed the deal that had successfully raised just over £4m from four very different sources of social finance in a sophisticatedly structured package of loans (see Table 10.1).

Challenges of early stage institutionalization

Despite the significant growth in recent years of the capital allocated through the social finance markets globally, this remains a field of action at an early stage of institutionalization. This is best understood in terms of the two sets of limitations: overall market development and the underpinning information architecture. Each will now be considered in turn.

Market development[18]

A number of studies of the social finance market have identified important structural challenges, particularly in terms of connecting supply and demand (Nicholls and Pharoah 2006; Emerson *el al.* 2007). In this context, Evenett and Richter (2011) identified seven persistent challenges to the further institutionalization of the social finance marketplace:

- Fragmentation of capital supply and the absence of joined-up and plural finance options. There is a need for more collaboration and co-investment in the sector as well as more players in the market to build competition. Furthermore, pooling demand-side investment opportunities could bring in players for whom the market is currently too small.
- Need for more bespoke business support with deeply embedded cultural and technical issues that need addressing.
- No universally agreed metrics for social outcomes and no single 'silver bullet' solution to this. A pernicious consequence of this lack of accounting standards

TABLE 10.1 Breakdown of HCT structured loan deal

Investor	Date	Social Loan	Fixed loan	Total Amount
Bridges Ventures				
Bridges Social Entrepreneurs' Fund (BSEF)	February 2010	£1m		£1m
Bridges Social Entrepreneurs' Fund (BSEF)	October 2010		£0.5m	£0.5m
Total: Bridges Social Entrepreneurs' Fund (BSEF)		£1m	£0.5m	**£1.5m**
Social Investment Business (SIB), Futurebuilders Fund	February 2010		£1m	£1m
Social Investment Business (SIB), Futurebuilders Fund	February 2010	£0.5m		£0.5m
Total: Social Investment Business (SIB), Futurebuilders Fund		£0.5m	£1m	**£1.5m**
Big Issue Invest (BII), Social Enterprise Investment Fund	October 2010	£417,000		£417,000
Big Issue Invest (BII) Social Enterprise Investment Fund and Loan Fund	October 2010		£208,000	£208,000
Total: Big Issue Invest (BII) Social Enterprise Fund and Loan Fund		£417,000	£208,000	**£625,000**
Rathbone Greenbank	October 2010		£420,000	£420,000
Total: Rathbone Greenbank			£420,000	**£420,000**
Total Social Loan		£1,917,000		**£1,917,000**
Total Fixed Loan			£2,128,000	**£2,128,000**
Total Investment Raised		**£1,917,000**	**£2,128,000**	**£4,145,000**

is high due diligence costs per deal and, therefore, high perceived risks in social investments (see further below).

- No clear market signals: the mix of instruments in social investment noted above (i.e. including grants, soft loans and so on) makes this a complex and difficult market for potential new entrants.
- Restrictive regulatory and legislative environment for foundation assets.
- Insufficient investor incentives such as tax breaks or government guarantees (though more creative structured finance deals can address this).
- Need for better deal-brokering to address illiquidity of the secondary market place for social investment.

There is also a significant need for building better financial literacy on the demand-side in terms of investment models, opportunities and financial instruments. As a report from Venturesome (Goodall and Kingston 2009) noted, social investees need to address a range of issues in terms of their own financial expertise before they can make the most effective use of the emergent social investment marketplace. The provision of capacity-building support (social and human capital) combined with financial capital is widely recognized as important to foster and grow the social finance investee market – something also acknowledged in the engaged or venture philanthropy model, for example (John 2006). Of particular significance is educating the demand-side to recalibrate expectations of the relationship between risk and return in terms of accessing non-grant funding (see further below). Overall, the report suggested that potential recipients of social finance should:

- identify their own financial needs more thoroughly
- be aware of all available finance mechanisms and instruments and their pros and cons (and risks)
- be aware of the different capital providers available to them and their requirements
- have confidence to seek new finance from multiple sources and to structure deals blending investors with multiple risk and return profiles
- distinguish between income and capital both in their accounting and investment plans
- understand that grants are not free money (the can cost up to 15–25 per cent of the capital raised: more than three times the typical cost of raising equity).

To address these issues it is clear that a series of market or institutional voids in the social finance eco-system will need to be filled. In terms of the overall market structure such voids are most apparent in the intermediary or market-making space. Shanmugalingam *et al.* (2011) identified five crucial roles for market intermediaries in terms of developing the social finance market:

- To provide finance.
- To provide access to people, networks and expertise.
- To provide market access and distribution (match-making).
- To provide support for innovation and start-ups.
- To provide investment monitoring and performance information to investors.

To date, the intermediary space has been the most fertile site for social finance innovation globally, but it remains fragmented and lacks coordination, cooperation or standardization. The two social stock exchange projects currently under development in London and Singapore should offer the first examples of potential models for better consolidation of intermediaries (see further Unwin 2006; NEF 2006; Hartzell 2007).

Finally, public policy represents another important element in the future institutionalization of the social finance ecosystem. Government can utilize several policy and practice levers to support the institutionalization of social finance, including regulation, fiscal policy, direct investment, direct purchasing/commissioning, acting as a champion, supporting research and development. For example, government capital can be used as risk capital or as a guarantee – taking the first loss – to secure mainstream investor interest for new social finance funds. Effectively, this is the logic behind the Big Society Capital project in the UK. Indeed, the British government has been the most proactive state in the world in terms of using policy to support and grow the social finance market. Since 2001, a range of initiatives has emerged to support the development of social finance, including: a new legal form for social enterprises (the Community Interest Company); a new fiscal measure, Community Investment Tax Relief; direct funding of around £1 billion in new vehicles, funds and support mechanisms; research and development within the Office of the Third Sector (that became the Office of Civil Society in 2010); public events; ministerial briefings across various departments (Nicholls and Pharoah 2007; Nicholls 2010a). In 2010, this wave of innovation moved forward again with the establishment of the world's first Social Impact Bond – a new contractual model that used private capital to support payment-by-results programmes (Social Finance 2009).

Subsequent to the pioneering policy agenda set by the UK government, other states have continued to innovate around the institutionalization of social finance, most notably Australia, Singapore, Brazil and South Africa.

Case study

Social Impact Bonds (SIBs)

In the UK in early 2008, as part of a wider policy consultation around introducing more *Payment by Results* contracts, the Young Foundation coined the term 'Social Impact Bonds' (SIBs) and published a short paper with that title setting out thinking on a new generation of financial tools to support investment in social solutions (Young Foundation 2008). The SIB represents a contract between a public sector body and third-party investors, in which the former commits to pay for an improved social outcome and investor funds are used to pay for a range of (social enterprise) interventions upfront to improve social outcomes and generate public goods more efficiently. The SIB was developed over several years by an independent organization, Social Finance, but with close discussion with the then New Labour government. By enabling non-government investment to be utilized, SIBs aim to increase spending on preventative services, such that these interventions can have a direct impact on costly health and social problems saving the state money over time. This measurable outcome, relating to cost savings, triggers the repayment to third-party investors in the SIB. Effectively, the SIB acts as a social futures contract rather than as a debt instrument.

The SIB structure aims to align the interests of key stakeholders around social outcomes including:

• *Government*: the public sector pays only for positive outcomes by releasing a proportion of savings to investors. Success payments are calculated such that, if

SIB-funded services improve outcomes, these payments will cover the costs of the interventions. This enables investors to make a return. Investors carry the risk that funded interventions may fail to improve outcomes.

- *Social investors*: investment by trusts and foundations, commercial investors and high net worth individuals offers an opportunity to generate a blended social and financial return on investment. The social and financial imperatives are aligned since investors receive greater financial return as social returns improve.
- *Social service providers*: investment is used to pay for service delivery. Enables providers of all sizes to participate. Providers are encouraged to innovate in order to maximize outcomes for their target populations. Focus is on the social value that service providers can offer, rather than on the cost of services alone.

Each SIB is structured around a well-defined social outcome in a clearly specified intervention area (e.g. youth offending, teenage pregnancy, young people not in education, employment or training). Appropriate outcomes and success metrics are negotiated and agreed between government and sector expert intermediaries. Having established the terms of the contract, the intermediary seeks investment from socially-oriented investors that have an interest in ensuring the defined outcomes. These investors are asked to take all the risk that the interventions lead to the target outcomes, but know that, in the event that the interventions are successful, they will make a return on their investment. Due to their lack of track record, it is likely that social finance institutions – which are driven primarily by achieving social impact – will support the first SIBs (Loder *et al.* 2010).

The first, pilot SIB was launched in collaboration with the Ministry of Justice on 18 March 2010 and had a six-year time-span (Strickland 2010). The initial social investors included charitable foundations such as the Esmée Fairbairn Foundation and the Monument Trust, as well as social venture funds. The investment closed at £5 million. The contract agreed that the Ministry would make payments to investors in the event that reoffending is reduced below an agreed threshold. Reoffending is an area where preventative work saves the taxpayer money: 60 per cent of 40,200 adults on short-term sentences will reoffend within a year of release. The pilot SIB offers intensive support to 3,000 short-term prisoners in Peterborough Prison over a six-year period, both inside prison and after release, to help them resettle into the community. Key social enterprise partners include St Giles Trust. If the SIB reduces reoffending by 7.5 per cent, investors will receive a share of the long-term savings. If the SIB delivers a drop in reoffending beyond the threshold, investors will receive an increasing return the greater the success at achieving the social outcome, capped at 13 per cent IRR. The total cost of the project is capped at £8m.[19]

Information architecture

Perhaps the most obvious challenge to growing the social finance market lies in the lack of consistent *blended* performance metrics that allow owners of capital to make comparative allocation judgements. It is well understood that in order to function efficiently capital markets require high levels of accurate, transparent, comparable and relevant data to price allocation options efficiently and reduce transaction costs. Over many years, accounting standards have developed to support capital allocation decisions in mainstream finance, but in social finance the process of institutionalizing standards around blended performance data is still at an early stage (Nicholls 2009). The consequence of this is a market characterized by high transaction costs, poor liquidity (and resultant difficulties with exit), and – often – capriciousness rather than rationality on the part of owners of capital (Weisbrod 2004, 2011; Foster and Bradach 2005). The main issue is not, however, a *lack* of blended performance metrics – there are many examples of this – but a lack of agreed standards across the whole market. The closest to an emergent standard globally is the Social Return on Investment (SROI) model that has had significant policy support in the UK and beyond for several years, but whilst this has proved useful as an internal performance management and accountability tool it has yet to function as a market-making data set (Nicholls 2004). Furthermore, SROI remains an absolute measure of monetized blended outcomes framed in a cost-benefit model. The more sophisticated data sets typical of mainstream capital allocation are unlikely to be driven by such a mechanism.

Hill (2011) suggested that the owners of capital often perceive the level of risk involved in social finance to be too high, relative to the prospective blended returns. In this respect, risk is seen in a very broad sense and encompasses:

- Investment risk: the relative immaturity of many social enterprises.
- Team risk: many of the management teams in this sector are relatively new and untested.
- Product risk: many of the financial vehicles proposed are new and have no track record.
- Liquidity and exit risk: the novelty of the marketplace and absence of developed secondary markets mean that exit routes are untested or unavailable.

As a consequence, a major issue in terms of the further institutionalization of social finance will be the development of effective models of blended/social risk and return. Such data allows investors not only to make absolute comparative choices based on projected outcomes, but also to assess the uncertainty of such performance being achieved. At its simplest level, the riskiness of social finance capital allocation can be assessed by the lifecycle stage of the organization or project that is to be financed. Thus, start-ups may be assessed as riskier than well-established organizations. However, this may be a false assumption since many well-established organizations in this sector have been financed by grants or government contracts over time – both inherently unstable sources of capital. More effective measures would include assessments of the overall risk of programme failure, reputational risk in collaborative settings, political risk (both in terms of key relationships with government and more local, grassroots power relations), and calculations concerning risk over time. It is also possible that measures of social performance risk could be developed that reflect the levels of uncertainty surrounding outcome calculations rather than absolute projections of blended value creation.

Taken together this range of risk and return approaches could lead to the development of Net Present *Social* Value models that would mirror the well-established discounting of future cash-flows used in Net Present Value assessments of capital allocation decisions in mainstream finance, but would calibrate the discount (risk-return) rate rather differently. For example, it is often the case that early and large interventions in welfare can produce better outcomes over time compared with consistent spending over several time periods. This means that the blended value creation resulting from upfront spending today may be much higher than that achieved by spending the same amount over time. A NPSV discount rate could be developed to capture this. Alternatively, the future blended value of outcomes may be seen as higher than present outcomes if the perspective of subsequent generations is taken into account – for example in the case of interventions to address climate change.

Such approaches would allow new *Social* Portfolio Theory to emerge that reflects conventional portfolio analyses but factors in some key differences between the impacts of social finance and mainstream capital allocation. This new Portfolio Theory would be of great utility in guiding social finance allocation decisions across the multiple markets of social finance, both in terms of individual portfolios and at the owner of capital level and in terms of structuring deals that blend multiple risk and return profiles across owners of capital. For example, the levels of financial return required by social angel investors and social venture capitalists could be achieved within a single deal if their capital allocation is underwritten or subsidized by finance from government or philanthropists that requires lower rates of financial return. The latter would also be attracted to such a deal because it allows their grant-making to leverage other capital into a deal that has their desired social outcomes. Such combinations of risk and return profiles can be seen as a form of *Social* Weighted Average Cost of Capital (WACC) in which the overall calculation of blended value returns is a composite of multiple preferences and perspectives across several owners of capital.[20]

Conclusions

Recent neo-institutional theory has focused particularly on how institutional fields form and are transformed in processes of contestation and collective action (Stryker 2000; Seo and Creed 2002; Lounsbury *et al.* 2003). From this perspective, the inchoate social finance market has parallels with Schneiberg and Lounsbury's categorization of social movements as driving institutional change via 'multiple logics, contradictions and ambiguities' (2008: 651). The analysis of social finance above clearly demonstrates the potentially unstable diversity of institutional elements currently in play across the field by suggesting that the field can be structured into multiple distinct markets, each with its own institutional norms, logics and rationalities. From a Kuhnian perspective (Kuhn 1962), the institutional voids that are still evident in this emergent market suggest the absence of an established epistemology of social finance that is likely to undermine wider perceptions of its normative and cognitive legitimacy for some time (Suchman 1995). This may ultimately prove to be a barrier to its continued growth and access to resources, not least because it undermines its credibility to a range of important actors including: the asset managers beyond 'core' social finance who control the majority of mainstream capital; government policymakers; the wider public; and academic researchers (see also Dart 2004). From this perspective, the most important prerequisite for the accelerated development of social finance is to establish its own distinct epistemology that institutionalizes around a defined set of norms, logics and rationalities. Such a process will most likely be something of a power struggle between different logics and rationalities as would be expected in the formation of any new paradigm. Thus, the final institutionalization of social finance is likely to produce losers as well as winners. Three possible future scenarios of institutionalization can be hypothesized.

Scenario 1: Absorption

The first possible future scenario for social finance would reflect the dominance of logics that give precedence to the owners of capital appropriating value creation, as in conventional finance. This would see social finance move into the mainstream of financial markets and, potentially, be absorbed by them. This scenario would be focused on a demand-side market of profitable social enterprises that could be integrated within SRI funds in mainstream portfolio management. The growth and success of clean energy investing may offer a precursor to such a trend, as may the growing interest in so-called *finance-first* impact investing (where financial returns are prioritized over social returns).

At present, however, it is unclear how many social enterprises can go to the necessary scale for such finance and, even in those that could, it remains to be demonstrated that growing in organizational size necessarily increases social or environmental impact. Furthermore, since many social enterprises act as contractual service-providers for the state, it is not clear in what ways these organizations could access mainstream funds. Finally, there remains the thorny issue of ownership. Many social entrepreneurs are unwilling to hand over ownership and control of their ventures – a prerequisite for most equity funding.

Despite these issues, there is already some evidence that this scenario is currently moving towards dominance. Since the early development of modern social finance, actors from within conventional finance have played a leading role, bringing market/business logics to its incipient institutionalization. An important element within this transition has been a particular focus on 'professionalizing' social investment along business lines in contrast to the traditions of gift-giving and grant-making. As Abbott (1988) has suggested, clearly delineated professions have acted historically as power constructs that attempt intellectual and organizational domination of areas of social action. Indeed, the professions have conventionally interacted as a system in competition for resources and influence defined by issues of control, power, and (often abstract, specialist) knowledge. In concrete terms, the drive towards (a particular sort of) professionalization of social finance is clearly demonstrated by the dominance of board members from a mainstream finance background currently in the major institutions of social investment in the UK. This suggests that such actors are, perhaps, positioning themselves to shape the institutionalization of social finance according to their own dominant investor rationalities and investment logics – those of mainstream markets and investment management.

Scenario 2: Parallel institutionalization

The second scenario suggests that social finance would continue to operate on the margins of the mainstream intersecting with it where mutual interest makes this viable (i.e. around social enterprises that are at scale), but also working as a separate, parallel system supporting the wider social economy in a traditional manner. This is the current status quo. The logics of gift-giving and mainstream investment would be kept balanced by a larger number of new, hybrid organizations and financial instruments that would gradually gain wider normative and cognitive legitimacy and, thus, access larger pools of philanthropic and investment capital.

In this scenario, venture philanthropy and the emerging collaborations between for-profit and not-for-profit organizations would play key roles in institutionalizing new relationships between formerly distinct logics and rationalities. A resurgence of mutualization would also be a distinctive feature of this scenario, seeing a return to regional stock markets, new local currencies (such as the Totnes pound in the UK), a new wave of friendly and building societies, and local cooperatives taking on significant roles in terms of public- and private-sector action. The UK government's attempts to transfer large parts of the welfare state into new social enterprises or mutuals may support this transition.

Scenario 3: Institutional transformation

In the third scenario social finance first institutionalizes a unique set of values-driven rationalities and then exports them into mainstream, capital markets. This scenario would generate systemic change across all investment via radical and disruptive action seeking a broader or deeper transformation of society marked by more explicitly political, critical and counter-cultural orientations (Davis *et al.* 2005). The rise of ethical consumption provides a possible template for this transformation (see Nicholls 2007). Whilst the market for ethical goods and services remains less than 1 per cent of all transactions in Europe (and less in the USA), its principles have proved to be far more influential. For example, in the North, the fairtrade model has inspired consumers to demand both increased supply chain transparency and better supply chain practices across the entire retail industry (see Nicholls and Opal 2005).[21]

In this scenario, social finance would act as both a symptom and a cause of a re-alignment of capital investment that would demand that risk and return calculations are re-embedded in their social and environmental context, something that is already happening in terms of the carbon footprint of many industrial businesses. The transformatory social finance scenario would combine with the continued growth of ethical consumption and state regulatory responses to the global financial crisis to synthesize a new Economy of Regard (see Offer 1997) 'after capitalism' (Mulgan 2009). This would respond to Sen's (1987) argument that ethics and economics have been theoretically separated for too long in an artificial representation of utility, rationality and efficiency that has conspicuously failed to deliver maximum welfare and has, in fact, exaggerated inequality. An economy built upon the virtues of fairness and interpersonal regard may offer not only a new economy better suited to the cultural complexity of today's global trade but also a return to a more humanistic model of exchange and economic interaction that has – temporarily – been displaced in the past century by the rise of corporate power and marketing. From this perspective, Marshall's (1907) call for 'economic chivalry' may yet be realized by the simple power of shifting market forces. Indeed, as mainstream markets lost 20 to 30 per cent of their worth during 2008/09, there is some evidence to suggest that social finance yielded returns of up to 6 per cent during the same period (Emerson 2009) – something that should be of considerable interest to a growing number of investors and asset managers alike.

Despite some evidence of a research agenda emerging for social finance (see, for example, Salamon 2013; Nicholls *et al.* 2013), there remains the opportunity for a wide range of new work on this emergent field both to build new academic theory and to inform practice. Key areas of potentially impactful future work can be grouped under the two headings noted above in the context of the under-institutionalization of the field:

- *Market development research*
  - To explore, test and quantify the various submarkets within social finance, particularly from the investor's point of view.
  - To develop new teaching and coaching materials to:
    - broaden the understanding of the field across the public, private and civil society sectors
    - enhance the financial literacy of the recipients of capital
    - improve government commissioning practices.
  - To build coordinated policy agendas that support the social finance landscape, looking particularly at cross-border policy transfer and policy learning.
- *Information Architecture Research*
  - To analyze the performance metrics currently in use in mainstream finance in terms of their relevance and utility in social finance.
  - To test new theoretical models of social risk and return to develop a suite of discount rates to price projected blended outcomes for different stakeholders.
  - To standardize blended accounting performance metrics and audit practices.
  - To analyze the role of grants and soft capital in structured deals and funds, particularly in terms of potential market distortions or crowding-out issues.

Whilst certainly not an exclusive list of research topics, it is proposed here that addressing this research agenda would both generate valuable new scholarship and materially move the field of practice forward.

This chapter has attempted to capture the distinctive boundaries and issues that are defining social finance today as both a new market of finance and as a new model of exchange and value creation. It has also identified some of the critical issues for the future institutionalization of the field. Despite limited research to date, the study of social finance offers rich promise, theoretically and practically. Today, questions concerning the reform of capital markets and the future role of financial institutions represent some of the most urgent agendas in policy and practice globally. It is suggested here that further analysis of the emergent social finance market can play an important and useful part in informing these critical debates concerning the future of modern capitalism.

Notes

1 Generally, issuing equity in social finance is very similar to issuing equity in mainstream companies. The main differences typically lie in the governance arrangements of the company. These might restrict the freedom of the shareholders in some way in order to ensure the continuance of a social mission or provide for a certain percentage of any surpluses to be invested socially or retained by the company, or other socially-oriented limitations such as a 'golden share' that prevents a hostile takeover.
2 Though this is only about 1 per cent of the value of all loans to small businesses in the UK.
3 This is a £10 million 'fund of funds' and is 'on balance sheet', i.e. the fund is financed internally and does not include external investors.
4 The report particularly noted the continuing need for: social investors to accept higher levels of risk; more specialization of intermediaries in distinct sectors such as health or education rather than focusing on operational sectors; new types of 'value sponsorship' or purchasing of social goods by governments and foundations, rather than using block grants to build social enterprise cash-flows and profit and loss accounts.
5 The capital allocation characterized as social 'investment' on the other hand, typically involves, at a minimum, the return of an investor's capital and, sometimes, also an additional return. This is the definition preferred in the impact investing market and also by some significant new institutional players such as Big Society Capital in the UK: 'Social investment is the provision and use of capital to generate social as well as financial returns. Social investors weigh the social and financial returns they expect from an investment in different ways. They will often accept lower financial returns in order to generate greater social impact. Some interpretations of social investment include the provision of capital without any expectation of financial return. When we refer to social investment, however, we mean investment mainly to generate social impact, but with the expectation of some financial return' (BSC 2012).
6 Social value creation is best understood in terms of the outputs and impacts of organizational action identified as 'social' or 'environmental' in terms of normative (and often localized) assessments of their positive effects across five dimensions: geography and demography (Nicholls and Schwartz 2013): who the target market or beneficiaries are and where they are located, for example a project working in a deprived area or within disenfranchised populations; organizational processes: how value is created within an organization for key stakeholders and beneficiaries, for example work integration social enterprises that aim to bring excluded groups into the labour market; goods and services produced: how mission objectives are achieved in terms of outputs, for example providing care services or low-cost irrigation pumps; sector: in which category of economic activity the

organization fits, for example health, education, clean energy/green technology, clean water (the main areas of activity identified in the emerging Impact Investing sector); financial or organizational structure: who appropriates the value created, for example mutual or cooperative enterprises or dividend-capped or asset-locked legal forms (such as UK Community Interest Companies).

7 See Harold *et al.* (2007), for example, and further below.

8 The definition of social finance used in this chapter excludes capital allocation to conventional businesses that simply employ people, pay corporate taxes or that create other social value as incidental benefits of a central focus on maximizing financial returns to shareholders or other investors/owners. Thus, the majority of *broad* SRI is excluded here with only *core* SRI considered part of social finance (see further below).

9 Such investors range from small-scale retail investors allocating capital via crowd-funding platforms such as Kiva or Buzzbnk or social finance institutions such as Charity Bank to high net worth individuals investing via private banks such as UBS.

10 Charities and charitable foundations typically give grants amounting to between 3 and 5 per cent of their total assets per annum (5 per cent is mandated by law in the USA). Since charitable foundations in the USA are estimated to have in excess of £324 billion invested (Emerson *et al.* 2007) and those in the UK approximately £60–£80 billion (Nicholls and Pharoah 2007) this suggests a figure between £12 and £20 billion. This is supported by data on UK foundations that show grants of around £3.3 billion in 2006.

11 With respect to the sectoral structure of impact investment demand, O'Donohoe *et al.* (2010) identified two markets: basic needs (agriculture, water, housing), and basic services (education, health, energy, financial services).

12 This is consistent with Freireich and Fulton (2009) who suggested that the market for impact investment would grow to £308 billion in the next five to ten years.

13 This has been calculated as four billion consumers each earning £1,230 per year.

14 This was the title of a policy programme designed to encourage the high street banks to increase the availability of debt to businesses in the UK after the financial crisis and subsequent credit crunch.

15 This account of the HCT deal is based upon a 2010 case study prepared for the Skoll Centre by Catalyst Consulting (Hill 2010).

16 Quasi-equity aims to give investors returns on debt that are similar to equity by being linked to an organization's underlying performance. This is typically done as some form of debt contract since quasi-equity is typically offered by organizations that cannot generally issue standard equity shares, for example a charity or other organization that is unable to grant investors any control over the organization's mission or operations. However, to secure investment capital for high-risk projects such organizations need to offer satisfactory returns to the investor. This is often done by tying the returns to the revenue growth of the firm as a whole, or an individual project. Whilst quasi-equity accounted for 5 per cent of social lending in 2011, it is forecast to grow to 15 per cent by 2015 (Brown and Swersky 2012).

17 As a matter of due diligence, Rathbone Greenbank insisted on the option to transfer ownership of the bond between clients if required (e.g. in the case of death, a client would have to realize his share of HCT holding).

18 Jackson and Harji (2012) identified six dimensions of crucial importance to the ongoing development of the impact investing market, which also apply to the larger social finance market: unlocking capital; placing and managing capital; demand for capital; assessing impact; creating an enabling environment; building leadership (2012: xii).

19 According to the Social Exclusion Unit every reoffender costs the state a minimum of £143,000 a year, not including the costs to the victims of their crimes. So for a group of 50 gang members if 38 (75 per cent) of them reoffend, this will cost the state 38 times £143,000 or £5,434,000. With the St. Giles Trust's intervention, only an estimated five will reoffend, saving society a remarkable £4,719,000.

20 It is interesting to note that one reason for the growing appeal of social finance to mainstream investors could be its low correlation with other asset classes. This low *social beta* is a consequence of the more diverse funding and income streams evident in organizations supported by social finance that makes them more resilient in times of market downturn.

21 This type of intervention is becoming increasingly mainstream and has been captured in a new set of corporate CSR strategies grouped under the general heading of *Creating Shared Value* (Porter and Kramer 2011).

References

Abbott, A. (1988) *The System of Professions*. Chicago: University of Chicago Press.

Advantage Ventures (2011) *Beyond the Margin: Redirecting Asia's Capitalism*. Hong Kong: Advantage Ventures.

Anheier, H. (2004) *Civil Society: Measurement, Evaluation, Policy*. London: Earthscan.

Biggart, N. and Delbridge, R. (2004) 'Systems of exchange', *Academy of Management Review*, 29(1): 28–49.

Billis, D. (2010) *Hybrid Organizations and the Third Sector*. London: Palgrave Macmillan.

Bishop, M. and Green, M. (2008) *Philanthrocapitalism: How the Rich Can Save the World and Why We Should Let Them*. London: A&C Black.

Bishop, M. and Green, M. (2010) 'The capital curve for a better world', *Innovations*, 5(1): 25–33.

Brown, A. and Norman, W. (2011) *Lighting the Touchpaper: Growing the Market for Social Investment in England*. London: Boston Consulting Group/Young Foundation.

Brown, A. and Swersky, A. (2012) *The First Billion. A Forecast of Social Investment Demand*. London: Boston Consulting Group/Big Society Capital.

BSC – Big Society Capital (2012) *What Is Social Investment?* Available at: www.bigsocietycapital. com/what-social-investment (accessed 1 December 2012).

Cabinet Office (2011a) *Growing the Social Investment Market: A Vision and Strategy*. London: Cabinet Office.

Cabinet Office (2011b) *The Big Society Bank ("BSB") Outline Proposal*. London: Cabinet Office.

Campanale, M. (2005) *Mission Related Investing and Charities*. London: Henderson Global Investors.

CDFA (Community Development Finance Association) (2007) *Community Investment Tax Relief: Call for Evidence*. London: CDFA.

Chavez, R. and Campos, J.-L. (2008) *The Social Economy in the European Union*. Brussels: CIRIEC Working Paper 2008/02.

Cockerham, W., Abel, T. and Lueschen, G. (1993) 'Max Weber, formal rationality, and health lifestyles', *The Sociological Quarterly*, 34(3): 413–25.

Cohen, J., Hazelrigg, L. and Pope, W. (1975) 'De-Parsonizing Weber: a critique of Parsons' interpretation of Weber's sociology', *American Sociological Review*, 40: 229–41.

Commission on Unclaimed Assets (2006) *A Social Investment Bank: Consultation Paper*. London: Commission on Unclaimed Assets.

Dart, R. (2004) 'The legitimacy of social enterprise', *Nonprofit Management and Leadership*, 14(4): 411–24.

Davis, G., McAdam, D., Scott, W. and Zald, M. (2005) *Social Movements and Organization Theory*. Cambridge: Cambridge University Press.

Defourny, J. and Nyssens, M. (2008) *Social Enterprise in Europe: Recent Trends and Developments*. Lieges: EMES Working Paper, no. 08/01.

Deutsche Bank Research (2007) *Microfinance: An Emerging Investment Opportunity*. Berlin: Deutsche Bank.

Edwards, M. (2008) *Just Another Emperor? The Myths and Realities of Philanthrocapitalism*. London: Young Foundation.

Emerson, J. (2003) 'The blended value proposition: integrating social and financial returns', *California Management Review*, 45(4): 35–51.

Emerson, J. (2009) *Beyond Good Versus Evil: Hedge Fund Investing, Capital Markets and the Sustainability Challenge*. Available at: www.blendedvalue.org/publications (accessed 10 July 2010).

Emerson, J. and Spitzer, J. (2007) *From Fragmentation to Functionality: Critical Concepts and Writings on Social Capital Market Structure, Operation, and Innovation*. Oxford: Skoll Centre for Social Entrepreneurship.

Emerson, J., Freundlich, T. and Fruchterman, J. (2007) *Nothing Ventured, Nothing Gained*. Oxford: Skoll Centre for Social Entrepreneurship.

Eurosif (2008) SRI Studies. Available from: www.eurosif.org/publications/sri_studies (accessed 20 September 2010).

Evenett, R. and Richter, K. (2011) *Making Good in Social Impact Investment: Opportunities in an Emerging Asset Class*. London: Social Investment Business and The City UK.

Evers, A. and Laville, J-L. (2004) *The Third Sector in Europe*. London: Edward Elgar.

FB Heron Foundation (2007) *2007 Annual Report*. New York: FB Heron Foundation.

Foster, W. and Bradach, J. (2005) 'Should nonprofits seek profits?', *Harvard Business Review*, 83(February): 92–100.

Freireich, J. and Fulton, K. (2009) *Investing for Social and Environmental Impact: A Design for Catalyzing an Emerging Industry*. New York: Monitor Group.

Goodall, E. and Kingston, J. (2009) *Access to Capital: A Briefing Paper*. London: Venturesome.

Hammond, A., Kramer, W., Katz, R., Tran, J. and Walker, C. (2007) *The Next Four Billion. Market Size and Business Strategy at the Base of the Pyramid*. New York: World Resources Institute/International Finance Corporation.

Harold, J., Spitzer, J. and Emerson, J. (2007) *Blended Value Investing: Integrating Environmental Risks and Opportunities into Securities Valuation*. Oxford: Skoll Centre for Social Entrepreneurship.

Hartzell, J. (2007) *Creating an Ethical Stock Exchange*. Oxford: Skoll Centre for Social Entrepreneurship.

Hill, K. (2010) *Hackney Community Transport: Case Study*. Oxford: Skoll Centre for Social Entrepreneurship.

Hill, K. (2011) *Investor Perspectives on Social Enterprise Financing*. London: City of London/Big Lottery Fund/ClearlySo.

Impact Investment Shujog (2011) *Impact Investors in Asia: Characteristics and Preferences for Investing in Social Enterprises in Asia-Pacific*. Singapore: Impact Investment Shujog and Asian Development Bank.

Jackson, E. and Harji, K. (2012) *Accelerating Impact. Achievements, Challenges and What's Next in Building the Impact Investing Industry*. New York: ET Jackson and Associates Ltd/Rockefeller Foundation.

John, R. (2006) *Venture Philanthropy: The Evolution of High Engagement Philanthropy in Europe*. Oxford: Skoll Centre for Social Entrepreneurship.

Joy, I., de Las Casas, L. and Rickey, B. (2011) *Understanding the Demand for and Supply of Social Finance: Research to Inform the Big Society Bank*. London: New Philanthropy Capital/NESTA.

Kuhn, T. (1962) *The Structure of Scientific Revolutions*. Chicago: University of Chicago Press.

Loder, J., Mulgan, G., Reeder, N. and Shelupanov, A. (2010) *Financing Social Value: Implementing Social Impact Bonds*. London: Young Foundation.

Lounsbury, M., Ventresca, M. and Hirsch, P. (2003) 'Social movements, fields frames and industry emergence: a cultural-political perspective on U.S. recycling', *Socio-Economic Review*, 1: 71–104.

Marshall, A. (1907) 'The social possibilities of economic chivalry', *The Economic Journal*, 17(65): 7–29.

Martin, M. (2009) 'Managing philanthropy after the downturn: what is ahead for social investment?', in Martin, M. and Ernst, A. (eds), *Viewpoint 2010*. Geneva: IJ Partners, pp. 11–21.

Mulgan, G. (2009) 'After capitalism', *Prospect Magazine*, 26 April, pp. 157–70.

Mutuo (2009) *The Mutuals Yearbook 2009*. London: Mutuo.

NEF (New Economics Foundation)/CAF (Charities Aid Foundation) (2006) *Developing a Social Equity Capital Market: Views from the Sector*. London: NEF/CAF.

New Energy Finance (2009) *Global Trends in Clean Energy Finance Q4 2009 Fact Pack*. London: New Energy Finance.

Nicholls, A. (2007) *What Is the Future of Social Enterprise in Ethical Markets?* London: Office of The Third Sector.

Nicholls, A. (2009) '"We Do Good Things Don't We?" Blended Value Accounting In Social Entrepreneurship', *Accounting, Organizations and Society*, 34(6–7): 755–69.

Nicholls, A. (2010a) 'The institutionalization of social investment: the interplay of investment logics and investor rationalities', *Journal of Social Entrepreneurship*, 1(1): 70–100.

Nicholls, A. (2010b) *The Landscape of Social Finance in the UK*. University of Birmingham: Third Sector Research Centre.

Nicholls, A. and Opal, C. (2005) *Fair Trade: Market Driven Ethical Consumption*. London: Sage.

Nicholls, A. and Pharoah, C. (2007) *The Landscape of Social Finance*. Oxford: Skoll Centre for Social Entrepreneurship.

Nicholls, A. and Murdock, A. (eds) (2011) *Social Innovation*. London: Palgrave Macmillan.

Nicholls, A. and Schwartz, R. (2013) 'The demandside of the social investment marketplace', in Salamon, L. (ed.), *New Frontiers of Philanthropy*. New York: Jossey Bass.

Nicholls, A., Paton, R. and Emerson, J. (eds) (2013) *Social Investment*. Oxford: Oxford University Press.

Nicholls, J. (2004) *Social Return on Investment: Valuing What Matters*. London: New Economics Foundation.

Nyssens, M. (2006) *Social Enterprise*. London: Palgrave Macmillan.

O'Donohoe, N., Leijonhufvud, C. and Saltuk, Y. (2010) *Impact Investments: An Emerging Asset Class*. New York: JP Morgan and Rockefeller Foundation.

Offer, A. (1997) 'Between the gift and the market: the economy of regard', *Economic History Review*, 50(3): 450–76.

OTS (Office of the Third Sector) (2009) *Social Investment Wholesale Bank: A Consultation on the Functions and Design*. London: Cabinet Office.

Porter, M. and Kramer, M. (2011) 'Creating shared value', *Harvard Business Review*, January–February: 1–17.

Prahalad, C. K. (2006) *The Fortune at the Bottom of the Pyramid: Eradicating Poverty Through Profits*. New Jersey: Wharton Business School Press.

Rayner, S. (2006) *Wicked Problems: Clumsy Solutions – Diagnoses and Prescriptions for Environmental Ills*. Jack Beale Memorial Lecture on Global Environment. Available at: http://www.sbs.ox.ac.uk/research/Documents/Steve%20Rayner/Steve%20Rayner,%20 Jack%20Beale%20Lecture%20Wicked%20Problems.pdf (accessed 13 March 2012).

Salamon, L. (ed.) (2013) *New Frontiers of Philanthropy*. New York: Jossey Bass.

Salamon, L. and Anheier, H. (1999) *The Emerging Sector Revisited*. Baltimore: John Hopkins University.

Saltuk, Y., Bouri, A. and Leung, G. (2011) *Insight into the Impact Investment Market*. London: J. P. Morgan Social Finance Research.

Schneiberg, M. and Lounsbury, M. (2008) 'Social movements and institutional analysis', in Greenwood, R., Oliver, C., Sahlin, K. and Suddaby, R. (eds), *The Sage Handbook of Organizational Institutionalism*. London: Sage, pp. 650–72.

Sen, A. (1987) *On Ethics and Economics*. Oxford: Blackwell.

Seo, M. and Creed, W. (2002) 'Institutional contradictions, praxis, and institutional change: a dialectic perspective', *Academy of Management Review*, 27: 222–47.

Shanmugalingam, C., Graham, J., Tucker, S. and Mulgan, G. (2011) *Growing Social Ventures*. London: NESTA/Young Foundation.

Social Finance (2009) *Social Impact Bonds: Rethinking Finance for Social Outcomes*. London: Social Finance.

Social Investment Forum (2008) *2007 Report on Socially Responsible Investing Trends in the United States*. Washington, DC: Social Investment Forum.

Stein, P., Goland, T. and Schiff, R. (2010) *Two Trillion and Counting: Assessing the Credit Gap for Micro, Small, and Medium-sized Enterprises in the Developing World*. Washington DC: IFC and McKinsey and Company.

Strickland, P. (2010) *Social Impact Bonds – the Pilot at Peterborough Prison*, Standard Note SN/HA/5758. London: House of Commons Library: Home Affairs Section.

Stryker, R. (2000) 'Legitimacy processes as institutional politics: implications for theory and research in the sociology of organizations', *Research in the Sociology of Organizations*, 17: 179–223.

Suchman, M. (1995) 'Managing legitimacy: strategic and institutional approaches', *Academy of Management Review*, 20(3): 571–610.

Unwin, J. (2006) *An Intermediary for the Social Investment Market?* London: CAF Venturesome/Futurebuilders.

Weber, M. (1978) *Economy and Society*, Roth, G. and Wittich, C. (eds). California: University of California Press.

Weber, M. (1987) *Rationality and Modernity*, Whimster, S. and Lash, S. (eds). London: Allen and Unwin.

Weber, M. (2002) *The Protestant Ethic and 'the Spirit of Capitalism*, Baehr, P. and Wells, G. (trans.). London: Penguin.

Weisbrod, B. (2004) 'The pitfalls of profits', *Stanford Social Innovation Review*, 2(3): 40–52.

Weisbrod, B. (2011) 'The nonprofit mission and its financing', *Journal of Policy Analysis and Management*, 17(2): 165–74.

Young Foundation (2008) *Social Impact Bonds*. London: Young Foundation.

11

IN FUTILE SEARCH OF EXCELLENCE

The 'muddling through agenda'
of service-providing social enterprises
in contemporary Europe

Ingo Bode

Introduction

More recently, academics dealing with nonprofits can barely avoid coming across the concept of 'social enterprise'. This is obvious in particular when browsing through recent management handbooks (e.g. Dees *et al.* 2001; Shockley *et al.* 2008; Seaman and Young 2010). Although the respective debate is coloured by specific (national) traditions,[1] it has become customary to view nonprofits as *entrepreneurial* collective actors, including where they are directly involved in the delivery of human services. In the same vein, there is a growing interest in social entrepreneurship, understood 'as a disciplined, innovative, risk-tolerant … process of opportunity recognition and resource assembly directed toward creating social value' by economic action (Hill *et al.* 2010: 21).

Through the lens of practitioners, this may make sense insofar as many of these organizations, after having been entrenched in a public sector culture over many years, are nowadays exposed to processes of 'market-based governance' (Donahue and Nye 2002; see also Bode 2008). They move towards a 'new organizational construct' (Hockerts 2006: 143) and conform to novel 'institutionalized constructions' (Levander 2010) according to which nonprofit action is about both raising market revenue and fostering social innovation. Irrespective of the conceptual pluralism to be found around the social enterprise model, the latter is based on the conjecture that agencies committed to social purposes already are, or should become, independent businesses generating revenue through selling products and services to individual consumers or public authorities operating as purchasers. This conjecture goes alongside the assumption that these agencies are able to develop a sound management model through which this approach can be pursued purposefully. At least implicitly, advocates of the 'social enterprise model' suggest that one can have the best of two worlds: the achievement of social value as known from 'good old charity' *and* profit-oriented management endemic to private business. Yet what does the reality of major service-providing nonprofits tell us regarding this vision? Do typical service-providing nonprofits dispose of managerial discretion in order to prosper in both worlds?

Answering these questions more profoundly would require rigorous empirical enquiry into what actually happens to those undertakings that the literature empathetic with the social enterprise model is looking at. To date, such empirical knowledge is rare. However, as more and more traditional nonprofits involved in the delivery of public (human) services have become 'entrepreneurial' as a matter of fact, it is possible to review their *general development* over a longer term and thus to check the *conceptual soundness* of the double bottom-line approach.

This chapter will illustrate that major contemporary nonprofits in Europe see their traditional objectives coming under pressure, with public (and civic) stakeholders articulating new expectations infused by the 'market logic'. Under these conditions, organizational success is contingent on factors that are, at least partially, out of managerial control. Hence the search for both micro-economic fitness and social value – that is: the race to 'double bottom-line excellence' – turns out to be futile at the end of the day. Contemporary nonprofits, rather than being in a position of steering their business according to a sophisticated management model, are left with a 'muddling through agenda' that makes mission-oriented action more demanding than in former times.

The chapter is composed of three sections. The first section provides a brief theoretical enquiry into why it actually makes sense to refer to the notion of 'social enterprise' when dealing with contemporary nonprofits. Moreover, conceptual problems of the aforementioned double bottom-line approach will be highlighted. The second section charts the situation in which major European nonprofit agencies have for some time now been obliged to operate with an eye on two fields of human service provision – one recent, the other more traditional; *organized work integration* as an area often referred to when scholars discuss the virtues of social enterprise (Kerlin 2006: 250); and *social care* which has become infused with entrepreneurial orientations more incrementally.[2] The section illuminates the changing conditions under which nonprofits in these fields provide services, with examples from three different European countries: UK, Germany and France; this is to demonstrate the international character of these changing conditions. The third section derives insights from this overview, maintaining that, in the current situation, the preservation and development of a nonprofit profile does not follow from the application of ingenious entrepreneurial toolkits (including those associated with the social enterprise model) but from both chance and skills in the art of muddling through. The conclusion will discuss the general rationale behind this new international configuration.

Why 'social enterprise'?

For some time now, the academic discourse around the nonprofit sector has been driven by the idea of 'social enterprise' internationally (Pestoff 1988; Evers and

Laville 2004; Ridley-Duff 2008; Robinson *et al*. 2009; Defourny and Nyssens 2010; Levander 2010; Hackenberg and Empter 2011). This is in line with major political and economic elites having put their faith in 'nongovernmental, market-based approaches to address social issues' (Kerlin 2006: 247). It is also true that there is a lot of conceptual pluralism around the 'social enterprise model'. Some authors sympathetic with the latter are primarily interested in better management devices (Battle Andersen and Dees 2006), others discover new ingredients of nonprofit action, such as an amalgamation of sociality, market orientation and innovation (Nicholls and Cho 2006: 99) or social capital as a concept to draw upon (Ridley-Duff 2008). The 'Emergence of Social Enterprise' (EMES) group places an extra emphasis on the *civic* origin of social enterprises (Nyssens 2006) even as Paton (2003: 33) stresses the mixed governance of what he understands as contemporary entrepreneurial nonprofits: embracing a substantial lay or non-executive element; value commitments brought in by professionals or staff; close public scrutiny; and a propensity to work through partnerships.

That said, most academics and practitioners empathetic with the 'social enterprise model' assume that, in the current societal settlement, there is a place for organizations bound to a dual bottom-line, that is, market success materializing in the generation of surplus revenue on the one hand, and the achievement of social value (in which the mainstream for-profit economy is not interested) on the other. This twofold agenda, it is argued, can be ensured by a *distinctive* pattern of managerial orientation. Regarding practical implications, such orientation can lead nonprofits to review the portfolio of deliverables and resort to 'product extensions' or the 'production of complementary goods' (Oster 2010: 197–8), with this entailing the challenge of 'managing multiple benefits streams' (ibid: 203).

Against the background of crisis-ridden capitalism, the idea of blending the virtues of market agency and social value sounds intriguing. It appears to be something new, given that, by tradition, nonprofits have been isolated from the 'world of business' from which they are supposed to take lessons now. One should note, however, that many nonprofits have long been involved in economic activities – materializing in a budget to be managed, in paid staff and the production of tangible outputs. In other words, there has always been an *economic* dimension to nonprofit agency (Bode 2010). Numerous nonprofits have grown from early on as formally *independent* entities, collaborating at arm's length with external stakeholders (such as pubic authorities or donors). What is more, many European countries exhibit a tradition of cooperative economic action and associations entrusted with human service production (see Katz and Sachße 1986; Evers and Laville 2004).[3] In that sense, their development was always predicated on innovative, entrepreneurial action.

Importantly, however, many of these nonprofits often became involved in formal agreements with welfare bureaucracies enabling them to hire staff, operate plants and deliver services on a permanent and reliable basis. They were sheltered from market dynamics and largely based on non-market resources. In current social enterprise literature, however, nonprofits are understood as 'an organization that aims to achieve profit, through market activity, and social benefit, through a second bottom line' (Reid and Griffith 2006: 2). Hence, it appears that nonprofits are nowadays conceived of as hybrid organizations with a market orientation *adding to* those various orientations that have shaped their social world from very early on (Brandsen *et al.* 2005; Billis 2010). Notably, this new understanding differs markedly from theories of the nonprofit sector that view the 'non distribution constraint' as its key characteristic (Hansman 1986).

This new line of thinking is fraught with some ambiguity, though. It is unclear which will be the *guiding* rationale in the day-to-day challenge of 'keeping managerial focus' (Oster 2010: 204), particularly when trade-off situations occur. Furthermore, most proponents of the 'social enterprise model' suggest that nonprofit undertakings, notwithstanding their hybrid character, can, and should, be understood as *self-sustaining market players* like those anchored in the world of private business (Battle Anderson and Dees 2006). They may rely on further (civic, moral, voluntary) resources but, after all, they will be successful only if they employ these resources in a similar way to the for-profit sector. From this perspective, the actual hierarchy of managerial orientations endemic to the 'social enterprise model' becomes salient and nonprofits conforming to it appear as *less* hybrid than their classical predecessors, that is, market-sheltered nonprofit agencies.

More generally, a double bottom-line approach sits uneasily with modern rational thinking which makes human beings, and those organizations they form for the sake of collective action, behave according to a hierarchical goal set. Indeed, a complete blurring of boundaries between the 'world of business' and those social spheres in which human beings have other priorities than making money is prone to engender a confusion of cognitive realms. Modern society has grown with a division of labour between the for-profit economy and organizational fields deemed to take care of social needs arising from the activity of the former. The very existence of for-profit enterprises entailed the emergence of *other types* of organizations focusing on non-market environments (see Presthus 1979; Luhmann 1982; Perrow 1991). The respective collective experience became part of the cognitive structure of modern society. With the aforementioned blurring of boundaries, however, this division of labour and its cognitive representations are called into question, with stakeholders of nonprofits no longer being sure of their actual priorities. Society wants nonprofits to make a difference to the 'business world' out there, yet simultaneously it expects them to deliver 'value for money'. From this perspective, too, there is little hope for a consistent management orientation to emerge.

That said, contemporary nonprofits often have *no other choice* than adopting a market-oriented entrepreneurial spirit. This is less because a growing number of nonprofits develop this spirit *from the very start*, seeking to rely *primarily* on sources handled on markets, including those infused with civic orientations (materializing in social sponsoring, political consumerism etc.). Such initiatives, when compared with the bulk of human-service providing agencies, have remained marginal throughout the nonprofit sector in most Western countries. Rather, nonprofits – although public resources remain crucial to their functioning – have increasingly become *dependent* on the generation of revenue from markets for goods and services, as international surveys have evidenced (Salamon *et al.* 2004). Increasingly, traditional non-market resources (formal and informal) prove insufficient to maintain their distinctive profile. While it remains imperative for them to cultivate their image of being *mission-driven* they have to open themselves towards 'the market' at the same time.

Contemporary nonprofits see themselves embedded in a 'disorganized welfare mix' (Bode 2006) in which not only public, but also major civic resources (volunteers, donations) have become much more volatile, less reliable and short-term. While still expected to stick to mission, they are facing pressures to deliver measurable outputs and ensure cost-efficiency at any moment[4] – even though the issues they address 'are frequently complex and the consequences of their intervention uncertain' (Paton 2003: 5). Unlike their predecessors during the post-war-decades, they incur considerable risks in their day-to-day operations. It is these conditions that make 'entrepreneurialism' a generalized attitude throughout the nonprofit sector.

This new configuration materializes most clearly in changing relations between the sector and the state (Ascoli and Ranci 2002; Carmel and Harlock 2008; Bode 2010). One expression of this change is nicely phrased by Nicholls who states that the 'grant funding landscape has become an increasingly competitive and demanding marketplace' (2006: 102). What is more, the new configuration is shaped by what has been referred to as *managerialism* (Clarke and Newman 1997; Maier and Meyer 2011). This notion reflects, first of all, a changing attitude of those public bodies that still provide the lion's share of the nonprofit sector's revenue. Under a managerialist regime, welfare bureaucracies, eager to economize on public expenditure, resort to various techniques of streamlining their relations with non-statutory agencies involved in human service provision, with this making them more 'business-like'. The techniques used include competitive tendering, output-based funding and contractual inducements to reduce organizational slack. With their proliferation, 'contract-entwined voluntary agencies now operate in increasingly similar supervisory and policy environments' (Paton 2003: 14) and experience similar 'pressures to conform to certain organizational standards and structures' (Reid and Griffith 2006: 3)

Within nonprofits, these pressures translate into novel managerial approaches, placing the emphasis on both micro-economic and administrative accountability. The new 'managerialism' features a strong belief in organizational steering based on numbers, incentives and sanctions (Edwards 1998). It also chimes with commercial attitudes becoming ever more salient (Young 1998) even as other traditional characteristics of nonprofit governance, such as lay involvement and democratic deliberation, are shifted to the margins. Accordingly, accountants and production managers take centre stage, at the expense of mission-driven activists and stakeholders.

The emphasis placed on 'entrepreneurship' does not yield a clear orientation regarding what nonprofits should do in a given situation. In any case, there is more to the recent 'entrepreneurial turn' in the nonprofit sector than the insight that economic management matters. While contemporary nonprofits do not engage with economic affairs for the first time in their life, the very *character* of their economic engagement is changing with environments that expect them to operate as market entrepreneurs – be it as junior partners of a managerialized public sector, be it as agencies driven by a 'business spirit' in any instance. This sits uneasily with the necessity of 'making a difference' to private business and with the expectation to produce social value in order to preserve their particular reputation. Against this background, the idea of the double bottom-line is 'fuzzy' as a matter of principle.

The actual evolution of entrepreneurial nonprofits

Evidence from the field

The aim of this section is to picture the conditions under which typical nonprofits involved in human service provision are nowadays operating as 'social enterprises'. The section does not go into greater details, nor is this the place to elaborate on the methodological background of the evidence presented (information on this is provided in the references cited throughout). Rather, the evidence from three European countries (UK, Germany and France) serves as an illustration of an overarching argument spelled out above. Two areas of 'entrepreneurial' nonprofit action are taken as examples – one more recent, one more traditional.

The more recent field is 'back-to-work' projects undertaken by *work integration social enterprises* (WISE).[5] WISE have grown as a new organizational field in many European countries (see Nyssens 2006; Aiken and Bode 2009; Levander, 2010). Their emergence goes back to the late 1970s, when social workers or community groups established organizations providing paid work, training and personal support to unemployed citizens. Conceptualized as self-sustaining social undertakings selling goods and services, they were settling in markets such as recycling, second-hand trade and public transport. However, over the years, most of them became involved in partnerships with the welfare state. The second variety of organizations under study, nonprofits involved in social care, has adopted the 'social enterprise model' more incrementally. Social care is a broad field of human services; involving nonprofits as service providers for a long time now, it targets citizens facing major problems in their social life-world (children, the homeless etc.). In what follows, the focus will be on care to the elderly as organizations busy in this area have become exposed to 'marketized' environments most vigorously over the past two decades.[6]

How have these two organizational fields evolved over time? To begin with, the *United Kingdom* has seen various types of *work integration social enterprises* emerging from the 1970s onwards. Their legal and social foundations varied considerably: some developed with stronger relations to statutory bodies,[7] others were growing with a greater reliance on niche markets (worker cooperatives in the recycling sector, for instance).[8] All were using a mix of resources, among which being revenue from the sale of services (transport, recycling products) to the wider public and to local or regional authorities (Aiken 2006). Niche markets (e.g. charity magazines, recycling) provided some of them with a stable flow of independent income yet this widely depended on the customers' willingness to prefer their offer over alternative consumption options. Grant-givers, such as the Big Lottery (formerly Community Fund), were a further source of funding but for many UK WISE, public service contracts became an essential source of revenue. Some of these contracts were subject to competitive tendering, most (especially those under the 'New Deal framework') imposed heavy administrative procedures on these undertakings. Managers felt at times squeezed by these contracts as they made it difficult to pay attention to the social needs of particular employees and to accept those with the lowest employability. Overall, income generation proved precarious as it had to be ensured within a competitive environment *and* with a handicapped workforce. Although these organizations seemed to embody the 'social enterprise model' in pure form, most of them had limited managerial control, also because their productive capacity proved lower than those of major competitors from standard business.

Regarding social care, the UK nonprofit sector has equally seen a stronger involvement in service provision over the past two decades, although in elderly care, voluntary agencies were a minority among the fast growing population of independent service providers. In this area as well, nonprofits have increasingly been run as both economically independent undertakings *and* delivery agents of the welfare state (Greengross 2011). The newly emerging care market was highly regulated, with an institutional framework based on national quality standards and inspection bodies. Local authorities were entrusted with the management of both commissioning and case management schemes, including need assessments and the oversight of care plans.[9] Service provision was concentrating on the poor strata of the population, with public support being means-tested. Many local authorities resorted to management by numbers both internally and towards provider organizations, selected after public tendering and price enquiry. Nonprofits delivering these services therefore became exposed to both encompassing external standards and intense market competition – although the degree of the latter depended on the existing policy of a local authority (which may have a preference for long-term contracts). Notably, volunteerism is ever more confined to particular activities at the margins of the sector, such as daycare. Again, the leeway for managing a nonprofit undertaking independently appears quite limited, given both strong market pressures and procedural constraints imposed by public bodies.

Things are not much different in Germany. Like in the UK, *organized work integration* has grown there as an organizational field on its own from the late 1970s onwards. At this time, social activists established undertakings with the explicit aim to create jobs for unemployed citizens or to foster their employability; initiatives of local authorities added to this (Bode *et al.* 2006). The portfolio of activities resembled those of their UK counterparts. However, compared to the UK, the sector was institutionalized much more forcefully. Most German WISE – of which many are holding a nonprofit status – became integrated in what is often referred to as *corporatist* (public) governance (Bode 2011), espousing cordial collaboration and highly formalized agreements between the (local) state and the nonprofit sector.

Although most German WISE generated some independent income by selling goods and services on niche markets, they soon developed into publicly subsidized 'temporary labour market integration' agencies. At the beginning of the 1990s, the policies of the job centres that were responsible for admitting and funding became more and more influenced by managerialist approaches. Funding was confined to mere wage subsidies[10] and ever more predicated on measured outputs (job placements mainly). Market risks and the expenses for investment were fully devolved onto the undertakings. German WISE increasingly relied on earned income to cover expenses the public programmes no longer reimbursed. This made them dependent on civic-minded consumers to a considerable extent. In fields such as the sale of second-hand-clothes, competition from private providers put additional strain on them. Accordingly, entrepreneurial mission statements proliferated, often modelled on those of private firms. Concomitantly, many (nonprofit) WISE felt caught in a straightjacket preventing them from fulfilling their mission of empowering disadvantaged groups. Cost-efficiency became a 'big issue', often at the expense of social support devoted to workers with particular handicaps.

The German *social care sector* has seen similar developments. Again, the case of domiciliary elderly care is telling (Bode *et al.* 2011). In this area, corporatist (cordial) collaboration between the welfare state and nonprofit agencies has certainly not disappeared. Yet growing sections of the industry are subject to a consumer-led quasi market in which providers compete for 'customers' who are granted direct (social insurance) payments they can use at their convenience on a mixed provider market (Rothgang 2010). The institutional framework is different from the English quasi-market model (as there are no purchasing agencies) yet the regulatory mode governing the German care system has been markedly influenced by managerialist orientations as well. The care package of social insurance is capped, with the bulk of care acts being prescribed by an agreement between funders and umbrellas of providers. External regulations have imposed severe procedural norms regarding time schedules, methods of working and specifications of the services by which the scope for managerial independence has been confined markedly. There is systematic quality inspection, the results of which are used to publish a (quasi) star-rating report. The non-profit sector – which currently holds 45 per cent of the market – was urged to resort to managerial policies geared towards attracting users and selling on-top services, with one consequence being that the connection with volunteers involved in befriending and social support became weaker. Providers felt squeezed between their commitment of being responsive to actual needs on the one hand, and the pressure to break even on the other. Their workers were urged to stick rigorously to the established service contracts, regardless of concerns expressed by the users. The latter (and their relatives) now tend to negotiate the conditions of service provision, with providers being tempted to both offer additional support for free and make actual service provision contingent on the clients' ability to evaluate the quality delivered. Like in the UK, then, strong limitations exist regarding a pro-active 'double bottom-line' management.

In *France*, the overall configuration looks similar although some particularities can be observed. In the field of *organized work integration*, a considerable number of undertakings were set up by social activists from the 1970s onwards (Bucolo 2006). Today, the sector is composed of different types of organizations, with one variety (the so-called *entreprises d'insertion*) representing its core. These 'integration firms' are not understood by the state as agencies entrusted with a public service. Rather, public policies are aimed at compensating, over some time, the disadvantage of hiring workers with low employability in a number of open service markets (recycling, second-hand trade, domestic services etc.). *De facto*, these undertakings fulfil a mission equal to the one pursued by their German and UK counterparts (Meyer 2002).

Importantly, 'integration firms' compete with for-profit companies in most cases. In spite of public support, granted for a limited period and for each disadvantaged worker taken on board, they can never be sure of being able to keep up with their rivals. They also compete with workers engaged on an individual basis by private households, with the latter equally being promoted by public subsidies and tax exemptions (Windebank 2009).[11] This is one reason for many 'integration firms' facing difficulties in preserving their business. Like their German counterparts, moreover, many of them depend on civic-minded customers they can never be sure of. Over the past years, French WISE have experienced tough challenges to which many have responded by developing into quasi-commercial firms (Pache and Santos 2010).

Due to the aforementioned public subsidies, the work integration sector overlaps with *social care* in the area of domestic services provided to frail elderly people. Similar to Germany, the latter are entitled to professional services by means of a quasi-public care allowance (Bode 2008: 48–50, 75–7; Le Bihan and Martin 2010). There is a long tradition of French nonprofits providing home help to the elderly, with volunteers ensuring domestic arrangements and some social support. Nowadays, all types of suppliers, including for-profit ones, are admitted to this field, provided that basic input standards are respected. Although competition is still in its infancy,[12] nonprofit providers and their umbrellas have embarked, for some time now, on marketing and market development strategies. Even as managerialist thinking is proliferating throughout the sector, the volunteer basis of many nonprofits is eroding. More recently, some providers have faced the risk of bankruptcy as the available income did not suffice to enable them to break even (Petrella 2012). While the providers' economic health still highly depends on informal relations with local public authorities, formerly established cordial relations can break up more easily than previously (e.g. when the political party in power changes). Thus, *post*-corporatism is an issue in France as well (Bode 2011). Again, given the new environments for nonprofit activity, the scope for managerial discretion is narrowed down considerably.

Muddling through as 'one best way'

As the evidence suggests, being a social enterprise is a reality for numerous nonprofits throughout the three countries under study. With changing environments, they exhibit a new sort of hybridity. Besides the multiple orientations brought in by traditional stakeholders (members, volunteers, users, political movements and the like), markets have become a key reference for them. In this sense, the 'social enterprise model' chimes with their day-to-day experience.

That said, the rise of this model has little to do with the ingenious idea of reconciling, once and for all, social value and micro-economic fitness. Rather, nonprofits resort to increasingly risky methods of managing their undertakings under the volatile conditions of market-driven environments. Contemporary non-profits have to cope with the ever less controllable interface between themselves and welfare bureaucracies on the one hand and civic stakeholders on the other. In many instances, *chance* is critical to their wider development as the effects of multi-level market interplay are barely predictable. Compared to the era in which markets were widely irrelevant to them, there are *more* trade-offs to handle and *less* clear-cut relations between micro-economic and mission-oriented issues.

Previously, the undertakings dealt with above were operating a sheltered business, with public policies protecting their domain and civic stakeholders ensuring additional robust support.[13] In the era of managerialism, however, service-providing nonprofits have to comply with policies benchmarking them against 'best-in-class organizations' including from the for-profit sector. Moreover, non-statutory stakeholders become less calculable, developing into capricious volunteers, donors and supporters, if not customers. This situation provokes a 'light' handling of a non-profit's wider social mission[14] – and also of its democratic foundations. What is more, the new environments do not mind organizational failure. They accept that there will be winners and losers in the market game – if one organization fails, there will be another to step in.

Granted, nonprofit agencies are not powerless in their relationships with both civic environments and public bodies. Regarding the former, they may deploy extra efforts to convince stakeholders of their performance in terms of mission, and some will succeed in attracting new stakeholders, although this may be expensive. Concerning public stakeholders, commissioners are at times dependent on a non-profit's expertise in order to develop programmes and targets; it may be difficult for them to replace experienced providers with others. Hence, the terms of trade regarding funding and performance evaluation are always subject to negotiations and institutional pressures may be tamed to some extent – but much depends on local conditions and the outcome of strategic power games in the long term. Even in the short run, contemporary nonprofits can never be *sure* of receiving support from external stakeholders.

More generally, they exhibit *structural* ambiguity regarding their governance and their management has to cope with *systemic* tensions. Environmental volatility is awkward for organizations pursuing longstanding mission-related goals. Part of the literature on social enterprises is aware of this, paying attention to tensions between revenue-generating activities and programmes geared towards creating social value which, by their very nature, are seldom profitable. The recent debate on 'mission drift' reflects this dilemma – although this drift can have several backgrounds (Jones 2007).

In the fields explored above, things are quite obvious. As for work integration, WISE have to decide whether to focus on easy-to-deal-with groups or on disadvantaged communities as major addressees – unless they achieve a 'social oligopoly' (temporarily), as in the case of street magazines sold by homeless people.[15] While it is true that many social enterprises still operate in institutionally-shaped environments (with public authorities treating them as 'preferred' providers, for instance), managerialist public policies make this protection ever more precarious. In social care, there is almost no shelter left as nonprofits busy in this area are urged to behave like for-profit competitors. They may have at their disposal extra resources such as a volunteer workforce, but the evidence suggests that many have problems in benefiting from these resources under present-day conditions, given an increasing instability of volunteers and growing challenges regarding their integration. For those preserving a strong involvement of civic stakeholders, governance structures are less 'lean' than those of private competitors, which is prone to outweigh any other competitive advantage.[16] In turn, those 'organizations that seek to become more like private sector entrepreneurs in how they operate and manage their business will increasingly distance themselves from the voluntary sector traditions' (Jones and Keogh 2006: 16–17).

The least one can say is that, under the afore-sketched conditions, a typical service-providing nonprofit organization faces problems in maintaining its character as a 'multi-purpose organization' (Hasenfeld and Gidron 2005). The 'social mission bottom-line' is difficult to hold without disruption as in marketized environments service provision is fraught with contradictory functional requirements. This pertains to various dimensions of nonprofit agency: the mobilization of volunteers, human resource management, a community-oriented composition of the board, the participation in consultations with government, and political advocacy. Contemporary nonprofits are obliged to both make money and demonstrate their difference from commercial organizations at some point. This however often means squaring the circle.

In general, it is hard to see why nonprofits selling goods and services should have a *solid* comparative edge over for-profit undertakings that do not prioritize social concerns. A conceptualization of nonprofits as smart, entrepreneurial collective actors combining market fitness and social value overestimates the managerial discretion at their disposal. While contemporary nonprofits may enjoy greater autonomy by raising revenue from markets, they are facing permanent difficulties in keeping their 'marketized' environments under control. It becomes more demanding to exert influence within their wider environment, and opportunism in both economic constraints and managerialist expectations tends to become the prevailing rationality.

In this overall configuration, the management of nonprofits can merely be more than a profane art of handling tensions on the spot. Under conditions of marketization and public managerialism, entrepreneurial action in the nonprofit sector cannot follow a magic master plan according to which contradictory management logics, that is, the two bottom-lines, are consistently reconciled. The quest for a 'social enterprise management model' on which to build a new generation of nonprofits is ignorant of the fact that undertakings that handle, or are expected to handle, both social needs neglected by mainstream markets *and* the generation of market revenue, have no better choice than selecting among those trade-offs that are the least problematic in a given situation. For most of them, the search for excellence by applying a sophisticated managerial toolkit will eventually turn out to be a futile endeavour.

The best real-life nonprofits can do is to accept their transformation into '*muddling through agencies*'. The notion of muddling through draws on Lindblom's theory of public administration (1959, see also Rothmary Allison and Saint-Martin 2011). The concept departs from the assumption that rational governance is impossible in complex administrative settings, given that these have limited resources for this. It posits that the basic challenge to organizational steering is finding second-best solutions spontaneously, with the involved actors drawing on prior experience and available routine (tweaking past practices here and there). Muddling through is particularly salient where actors have limited environmental control and where they manage to evaluate only a few alternatives at one point in time, with the outcomes of decisions taken being hard to predict. This is precisely the configuration in which service-providing nonprofits (have to) operate at present. Muddling through is required in the relationship with managerialist welfare bureaucracies, and it is also in demand when the challenge is to raise resources from ever-more capricious stakeholders.

The muddling through agenda is also comprised of the efforts of lobbying for public shelter and informal institutional protection (hidden subsidies, indirect funding etc.). Internally, nonprofits mutating into social enterprises will permanently have to resort to compromises and exhibit high cognitive flexibility, if not schizophrenia. They need workers (and volunteers) ready to forego a long-term perspective in terms of career and personal development, given the ups and downs of market opportunities. They will also have to exhibit a certain laxity regarding their goal set and their organizational ethos. Whether this will, over the long run, endorse their institutional standing vis-à-vis critical stakeholders is another question, however.

Conclusion

The tendency towards the 'social enterprise model' appears as a *transnational* movement. Obviously, nonprofits from different nations and from different fields are currently facing *similar* challenges. In the three countries and two sub-sectors under review here, being a 'social enterprise' is not only a material reality but also a normative vision entrenched in the wider environment. Civic and public stakeholders sympathize with social entrepreneurship, and many expect 'their' nonprofits to generate independent income instead of relying on public subsidies (Jones and Keogh 2006: 20). This is illusionary to some extent as major service-providing nonprofits will never be able to forego partnerships with welfare bureaucracies. Yet, as a *cultural agenda*, such expectations are a matter of fact.

This development is consistent with institutionalist organization studies (Powell and DiMaggio 1991) according to which collective undertakings, especially those located outside the capitalist market economy, operate in environments that impose particular *normative* frames on them. As others have already noted (Dart 2004; Reid and Griffith 2006; Levander 2010), the discourse (and practice) of social entrepreneurship echoes change in the way current opinion leaders conceive of social welfare provision in general. The (welfare) state has been affected by a crisis of legitimacy throughout Western Europe (Offe 1996) even as European societies have lost faith in traditional forms of civic action, materializing, among other things, in the 'decline of public confidence in charities' (Paton 2003: 8) throughout the Anglo-Saxon world. At least in some quarters of the nonprofit sector, new generations of volunteers and donors seem to prefer 'value for money', or compensation for personal effort, over the mere promise of outcomes beneficial to the wider community in the long term (Hustinx 2010). Thus, the notion of social enterprise encapsulates a profound ideological change within the environments of the nonprofit sector. While the 'rejection of profit' can be still viewed as a widely shared 'social economy cultural position' (Jones and Keogh 2006: 15), it is obvious that, throughout the Western world, today's nonprofits are pressured to 'deliver' according to a logic of return-on-investment.

This chapter has argued that the social enterprise 'hype' echoes material developments through which service-providing nonprofit agencies increasingly adopt, or have to adopt, characteristics of market-oriented firms. However, they operate in an environment leaving little scope for managerial discretion, let alone for pursuing a management concept through which a double bottom-line can be addressed consistently. Ironically, the boom of the 'social enterprise model' goes alongside a *decreasing* scope for (mission-driven) entrepreneurial initiative throughout large sections of the contemporary nonprofit sector(s). From this perspective, our societies may see a new bubble bursting sooner or later.

Notes

1 Overviews are provided by Kerlin (2006) and Hill *et al.* (2010). Some of these traditions refer to the long history of collectively-owned undertakings such as mutuals and cooperatives (Duelfer and Laurinkari 1994; Evers and Laville 2004).
2 Social care embodies a classical area of nonprofit service provision in numerous Western countries and is defined differently throughout Europe (Anttonen and Sipilä 2005). It includes services provided to citizens who are facing major problems in their social life-world (children, the elderly, the homeless etc.).
3 True, in some countries (like the UK), the material involvement of nonprofits in public service provision has only recently appeared to be more substantial. However, there is evidence that even during the 'heyday' of the service-delivering welfare state, the voluntary sector was collaborating with public authorities at local level (see Bode 2006, 2010).
4 This is very obvious regarding present-day philanthropy where donors expect a direct social impact for a given unity of donation, 'on the spot', that is, in accordance with quantified measures and in a given time-frame. Yet it also applies to other sections of the nonprofit sector.

5 The evidence partly stems from a European project researching this organizational field comparatively. Results are provided at greater length in Nyssens (2006); see also Aiken and Bode (2009).

6 The findings presented hereafter are derived from several research activities, among which is a project labelled 'Care Regimes on the Move in Europe' (CROME), coordinated by 'Centre Interdisciplinaire de Recherche – Travail, État et Société' at the Université catholique de Louvain.

7 This was the case of the so-called Intermediate Labour Market organizations or the state-sponsored REMPLOY, established after the Second World War to assist with disabled veterans, or those voluntary agencies involved in New Labour's 'New Deal' programmes.

8 This business orientation was corroborated by a new legal form (the Community Interest Company, CIC) invented by 'New Labour', and the creation of a 'Social Enterprise Unit' established by the Department of Trade and Industry (DTI).

9 More recently, there are plans to replace the commissioning role of local authorities by direct payment schemes within which they would play the role of a moderator.

10 Public subsidies became concentrated on short-term 'One-Euro-Jobs' (with a salary of 1€ per hour plus social assistance) imposed on those claiming social assistance.

11 Reforms have sought to make private households, including those providing personal care to frail elderly people, employers of home helps. Major incentives include tax exemptions and the introduction of pre-paid service vouchers deemed to ease the administrative burden associated with the recruitment of private employees. Existing (and new) nonprofit agencies have been given the opportunity to embark in this market as broker agencies. As of mid-2006, however, only 20 per cent of the domestic workforce was employed by a nonprofit provider.

12 Commercial firms held only 2 per cent of the market in 2009. Yet in some areas, public authorities have introduced tenders in order to select providers to be entrusted with service provision.

13 This includes the early years of the organizations under study here. For instance, they benefited from an exclusive waste recycling contract or a monopolistic remit for providing domiciliary care in a given area.

14 In the aforementioned fields, for example: working with 'hopeless' or 'complex' cases or devoting time to spontaneous (and unknown) social needs.

15 Regarding these configurations, see Aiken (2006). These charitable markets are less open to competitors than mainstream markets. However, they may overlap with the latter (e.g. in the area of second-hand clothes) and be sensitive to pervasive strategies of for-profit imitators as well as fads and fashions.

16 Following some proponents of the 'social enterprise model' (e.g. Pestoff 1998), this is by intention as cooperatives are deemed to take decisions after democratic deliberation.

References

Aiken, M. (2006) 'Towards market or state?', in M. Nyssens (ed.), *Social Enterprises. Between Markets, Public Policies and Community*. London: Routledge.

Aiken, M. and Bode, I. (2009) 'Killing the golden goose? Third Sector organizations and back-to-work programs in Germany and the UK', *Social Policy and Administration*, 43: 209–25.

Anttonen, A. and Sipilä, J. (2005) 'Comparative approaches to social care: diversity in care production modes', in B. Pfau-Effinger and B. Geissler (eds), *Care Arrangements and Social Integration in European Societies*. Bristol: Policy Press.

Ascoli, U. and Ranci, C. (eds) (2002) *Dilemmas of the Welfare Mix. The New Structure of Welfare in an Era of Privatization*. New York: Kluwer Academic/Plenum Publishers.

Battle Anderson, B. and Dees, G. (2006) 'Rhetoric, reality and research: building a social foundation for the practice of social entrepreneurship', in A. Nicholls (ed.) *Social Entrepreneurship*. Oxford: Oxford University Press.

Billis, D. (ed.) (2010) *Hybrid Organizations and the Third Sector: Challenges for Practice, Theory and Policy*. Basingstoke: Palgrave Macmillan.

Bode, I. (2006) 'Disorganized welfare mixes. Voluntary agencies and new governance regimes in Western Europe', *Journal of European Social Policy*, 19: 346–59.

Bode, I. (2008) *The Culture of Welfare Markets. The International Recasting of Pension and Care Systems*. New York: Routledge.

Bode, I. (2010) 'Thinking beyond borderlines. A German gaze on a changing interface between society and the voluntary sector', *Voluntary Sector Review*, 1: 139–61.

Bode, I. (2011) 'Creeping marketization and post-corporatist governance: the transformation of state–nonprofit relations in continental Europe', in Phillips, Susan D. and Steven Rathgeb Smith (eds), *Governance and Regulation in the Third Sector*. London: Routledge, pp. 115–41.

Bode, I., Evers, A. and Schulz, A. D. (2006) 'Where do we go from here? The unfinished story of relations between social enterprises and public policies in Germany', in M. Nyssens (ed.), *Social Enterprises. Between Markets, Public Policies and Community*. London: Routledge.

Bode, I., Gardin, L. and Nyssens, M. (2011) 'Quasi-marketization in domiciliary care: varied patterns, similar problems?', *International Journal of Sociology and Social Policy*, 31(3/4): 222–35.

Brandsen, T., van de Donk, W. and Putters, K. (2005) 'Griffins or chameleons? Hybridity as a permanent and inevitable characteristic of the third sector', *International Journal of Public Administration*, 28: 749–65.

Bucolo, E. (2006) 'French social enterprises. A common ethical framework to balance various objectives', in M. Nyssens (ed.), *Social Enterprise. At the Crossroads of Market, Public policies and Civil Society*. London: Routledge.

Carmel, E. and Harlock, J. (2008) 'Instituting the 'third sector' as a governable terrain: partnership, procurement and performance in the UK', *Policy and Politics*, 36: 155–71.

Clarke, J. and Newman, J. (1997) *The Managerial State. Power, Politics and Ideology in the Remaking of Social Welfare*. London: Sage.

Dart, R. (2004) 'The legitimacy of social enterprise', *Nonprofit Management and Leadership*, 14: 411–24.

Dees, J. G., Emmerson, J. and Economy, P. (2001) *Enterprising Nonprofits: A Toolkit for Social Entrepreneurs*. New York: John Wiley & Sons.

Defourny, J. and Nyssens, M. (2010) 'Conceptions of social enterprise and social entrepreneurship in Europe and the United States: convergences and divergences', *Journal of Social Entrepreneurship*, 1: 32–53.

Donahue, J. D. and Nye, J. S. J. (eds) (2002) *Market Based Governance: Supply Side, Demand Side, Upside, Downside*. Cambridge: Brookings Institutions Press.

Duelfer, E. and Laurinkari, J. (ed.) (1994) *International Handbook of Cooperative Organizations*. Göttingen: Vandenhoek & Ruprecht.

Edwards, J. D. (1998) 'Managerial Influences in Public Administration', *International Journal of Organizational Theory and Behavior*, 1: 553–83.

Evers, A. and Laville, J.-L. (eds) (2004) *The Third Sector in Europe*. Cheltenham: Edward Elgar.

Greengross, S. (Lead Commissioner: Equality and Human Rights Commission) (2011) *Close to Home. An Inquiry into Older People and Human Rights in Home Care*. Manchester: EHRC.

Hackenberg, H. and Empter, S. (eds) (2011) *Social Entrepreneurship – Social Business: Für die Gesellschaft unternehmen*. Wiesbaden: Verlag für Sozialwissenschaften.

Hansman, H. B. (1986) 'The role of nonprofit enterprise', in S. Rose-Ackerman (ed.) *The Economics of Nonprofit Institutions. Studies in Structure and Policy*. Oxford/New York: Oxford University Press.

Hasenfeld, Y. and Gidron, B. (2005) 'Understanding multi-purpose hybrid voluntary organizations: the contributions of theories on civil society, social movements and non-profit organizations', *Journal of Civil Society*, 1: 97–112.

Hill, T. L., Kothari, T. H. and Shea, M. (2010) 'Patterns of meaning in the social entrepreneurship literature: a research platform', *Journal of Social Entrepreneurship*, 1: 5–31.

Hockerts, K. (2006) 'Entrepreneurial opportunity in social purpose business ventures', J. Mair, J. Robinson and K. Hockerts (eds), *Social Entrepreneurship*. Basingstoke: Palgrave Macmillan.

Hustinx, L. (2010) 'Institutionally individualized volunteering: towards a late modern re-construction', *Journal of Civil Society*, 6: 165–79.

Jones, D. and Keogh, W. (2006) 'Social enterprise: a case of terminological ambiguity and complexity', *Social Enterprise Journal*, 2: 11–26.

Jones, M. B. (2007) 'The multiple sources of mission drift', *Nonprofit and Voluntary Sector Quarterly*, 36: 299–307.

Katz, M. B. and Sachße, C. (eds) (1986) *The Mixed Economy of Social Welfare. Public-private Relations in England, Germany and the United States*. Baden-Baden: Nomos.

Kerlin, J. A. (2006) 'Social Enterprise in the United States and Europe: understanding and learning from the differences', *Voluntas*, 17: 247–63.

Le Bihan, B. and Martin, C. (2010) 'Reforming long-term care policy in France: private–public complementarities', *Social Policy and Administration*, 44: 392–410.

Levander, U. (2010) 'Social enterprise: implications of emerging institutionalized constructions', *Journal of Social Entrepreneurship*, 1: 213–30.

Lindblom, C. E. (1959) 'The science of muddling through', *Public Administration Review*, 19: 79–88.

Luhmann, N. (1982) 'Interaction, organization, and society', in id., *The Differentiation of Society* (trans. S. Holmes and C. Larmore). New York: Columbia University Press.

Nicholls, A. (ed.) (2006) *Social Entrepreneurship*. Oxford: Oxford University Press.

Nicholls, A. and Hyunbae Cho, A. (2006) 'Social entrepreneurship', in A. Nicholls (ed.) (2006) *Social Entrepreneurship*. Oxford: Oxford University Press.

Nyssens, M. (ed) (2006) *Social Enterprises. Between Markets, Public Policies and Community*. London: Routledge.

Maier, F. and Meyer, M. (2011) 'Managerialism and beyond: discourses of nonprofits and their governance implications', *Voluntas*, 22: 731–54.

Meyer, J.-L. (2002) 'Organisation de la solidarité et insertion par l'activité économique', in G. Hénaff (ed.), *Concurrence et services publics: Enjeux et perspectives*. Rennes: Presses Universitaires de Rennes.

Offe, C. (1996) *Modernity and the State. East, West*. Cambridge: Polity Press.

Oster, S. M. (2010) 'Product diversification and social enterprise', in B. A. Seaman and D. R. Young (eds), *Handbook of Research on Nonprofit Economics and Management*. Cheltenham: Edward Elgar, pp. 195–207.

Pache, A. C. and Santos, F. (2010) Inside the Hybrid Organization: An Organizational Level View of Responses to Conflicting Institutional Demands. INSEAD Working Paper 2010/57, Paris.

Paton, R. (2003) *Managing and Measuring Social Enterprises*. London: Sage.

Perrow, C. (1991) 'A society of organizations', *Theory and Society*, 20: 725–62.

Pestoff, V. (1998) *Beyond the Market and the State. Social Enterprises and Civil Democracy in a Welfare Society*. Aldershot: Ashgate.

Petrella, F. (ed.) (2012) *Aide à domicile et services à la personne. Les associations dans la tourmentee*. Rennes: Presses Universitaires de Rennes.

Powell, W. W. and DiMaggio, P. J. (eds) (1991) *The New Institutionalism in Organizational Analysis*. Chicago: Chicago University Press.

Presthus, R. (1979) *The Organizational Society*, Revised Edition. New York: St Martin's.

Reid, K. and Griffith, J. (2006) 'Social enterprise mythology: critiquing some assumptions', *Social Enterprise Journal*, 2: 1–10.

Ridley-Duff, R. (2008) 'Social enterprise as a socially rational business', *International Journal of Entrepreneurial Behaviour and Research*, 14: 291–312.

Robinson, J., Mair, J. and Hockerts, K. (eds) (2009) *International Perspectives on Social Entrepreneurship Research*, Revised Edition. Basingstoke: Palgrave Macmillan.

Rothgang, K-H. (2010) 'Social insurance for long-term care: an evaluation of the German model', *Social Policy and Administration*, 44: 436–60.

Rothmary Allison, C. and Saint-Martin, D. (2011) 'Half a century of "muddling": Are we there yet?', *Policy and Society*, 30: 1–8.

Salamon, L. M., Sokolowsky, S. W. and associates (2004) *Global Civil Society: Dimensions of the Nonprofit Sector*, Volume 2. Bloomfield, CT: Kumarian Press.

Seaman, B. A. and Young, D. R. (eds) (2010) *Handbook of Research on Nonprofit Economics and Management*. Cheltenham: Edward Elgar.

Shockley, G. E., Frank, P. M. and Stough, R. R. (eds) (2008) *Non-market Entrepreneurship. Interdiscplinary Approaches*. Cheltenham: Edward Elgar.

Windebank, J. (2009) 'State support for domestic services: a comparison of the outsourcing of domestic cleaning in France and Britain', *Journal of Contemporary European Studies*, 17: 437–49.

Young, D. (1998) 'Competition, commercialization, and the evolution of nonprofital structures', in B. A. Weisbrod (ed.), *To Profit and Not to Profit. The Commercial Transformation of the Nonprofit Sector*. Cambridge: Cambridge University Press.

12

SOCIAL ENTERPRISE THROUGH A CRITICAL APPRECIATIVE LENS[1]

Suzanne Grant

Introduction

Grant and Dart (2008) observe how political, social, economic, historical and cultural contexts potentially influence our interactions and hence the social construction of a shared understanding of social enterprise (SE).[2] While the extent to which context might influence the balance between social and enterprise ideologies varies according to geographical and political circumstance (Grant 2008), I suggest continued development of social enterprise theory and practice can be enhanced through critical consideration of these dimensions, either individually or collectively, and their subsequent interaction.

Enthusiasm amid policymakers, practitioners and others that social enterprise may be a panacea to address many of the challenges facing society today (see for example Bornstein 2004; Dees *et al.* 2004; Drayton 2006; Martin and Osberg 2007) must be balanced by careful consideration of the underlying assumptions that are embedded in our negotiated understand of 'what social enterprise is'. The aim of this chapter is to encourage the reader to look beyond the 'positive' and 'glowing' accounts of social enterprise proffered by a mix of policymakers, practitioners and academics so that we may develop a deeper understanding of how social enterprise is socially constructed within our respective contexts, hence increasing our awareness of potential opportunities AND pitfalls that may be encountered by those engaging in social enterprise activities.

In this chapter I introduce a conceptual framework to assist our understanding of the social construction of social enterprise. Drawing inspiration from the apparent paradox between social and enterprise (Alter 2006; Peattie and Morley 2008), I apply another seemingly paradoxical development, 'critical appreciative processes' (Grant 2006) as a means of deepening our understanding of social enterprise and potentially its outcomes. I recognize social enterprise to be a socially constructed concept, with a plethora of interpretations and definitions existing to accommodate theoretical, geographic, economic, political, social and cultural differences (see for example Defourny and Kim 2011; Defourny and Nyssens 2006; Grant 2008; Kerlin 2006a, 2010; Thompson and Doherty 2006). For this reason, while guided by Seanor *et al.*'s (2007: 16) proposal that social enterprise 'is a heterogeneous movement located at cross-over points between three distinctly different sectors', my focus here is not on a specific definition of SE, but rather on the tenuous balance between two seemingly different value systems. 'Social' invites a sociological perspective, considering interactions and/or relationships which desire to benefit society, or enhance the wellbeing of its members in some way (Diochon and Anderson 2009; Peredo and McLean 2006). In contrast, 'enterprise' may be interpreted as the application of 'business-like' and/or profit-orientated approaches to organization activities (Dees 1998; Kerlin 2006b, 2010; Young 2001), activities which some (such as those wary of capitalist intentions) may perceive to put profit before people.

The conceptual framework proposed develops as this chapter progresses. I begin with 1) a brief overview of appreciative inquiry to orientate those readers unfamiliar with this action research approach, followed by 2) a similarly focused brief overview of critical theory, which in this instance draws on Habermas' conception of the lifeworld and system. An introduction to critical appreciative processes (CAPs) is provided in 3), and then CAPs are applied to social enterprise to demonstrate insights that can be gained through this conceptual framework 4). Such application is developed from a review of relevant social enterprise scholarship, which includes consideration of key themes such as policy capture, heroic and deliverance claims, and increased marketization. I conclude this chapter with a proposal 5) to further this work through critical appreciation of dimensions within social enterprise such as culture. Areas for further research are also identified.

Appreciative inquiry

Often applied as a change management and/or evaluation process, appreciative inquiry (Ai) focuses our attention on 'what is good' (Cooperrider and Whitney 2000) and depicts an organization as a living system which has 'a mystery to be embraced' (Cooperrider and Srivastva 1987). The Ai process is often portrayed in a circular form, and may be described through models such as Cooperrider and Whitney's (2000) 4D cycle depicted in Figure 12.1 (discovery, dream, design, destiny) or Mohr and Jacobsgaard's 4-I (initiate, inquire, imagine, innovate) model noted in Watkins and Mohr (2001).

Working through each phase, participants identify what is working well in the organization so that this foundation of strength can be built upon to achieve the organization's dreams. Reports of fruitful applications across of range of settings (including individuals, families, organizations and even cities) are plentiful in both practitioner and academic literature (see for example Bushe 1998; Jacobsgaard 2003; Mantel and Ludema 2000; Rogers and Fraser 2003; Ryan *et al.* 1999). However, often the value in Ai lies beyond formal processes, resting instead in the

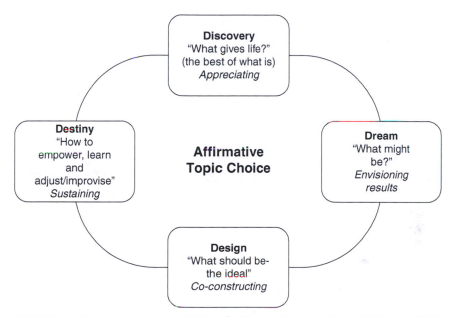

FIGURE 12.1   Appreciative inquiry 4-D cycle (Source: Cooperrider and Whitney, 2000)

positive intent informing a desire for change (Barge and Oliver 2003; Bushe and Khamisa 2004; Grant 2006). Application of Ai as a means of achieving change brings a strong transformational intent and emancipatory potential to a situation. The pursuit of positive change to enhance wellbeing is hence an aspiration common to both Ai and social enterprise activity.

Ai encourages participants to engage in 'vocabularies of hope' (Ludema 2001; Ludema *et al.* 2001), recognizing that the language we use creates/influences the reality we perceive. Storytelling is encouraged within Ai processes. As participants share their stories, values and aspirations, insight is gained into those aspects which are most important and/or influential to their circumstances (Diochon and Anderson 2011). Application of Ai as an evaluation process may be targeted to evaluate a specific programme or more holistically adopted as an approach to shape and manage positive change. Examples of Ai evaluations of not-for-profit/community organizations abound, including Elliot's (1999, as cited in Coghlan *et al.* 2003) evaluation of programmes working with street children in Africa, the evaluation of the Girl Scouts' Beyond Bars programme (Preskill and Catsambas 2006; Smart and Mann 2003) and Odell's (2002) evaluation of Habitat for Humanity. Catsambas and Webb (2003) note the compatibility between the asset-based and participatory approaches of Ai and the strategic mission and democratic structures of such not-for-profit/community organizations. Building on this observation I suggest similar compatibility might be expected for appreciative applications within social enterprises.

Ai and its positive orientation is not without its critics however; and has variously been portrayed as 'too Pollyannaish' or excessively focused on 'warm fuzzy group hugs' (Fitzgerald *et al.* 2001). Pratt (2002: 119) calls our attention to 'the need to honour the multiple and undivided realities of human experience in organisations', and Reason (2000) questions the 'danger of ignoring the shadow'. Rogers and Fraser (2003: 77) question whether Ai encourages 'unrealistic and dysfunctional perceptions, attitudes and behaviour'. Golembiewski (2000) purports that Ai is under-evaluated and discourages analysis. Other shortcomings of Ai identified by Golembiewski include a lack of linkages to other theory and practice, lack of a critical imperative and sparse availability of research literature. More recently, Aldred (2011) highlights concerns that the Ai process might conceal structural inequalities and encourage problematic notions of empowerment.

Critical theory

Just as Ai can be more than looking at the positive (Rogers and Fraser 2003), critical theory need not be equated with negativity (Alvesson and Deetz 2000; Alvesson and Sköldberg 2000). Rather, critical theory encourages us to consider more deeply that which we might otherwise take for granted. Critical theory encompasses a vast range of concepts, often amalgamated together under a common label (Alvesson and Sköldberg 2000). Here I draw on processes that seek to realize emancipatory interests, specifically through critique of consciousness and ideology (Carr 2000). Application of critical theory in this way assists in developing insights into the everyday, practical manner in which power is deployed and potential conflicts suppressed (Alvesson and Willmott 2003 as cited in Grant 2006). Habermas' programme of social theory and later theory of communicative action is proposed as a useful framework for any critical analysis (Forester 2003) and specifically within action research such as an appreciative inquiry (Kemmis 2001). The lifeworld and system, key concepts within Habermas' theory of communicative action, are briefly introduced here to assist the reader.

The lifeworld and system

Habermas identifies society as comprising two distinct spheres, each with its own rules, institutions, discourse and patterns of behaviour (Finlayson 2005). The first sphere, the lifeworld, comprises informal and non-market domains of life, such as family, households, culture and voluntary organizations. Unregulated in a formal sense, but influenced through traditions and other aspects of culture, the lifeworld is the home of communication and discourse (Finalyson 2005) and provides a backdrop in which meaningful social action is realized through meaningful communicative action (Ahn 2009). The second sphere, the system, embodies structures in society; more specifically those related to money and power and typically identified as the capitalist economy, state administration and related institutions. Through the production and circulation of goods and services, 'system integration' contributes towards 'holding society together' and is hence the home of instrumental and strategic actions (Finlayson 2005). Interestingly, this binary portrayal of society does not portray the activities of government as a separate entity. Habermas' conception of the public sphere is a somewhat idealistic realm which resides within the lifeworld, distinct from state and civil society where matters of general interest could be discussed (Thompson and Held 1982). As business organizations continue to grow, and state intervention in economic activity increases, the public sphere (within the lifeworld) becomes restricted and compressed (Thomson and Held 1982).

While the lifeworld and system spheres of society are recognized as overlapping, neither is seen by Habermas to be more important than the other – it is the interconnection between the two environments and the resulting tension which he deems to be important. Just as the system provides structure to the lifeworld, the lifeworld also provides an anchor within the system through which lifeworld values and norms might formally influence organized action (Ahn 2009). Balance between the spheres is tenuous and fragile. Should tradition become unsettled causing societal norms to be brought into question and contested a 'legitimation' crisis may occur within the lifeworld. Similarly 'economic' and/or 'rationality' crises pose risk to the stability of the system.

Critical appreciative processes

Concerns (such as those noted earlier in this chapter) about the potential for the overtly positive orientation evident within Ai to distort both process and perception are addressed by Grant (2006) and Grant and Humphries (2006) who demonstrate how the apparent paradox between the negativity often associated with critical theory (Alvesson and Deetz 2000) and the positive focus of Ai (Cooperrider and Srivastva 1987; Cooperrider and Whitney 2000; Fitzgerald *et al.* 2001) may provide a reflexive lens, termed critical appreciative processes (CAPs) (Grant 2006; Grant and Humphries 2006). Ai and critical theory share an epistemological base in the premises of social constructionist theories. Both paradigms deem language to be central to all action while meaning is negotiated between participants (Grant 2006; Grant and Humphries 2006). Even though each lens approaches the situation in question from a seemingly different direction, both bring emancipatory and transformational intentions. In combination, both lenses have the potential to provide balance to their respective applications, reducing the risk of distortion which may occur should only one theoretical lens be applied. Just as 'breaking up established ways of using language is a vital task for critical research' (Alvesson and Deetz 2000: 55 as cited in Grant and Humphries 2006), Ai challenges researchers and participants to move beyond the problematic discourse often associated with research and/or evaluation (Grant 2006). Building on, and recognizing how power may be gained (or lost) through applications of language, both approaches also highlight the importance of reflection, opening doors to new possibilities (Carr 2000 as cited in Grant and Humphries 2006; Grant 2012).

Critical appreciative processes encourage us to apply an enhanced definition of appreciation. Appreciation can be much more than a focus on what is good. In addition to signifying value, appreciation also encourages us 'to know, to be conscious of, and take full and sufficient account of' (Grant 2006; Grant and Humphries 2006: 414). Application of a heightened (i.e. critical) sense of appreciation in this way may deepen our insight and recognition of the complexity of human endeavours such as social enterprise.

Application of both appreciative and critical lenses need not be as contradictory as first impressions may suggest. Habermas' conception of the lifeworld, the everyday sphere where social interaction takes place amid cultural, social and personal influences, sits well with the aspirations of Ai. Indeed, his positing of an ideal lifeworld – a state of free and equal, undistorted communication (Swingewood 2000) complements the dream phase of the 4D Ai cycle presented earlier in Figure 12.1 (Cooperrider and Whitney 2000) where participants are encouraged to 'dream what might be achieved if anything was possible'. It is the influence of system imperatives such as power, perceived status and/or money which complicate interactions. Continuing the example of the 4D cycle of Ai, the potential tension between lifeworld and system spheres identified by Habermas, must be taken into account as an Ai enters the design and destiny phases. Dreams may be revised to accommodate system limitations and/or resource constraints, but the focus on organizational strengths remains.

Critical appreciation of social enterprise as a socially constructed concept

Applying a traditional appreciative perspective to the concept of social enterprise is consistent with Gilligan and Golden's (2009) proposition that such organizations benefit society through the creation of 'social profit'. To this end, those initiating Ai processes and/or social enterprise activities both seek to facilitate positive change. Ai can help us 'unpack' our understanding of a social enterprise's mission and motivation. Recognizing that there is something of value in a situation (akin to the discovery phase of the 4D cycle portrayed in Figure 12.1 [Cooperrider and Whitney 2000] as described above), no matter how dire or downtrodden it may appear at first glance is key to an Ai and equally a motivating factor behind most social enterprises. Indeed, Diochon and Anderson (2009: 15) observe how those engaged in social enterprise are 'opportunity driven', while Trivedi and Stokols (2011: 9) suggest 'market failure, which is a problem for corporate enterprises, is an opportunity for social enterprises'. Similarly dreaming 'the best that might be' may assist the social enterprise gain momentum and garner support from stakeholders. Continuing on to consider implementation and evaluation processes of social enterprise, Young encourages us to look beyond economic measures and encourages reflection on social enterprise participants' experiences and 'whether they felt empowered or disempowered' (2006: 57). The narrative foundations of Ai, which encourage storytelling, could facilitate such reflection.

However, a commitment to, and subsequent achievement of, positive social change is easier said than done. Just as Ai has been challenged as 'too good to be true', Dey and Steyaert (2010) identify an almost messianistic aura present in the more optimistic versions of social entrepreneurship (as cited in Steyaert and Dey (2010: 239), implying a need for insightful critique of the concept. Good intentions may be implicit or accepted indubitably by stakeholders with minimal consideration of extenuating influences or outcomes achieved. Brackertz (2012) identifies a normative influence amid such intentions, with 'doing good' potentially value-laden with judgements of what 'is good'. Steyaert and Dey (2010: 233) encourage researchers to consider how we highlight certain themes or topics over others when we speak or think of social entrepreneurship.

Further, the drive to 'do good' or create positive change may be admirable, but we must also consider the influences which not only create the 'opportunity' in the first place, but also those which seek to shape our approach and subsequent activity. Identification of potential influences in the social construction of a concept such as social enterprise is by no means a simple process. Cho (2006: 38) identifies social enterprise as an inherently political enterprise which operates 'somewhere in the space between the state and market'. In light of such positioning, Mason (2012) suggests political actors may in turn be moulding social enterprise into a pseudo-corporate form. Yet a market-based ideology may have contributed towards the creation of the social need/issue in the first place; consider for example poverty and the unequal distribution of wealth in society – are we facing a perpetual cycle? Will the same system which generates need also be able to provide a solution? (Humphries and Grant 2005).

It is at this point that critical consideration of social enterprise becomes pertinent. In taking such consideration we begin to address Curtis' (2008) concerns regarding the paucity of research, and indeed discussion, focused on the problems faced by social enterprise. Recognition and appreciation of weaknesses and failures in social enterprise processes along with the success stories is essential if we are to truly understand, i.e. appreciate (as defined above and in Grant [2006] and Grant and Humphries [2006]), this developing field. Cho (2006: 44) draws our attention to 'the multiplicity of potentially incompatible visions at play' in the realm described ambiguously as 'social'. Amid such fragmentation, he warns that social enterprise initiatives may divide rather than integrate society. If we are to heed such caveats to avoid further harm to people and planet, we must first deepen our understanding of social enterprise. Critical appreciative processes may facilitate this awareness. Building on the appreciative lens applied thus far, I now adopt a more critical stance.

In this instance Habermas' conception of the lifeworld and system introduced above provides an informative lens for deeper reflection. Insightful applications of Habermas' work are already evident in critical consideration of management discourse (see for example Lehman 2006; Power and Laughlin 1996), although Calhoun (1992) and Mason (2012) suggest a Habermasian perspective to be somewhat idealistic and egalitarian. As such, it could be argued that this application 'fits' more comfortably with an Ai than might some alternative critical theory concepts; however I suggest analysis guided by alternatives such as Foucault's analysis of power might be equally insightful. Such opportunities are worthy of future research as my focus in this chapter is limited to application of Habermas' conception of the lifeworld and system.

Albeit a somewhat simplistic view, the lifeworld and system can be applied to illustrate the relationships between social and enterprise; with the lifeworld signifying 'social' and the system 'enterprise' activities respectively (see Figure 12.2). 'The tension between the lifeworld and the system is both an index of potential crisis and emancipation' (Swingewood 2000: 234). To this end, one might consider the tension between the two spheres to be representative of the transformative aspirations of social enterprise. Dialogue and communicative action are identified by Corner and Zorn (2012) as crucial to the entrepreneurial process. Further, Mason (2012) notes how communicative action is influenced by actors as each seeks to shape understanding (potentially of others) of a given context. Simply put, the relational ethics of the social/lifeworld and the instrumental ethics of the enterprise/system are seeking equilibrium. Construction and re-construction of social enterprise takes place as dialogue develops. This interplay is important, and reflects the fluid or varied nature of social enterprise currently portrayed across literature.

Colonization of the lifeworld

Habermas is also concerned with the processes through which lifeworld imperatives may be dominated/overcome by the instrumental intentions within the system. Commodification, where the economy extends into everyday life so that activities such as leisure or education become 'produced, packaged, promoted and sold' as items for consumption (Staats 2004), is but one example of how instrumental rationality may erode or obscure the fragile equilibrium between the two spheres. Habermas describes such domination as the 'colonization of the lifeworld'. Continuing a social enterprise application then, social enterprise activity initiated in

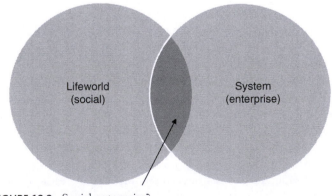

FIGURE 12.2 Social enterprise?

response to outcomes from such problematic circumstances may be interpreted by SE champions and/or agents as attempts to redress system imbalance or 'decolonize' the lifeworld. However a contrasting view can also be taken. Seanor *et al.* (2007) identify concerns that social enterprise may be encroaching upon the voluntary sector. If this is the case, it might be argued that further market-based activity such as that which underpins many social enterprise activities may simply be adding to the commodification issue – potentially embodying Cho's (2006) warning observed earlier, that SE initiatives may divide rather than integrate society. Clearly, colonizing system influences, such as power, perceived status, and money, must be contained if social enterprise is to successfully contribute towards human flourishing. How best to achieve such control/resolution seems to depend on who you ask. Analysis of some of the dominant themes evident within social enterprise scholarship, informed by the critical appreciative perspective introduced above, provides a helpful starting point.

Thematic analysis: the lifeworld and system of SE

The theoretical foundations informing Ai highlight how the language adopted and employed helps shape the context we operate in – now and in the future. Hence it is important to consider the lexicon evoked within social enterprise. If political and/or business language dominates, will the human element be stripped away from social enterprise? Concern for preservation of the 'social' dimension in social enterprise is evident in work such as Arthur *et al.* (2006) and Teasdale (2012) while the 'enterprise' orientation is accommodated by a range of scholars (see for example Dart 2004; Harding 2004; Martin and Osberg 2007; Seelos and Mair 2005). But to what degree is this all important balance between the two paradigms achieved? Awareness of potential domination and its influences is growing amid social enterprise scholarship. Consistent with the social constructionist epistemology underlying social enterprise, critical consideration of the discourse which shapes social enterprise provides insight into how the lifeworld/social and system/enterprise ideologies integrate.[3] What follows is a brief overview of key themes identified within social enterprise/entrepreneurship discourse.

Policy capture

Suggesting that while the organizational forms of social enterprise may not be new, Teasdale (2012) proposes the language used to describe them is. Competing interests are recognized as embracing different discourses to accommodate diversity in both individual/collective and economic/social orientations of social enterprise. With a specific focus on the United Kingdom, Teasdale (2012) observes how each widening of the social enterprise construct coincided with changing policy emphases during different periods of political office. Mason (2012) continues this political focus and considers how political discourse hegemonically exploits an imbalance of power to control and shape social enterprise with a seeming 'business-like' lexicon; which in turn may see non-government actors reject or even distance themselves from the concept and/or activity – opening the door to potentially greater control by political entities. In terms of Habermas' framework, the public sphere resides within the lifeworld. Hence such policy capture may be interpreted not as further colonization of the lifeworld, but indicative of restriction and compression of lifeworld processes (Thompson and Held 1982). Mason (2012) thus encourages us to respond by considering more deeply the impact of discord in social enterprise ideologies so we might draw on disagreement AND consensus to inform our understanding and continued development of social enterprise. Application of critical appreciative processes can inform such analysis by encouraging reflective consideration of both positive and negative attributes within social enterprise.

Heroic and deliverance claims

Ogbor (2000) considers the myths and reifications expressed through entrepreneurship discourse and ideology, noting ethnocentric and paternalistic themes as tales of white male 'heroes' are presented as archetypal entrepreneurs bringing about innovative change. Evidence of potential for such bias and inequality continues through to the discourse of social enterprise/entrepreneurship as through their analysis of social enterprise/entrepreneurship discourse Dey and Steyaert (2010) identify an almost messianistic/religious framing of the grand narrative of SE. The 'salvation' of 'doing well while doing good' presents social enterprise as positive, unthreatening activity leading the authors to question what traditional and/or alternative narratives may be silenced along the way (Dey and Steyaert 2010). Presented in such a way as to contribute towards the idea that 'social change can be achieved without causing debate, tensions or disharmony' (Dey and Steyaert 2010: 88), the importance of context is overlooked and potentially trivialized as social entrepreneurship is conceptualized as 'a universal means to universal problems' (ibid: 89). Dey and Steyaert (2010) propose such a salvation-oriented portrayal positions social enterprise as a concept 'which cannot be thought of without the existence of an "other", its inferior supplement' (ibid: 96). The authors identify 'the poor' as an example of a marginalized 'other' within this context. In terms of our application of Habermas' framework, every society can be conceived as simultaneously comprising a unique lifeworld/ social and system/enterprise realm. Each sphere provides context for communicative and instrumental action respectively. Compliant and uncritical acceptance of grand narratives such as those identified by Dey and Steyaert (2010) may result in this unique context being overlooked, such that the resulting balance/tension between the two spheres may be more colonizing than emancipatory and transformational.

Increased marketization

Although not specifically focused on social enterprise, Eikenberry (2009) adopts a critical or normative stance, challenging the marketization of the nonprofit or voluntary sector overall and discussing its implications. She observes how 'normative ideology surrounding market based solutions and business like models have become pervasive in the thinking and management of nonprofit and voluntary organisations' (Eikenberry 2009: 586). This theme is similarly apparent within social enterprise scholarship as Trivedi and Stokols (2011: 7) identify limitations in many SE definitions which rely on traditional corporate language and concepts.

The alternative discourses identified by Nicholls (2010) reinforce these concerns. Nicholls (2010) identifies two dyadic clusters in social entrepreneurship discourse. The first, located within the traditions of the third sector and not-for-profit organizations, is noted to resonate with cooperative and communitarian ideologies for social change and social justice and is therefore disengaged from commercial narratives. The second cluster, while still linked with third-sector initiatives, draws upon ideals of new public management and contracts between third sector and state organizations. Influenced by aspirations of marketization, this approach underlines the concept of 'businesses trading for a social purpose'. Actors in the second cluster are noted by Nicholls to be 'resource rich' and hence their business-like discourse is better able to dominate (as our understanding of social enterprise is negotiated), potentially marginalizing alternative discourses linked to social justice and change (Nicholls 2010).

Suggesting that the neoliberal ideology of the market is essentially antisocial through the political and economic promotion of individual freedom, Eikenberry (2009) identifies such influence as a threat to the development and maintenance of democracy, as consumers are increasingly promoted over citizens (Purcell 2008 as cited in Eikenberry 2009). Such outcomes appear contrary to the aspirations of social enterprise, and may even be indicative of the consumerism/commodification crisis identified by Habermas as potentially colonizing the lifeworld. Eikenberry (2009) also encourages the development of a counter-narrative, specifically counter-discourse within nonprofit organizations that encourages democratic participation, building social relationships and networks. The incorporation of democratic values into management strategy is identified as a starting point by Eikenberry, although such activity appears to still be framed within the management rhetoric that scholars such as Eikenberry have been questioning.

Theory into practice?

Conceptualization and analysis such as that presented above may progress our understanding of events and activities which develop in our everyday environments. For example, the opposition to capitalism as per the 'Occupy' movement which took place around the globe in the later part of 2011 (Boydston 2012; Gupta and Fawcett 2012; Rathke 2012) might be considered as an example of democratic participation and the building of social relationships and networks as encouraged by Eikenberry (2009); but in terms of Habermas' conceptualization they may also signify economic and legitimation crises, hence challenging the balance between lifeworld and system spheres. Habermas predicts that new social movements may develop to aid replenishment of the lifeworld (Fields 1991). Is it possible that such social movements are an example of social enterprise? Once again, there appears to be no simple answer. Although Touraine (2004: 719) distinguishes social movements from 'crises or forms of systemic evolution', links between these two approaches to social change are evident in scholarship. For example, Douglas (2008) draws our attention to the convergence between social movements and social entrepreneurship when both seek to achieve positive social change. However Curtis (2008), drawing on Tilly (2004), identifies links between social enterprise and social movements in a seemingly opposite direction, noting how social enterprises which contract to deliver services on behalf of the state may potentially be seen as 'a movement that depoliticises decisions around public service delivery' (Tilly 2004: 286). Although the brief review of literature earlier in this chapter might suggest the latter, i.e. that the politically dominated, power/system outcome is more likely to prevail, the variety of activity evident within social enterprise appears, at least in principle, to potentially develop from *both* lifeworld and system influences. Indeed, Cho (2006: 50) suggests that 'the market analogy implicit in SE invites comparison to the colonisation of the lifeworld'. Once again Cho's (2006) warning that social enterprise initiatives may divide rather than integrate society seems to be demonstrated.

Moving forward: critical appreciation of culture within social enterprise

Appreciating the good, but also critically reflecting on other issues, allows us to conceptually evaluate and understand the social construction of social enterprise more deeply. Although brief, the critical appreciative review above highlights the dominance of neoliberal voices in the articulation of the discourse of social enterprise – a voice so often projected within Western, colonial environments (Grant 2008), typically to the detriment of 'the other' (Dey and Steyaert 2010). Framed within Habermas' schema of the lifeworld and system such articulation demonstrates that the risk of colonization of the (social) lifeworld is very real, suggesting the 'success' of social enterprise may not be as readily achieved as some policy advocates and scholars might imply or even hope.

Culture, as one dimension within social enterprise and the lifeworld, provides a case in point for further consideration. Although a strong focus on the socio-economic dimension and its subsequent influence in social enterprise scholarship generally prevails (Dees and Anderson 2003; Defourny and Kim 2011), a brief review of literature suggests recognition of 'culture' as a driving influence in the social construction of social enterprise seems notably absent. If invoked at all, statements regarding culture may be potentially misleading. For example, framing social enterprise as an organizational culture, Bull (2008: 269) observes a focus on a culture 'that emphasises self reliance and personal responsibility and the rise of entrepreneurship generally'. Such usage fails to acknowledge and account for the contribution of the values and beliefs of a collective (often indigenous) group separate from the organization; and in doing so I suggest potentially constrains our negotiated under-standing of social enterprise, further colonizing the concept by Western, neo-liberal ideologies (Dey and Steyaert 2010; Eikenberry 2009; Teasdale 2010). For example, Western notions of social enterprise are identified by Curtis (2011) as eclipsing more embedded concepts grounded within the Chinese political economy. Historical significance appears not be taken into account as social enterprise is (mis) represented to China as a portable, context-less concept – easily transplanted between nations. Combined with the literature reviewed earlier, such misrepresenta-tion further reinforces the risk of uncritically accepting social enterprise as a politically neutral or uncontested concept.

Recognition of the significance of culture and its subsequent contributions is an important step towards a critical appreciation of social enterprise (Alvesson and Deetz 2000; Curtis 2008; Grant and Humphries 2006). If a market-driven discourse as identified earlier is allowed to dominate and potentially shape our understanding of social enterprise those people/communities deemed 'poor' (in a monetary sense) may be incorrectly assumed to be 'poor' in every sense – regardless of the wealth kinship and community (i.e. social capital, culture) may bring. Applying a critical appreciative lens we begin to appreciate how social enterprise activities, which fail to take sufficient account of culture, may be less effective, or may even bring more harm to their targeted communities than good. For example drawing from the growing field of indigenous entrepreneurship, community devel-opment nurtured by well-meaning outside agencies through policies, strategies and advice based on neoclassical economic ideology alone is shown by Tisdell (2002) to be inadequate in the Vanuatu context as it fails to take into account the institutional and cultural background of the country. In contrast, Tapsell and Woods (2010) and Overall *et al.* (2010) demonstrate how recognition of the significant influence of culture within Maori social entrepreneurship activities contributes towards eman-cipation and self-determination of the Maori people of Aotearoa, New Zealand. As Mason (2012) noted earlier, we can learn from both disagreement AND consensus within social enterprise discourse. Appreciating the value held in traditional societies while at the same time being critically aware of the limits our Western ideologies may inflict is an important step when considering the introduction and subsequent impact of social enterprises in/on communities.

Conclusion and future research

As our conceptual understanding of social enterprise continues to develop, we have the opportunity (and indeed I suggest obligation) to ensure this knowledge also informs social enterprise practice. Although relatively exploratory the discussion presented here highlights how elements of both social/lifeworld AND enterprise/ system are crucial to the success of social enterprise. 'The tension between the life-world and the system is both an index of potential crisis and emancipation' (Swingewood 2000: 234). However, the discussion also reinforces that no matter how well-intentioned a social enterprise's mission might be, if the delicate balance between social and enterprise is not achieved and maintained, if the tension between lifeworld and system colonizes rather than emancipates, then any aspirations to transform society through the creation of positive social value may be misguided, and potentially detrimental to the wellbeing of our planet and its inhabitants. There is much scope for further research. Future research may utilize other critical lenses (such as Foucault's conceptualization of power) to further understand the impact of the dominant business and political ideologies identified here; or may choose to consider further other dimensions within social enterprise beyond culture, values for example. Regardless of the focus taken, continued critical reflection on the influences that shape social enterprise theory and practice through lenses such as the critical appreciative application introduced here, can not only deepen our awareness and understanding of the complex interactions and ideologies which shape social enterprise, but perhaps also encourage us to better value (appreciate) the tension between these two ideologies.

Acknowledgements

I would like to thank Alex Nicholls, Chris Mason and other participants at the 2012 Social Entrepreneurship Theory Symposium, RMIT University, Melbourne, Australia, February 2012 for their helpful feedback and comments in the development of this chapter. I would also like to thank my co-authors in this book for their peer review.

Notes

1 This chapter further develops papers presented at the Fifth European Conference on Research Methodology for Business and Management Studies, Trinity College, Dublin, Ireland, July 2006, and Social Entrepreneurship Theory Symposium, RMIT University, Melbourne, Australia, February 2012.
2 Although my focus here is on social enterprise, I have also drawn on social entrepreneurship literature given that many scholars consider the two terms collectively under the social entrepreneurship umbrella.
3 Although still relatively small, critical consideration of social enterprise is growing. See for example the chapter by Chris Mason in this volume, and Vol 8(2) Special Issue of *Social Enterprise Journal*: Critical perspectives on social enterprise.

References

Ahn, I. (2009) 'Decolonization of the lifeworld by reconstructing the system: A critical dialogue between Jurgen Habermas and Reinhold Niebuhr', *Studies in Christian Ethics*, 22(3): 290–313.
Aldred, R. (2011) 'From community participation to organization therapy? World cafe and appreciative inquiry as research methods', *Community Development Journal*, 46(1): 57–71.
Alter, K. (2006) *Social Enterprise Typology*, Revised Edition. Washington DC: Virtue Ventures, LLC.
Alvesson, M. and Deetz, S. (2000) *Doing Critical Management Research*. London: Sage.
Alvesson, M. and Sköldberg, K. (2000) *Reflexive Methodology: New Vistas in Qualitative Research*. London: Sage.

Alvesson, M. and Willmott, H. (2003) *Studying Management Critically*. London: Sage.

Arthur, L., Keenoy, T., Scott Cato, M. and Smith, R. (2006) 'Where is the "social" in social enterprise?' Paper presented at the Third Annual Social Enterprise Conference, London South Bank University, London.

Barge, J. K. and Oliver, C. (2003) 'Working with appreciation in managerial practice', *Academy of Management Review*, 28(1): 124–42.

Bornstein, D. (2004) *How to Change the World: Social Entrepreneurs and the Power of New Ideas*. Oxford: Oxford University Press.

Boydston, B. (2012) 'What exactly does the Occupy movement want?', *The Humanist*, January/February: 20–23.

Brackertz, N. (2012) '"It's a good thing all the same" Social entrepreneurship and social innovation – theoretical underpinnings and policy appeal', Paper presented at the Social Entrepreneurship Theory Symposium, 9–10 February, RMIT University, Melbourne, Australia.

Bull, M. (2008) 'Challenging tensions: critical, theoretical and empirical perspectives on social enterprise', *International Journal of Entrepreneurial Behaviour and Research*, 14(5): 268–75.

Bushe, G. R. (1998) 'Appreciative inquiry with teams', *Organization Development Journal*, 16(3): 41.

Bushe, G. R. and Khamisa, A. (2004) *When is Appreciative Inquiry Transformational? A Meta-case Analysis*. Available at http://www.gervasebushe.ca/aimeta.htm (accessed 5 January 2005).

Calhoun, C. J. (1992) *Habermas and the Public Sphere*. Cambridge, MA: MIT Press.

Carr, A. (2000) 'Critical theory and the management of change in organisations', *Journal of Organizational Change Management*, 13(3): 208.

Catsambas, T. T. and Webb, L. D. (2003) 'Using appreciative inquiry to guide an evaluation of the International Women's Media Foundation Africa Program', *New Directions for Evaluation*, 100(Winter): 41–51.

Cho, A. H. (2006) 'Politics, values and social entrepreneurship: a critical appraisal', in J. Mair, J. Robinson and K. Hockerts (eds), *Social Entrepreneurship*. New York: Palgrave Macmillan, pp. 34–56.

Coghlan, A. T., Preskill, H. and Catsambas, T. T. (2003) 'An overview of appreciative inquiry in evaluation', *New Directions for Evaluation*, 100(Winter): 5–22.

Cooperrider, D. and Srivastva, S. (1987) 'Appreciative inquiry in organisational life', in W. A. Pasmore and R. W. Woodman (eds), *Research in Organisational Change and Development*. Greenwich, CT: JAI Press.

Cooperrider, D. and Whitney, D. (2000) 'A positive revolution in change: appreciative inquiry', in D. Cooperrider, P. F. J. Sorensen, D. Whitney and T. F. Yaeger (eds), *Appreciative Inquiry: Rethinking Human Organisation Towards a Positive Theory of Change*. Champaign, IL: Stipes Publishing LCC.

Corner, P. and Zorn, T. (2012) 'Interpersonal capital in entrepreneurship', Paper presented at the Social Entrepreneurship Theory Symposium, 9–10 February, RMIT University, Melbourne, Australia.

Curtis, T. (2008) 'Finding that grit makes a pearl. A critical re-reading of research into social enterprise', *International Journal of Entrepreneurial Behaviour and Research*, 14(5): 276–90.

Curtis, T. (2011) '"Newness" in social entrepreneurship discourses: the concept of "Danwei" in the Chinese experience', *Journal of Social Entrepreneurship*, 2(2): 198–217.

Dart, R. (2004) 'Being "business-like" in a nonprofit organisation: A grounded and inductive typology', *Nonprofit and Voluntary Sector Quarterly*, 33(2): 290–310.

Dees, J. G. (1998) 'Enterprising nonprofits', *Harvard Business Review*, 76(1): 55–67.

Dees, J.G. and Anderson, B. B. (2003) 'Sector-bending: blurring lines between nonprofit and for-profit', *Society*, 40(4): 16–27.

Dees, G., Anderson, B. B. and Wei-Skillern, J. (2004) 'Scaling social impact: strategies for spreading social innovations', *Stanford Social Innovation Review*, 1(4): 24–32.

Defourny, J. and Kim, S. (2011) 'Emerging models of social enterprise in Eastern Asia: a cross country analysis', *Social Enterprise Journal*, 7(1): 86–111.

Defourny, J. and Nyssens, M. (2006) 'Defining social enterprise', in M. Nyssens (ed.), *Social Enterprise: At the Crossroads of Market, Public Policies and Civil Society*. London: Routledge.

Dey, P. and Steyaert, C. (2010) 'The politics of narrating social entrepreneurship', *Journal of Enterprising Communities: People and Places in the Global Economy*, 4(1): 85–108.

Diochon, M. and Anderson, A. R. (2009) 'Social enterprise and effectiveness: a process typology', *Social Enterprise Journal*, 5(1): 7–29.

Diochon, M. and Anderson, A. R. (2011) 'Ambivalence and ambiguity in social enterprise; narratives about values in reconciling purpose and practices', *International Entrepreneurship and Management Journal*, 7(1): 93–109.

Douglas, H. (2008) 'Creating knowledge: a review of research methods in three societal change approaches', *Journal of Nonprofit and Public Sector Marketing*, 20(2): 141–63.

Drayton, B. (2006) 'Everyone a changemaker. Social entrepreneurship's ultimate goal', *Innovations* (Winter).

Eikenberry, A. M. (2009) 'Refusing the market: a democratic discourse for voluntary and nonprofit organisations', *Nonprofit and Voluntary Sector Quarterly*, 38(4): 582–96.

Fields, E. E. (1991) 'Understanding activist fundamentalism: capitalist crisis and the "colonization of the lifeworld"', *Sociology of Religion*, 52(2): 175–90.

Finlayson, G. (2005) *Habermas: A Very Short Introduction*. New York: Oxford University Press.

Fitzgerald, S. P., Murrell, K. L. and Newman, H. L. (2001) 'Appreciative inquiry: the new frontier', in J. Waclawski and A. H. Church (eds), *Organisational Development: Data Driven Methods for Change*. San Francisco: Jossey-Bass.

Forester, J. (2003) 'On fieldwork in a Habermasian way: critical ethnography and the extraordinary character of ordinary professional work', in M. Alvesson and H. Willmott (eds), *Studying Management Critically*. London: Sage.

Gilligan, C. and Golden, L. (2009) 'Re-branding social good: Social profit as a new conceptual framework', *Academy of Marketing Studies Journal*, 13(2): 97–117.

Golembiewski, R. (2000) 'Three perspectives on appreciative inquiry', *OD Practitioner*, 32(1): 53–8.

Grant, S. L. (2006) 'A paradox in action? A critical analysis of an appreciative inquiry', PhD Thesis, University of Waikato.

Grant, S. L. (2008) 'Contextualising social enterprise in New Zealand', *Social Enterprise Journal*, 4(1): 9–23.

Grant, S. L. (2012) 'Enhancing community policing through critical appreciative processes', *AI Practitioner. International Journal of Appreciative Inquiry*, 14(3): 21–5.

Grant, S. L. and Dart, R. (2008) *Social Construction of Social Enterprise. ISTR Eighth* International Conference; Seconed EMES-ISTR European Conference in partnership with CINEFOGO University of Barcelona, Barcelona, Spain, 9–12 July 2008.

Grant, S. L. and Humphries, M. (2006) 'Critical evaluation of appreciative inquiry', *Action Research*, 4(4): 401–18.

Gupta, A. and Fawcett, M. (2012) 'Inside the occupy movement', *The Progressive*, 76(2): 30–3.

Harding, R. (2004) 'Social enterprise. The new economic engine?', *Business Strategy Review*, 15(4): 39–43.

Humphries, M. and Grant, S. (2005) 'Social enterprise and re-civilization of human endeav-ours: re-socializing the market metaphor or encroaching colonization of the lifeworld?', *Current Issues in Comparative Education*, 8(1): 41–50.

Jacobsgaard, M. (2003) 'Using appreciative inquiry to evaluate project activities of a nongov-ernmental organization supporting victims of trauma in Sri Lanka', in H. Preskill and A. T. Coghlan (eds), *Using Appreciative Inquiry in Evaluation*. San Francisco: Jossey-Bass.

Kemmis, S. (2001) 'Exploring the relevance of critical theory for action research: emancipa-tory action research in the footsteps of Jurgen Habermas', in P. Reason and H. Bradbury (eds), *Handbook of Action Research*. London: Sage.

Kerlin, J. A. (2006a) 'Social enterprise in the United States and abroad: learning from our differences', in R. Mosher-Williams (ed.), *Research on Social Entrepreneurship: Understanding and Contributing to an Emerging Field*. Indianapolis, IN: Association for Research on Nonprofit Organizations and Voluntary Action, pp. 1, 105–25.

Kerlin, J. A. (2006b) 'Social enterprise in the United States and Europe. Understanding and learning from the differences', *Voluntas*, 17(3): 247–63.

Kerlin, J. A. (2010) 'A comparative analysis of the global emergence of social enterprise', *Voluntas*, 21(2): 162–79.

Lehman, G. (2006) 'Perspectives on language, accountability and critical accounting: an inter-pretive perspective', *Critical Perspectives on Accounting*, 17: 755–79.

Ludema, J. (2001) 'From deficit discourse to vocabularies of hope: the power of apprecia-tion', in D. Cooperrider, P. F. J. Sorensen, T. F. Yaeger and D. Whitney (eds), *Appreciative Inquiry: An Emerging Direction for Organisational Development*. Champaign IL: Stipes Publishing LCC.

Ludema, J., Cooperrider, D. and Barrett, F. (2001) 'Appreciative inquiry: the power of the unconditional positive question', in P. Reason and H. Bradbury (eds), *Handbook of Action Research*. London: Sage, pp. 189–99.

Mantel, M. J. and Ludema, J. (2000) 'From local conversations to global change: experienc-ing the worldwide web effect of appreciative inquiry', *Organization Development Journal*, 18(2): 42–53.

Martin, R. and Osberg, S. (2007) 'Social entrepreneurship: the case for definition', *Stanford Social Innovation Review*, 5(2): 28.

Mason, C. (2012) 'Up for grabs: A critical analysis of social entrepreneurship discourse in the United Kingdom', *Social Enterprise Journal*, 8(2): 123–40.

Nicholls, A. (2010) 'The legitimacy of social entrepreneurship: reflexive isomorphism in a pre-paradigmatic field', *Entrepreneurship, Theory and Practice*, 34(4): 611–33.

Odell, M. (2002) Beyond the Box: An Innovative Habitat for Humanity Paradigm for Participatory Planning, Monitoring and Evaluation – Measuring and Increasing Program Impacts with Appreciative Inquiry. Americus, GA: Habitat for Humanity International.

Ogbor, J. O. (2000) 'Mythicizing and reification in entrepreneurial discourse: ideology-critique of entrepreneurial studies', *Journal of Management Studies*, 37(5): 605–35.

Overall, J., Tapsell, P. and Woods, C. (2010) 'Governance and indigenous social entrepre-neurship: When context counts', *Social Enterprise Journal*, 6(2): 146–61.

Peattie, K. and Morley, A. (2008) 'Eight paradoxes of the social enterprise research agenda', *Social Enterprise Journal*, 4(2): 91–107.

Peredo, A. M. and McLean, M. (2006) 'Social entrepreneurship: a critical review of the concept', *Journal of World Business*, 41: 56–65.

Power, M. and Laughlin, R. (1996) 'Habermas, law and accounting', *Accounting, Organizations and Society*, 21(5): 441–65.

Pratt, C. (2002) 'Creating unity from competing integreties: a case study in appreciative inquiry methodology', in R. Fry, F. Barrett, J. Seiling and D. Whitney (eds), *Appreciative Inquiry and Organisational Transformation. Reports from the Field.* Westport, CT: Quorum Books.

Preskill, H. and Catsambas, T. T. (2006) *Reframing Evaluation through Appreciative Inquiry.* Thousand Oaks, CA: Sage.

Rathke, W. (2012) 'The global structure beneath the Occupy movement', *Social Policy*, 41(4): 84.

Reason, P. (2000) *Action Research as Spiritual Practice.* Available at: http://www.peterreason.eu/Papers/AR_as_spiritual_practice.pdf (accessed 26 February 2013).

Rogers, P. J. and Fraser, D. (2003) 'Appreciating appreciative inquiry', in H. Preskill and A. T. Coghlan (eds), *Using Appreciative Inquiry in Evaluation.* San Francisco: Jossey-Bass, pp. 75–84.

Ryan, F. J., Soven, M., Smither, J., Sullivan, W. M. and van Buskirk, W. (1999) 'Appreciative inquiry: using narratives for initiating school reform', *The Clearing House*, 72(3): 164.

Seanor, P., Bull, M. and Ridley-Duff, R. (2007) 'Contradictions in social enterprise: Do they draw in straight lines or circles?', Paper presented at the Institute for Small Business and Entrepreneurship Conference, Glasgow, United Kingdom.

Seelos, C. and Mair, J. (2005) 'Social entrepreneurship: creating new business models to serve the poor', *Business Horizons*, 48: 241–6.

Smart, D. H. and Mann, M. (2003) 'Incorporating appreciative inquiry methods to evaluate a youth development program', *New Directions for Evaluation*, 100(Winter): 63–74.

Staats, J. L. (2004) 'Habermas and democratic theory: the threat to democracy of unchecked corporate power', *Political Research Quarterly*, 57(4): 585–94.

Steyaert, C. and Dey, P. (2010) 'Nine verbs to keep the social entrepreneurship research agenda "dangerous"', *Journal of Social Entrepreneurship*, 1(2): 231–54.

Swingewood, A. (2000) *A Short History of Sociological Thought.* Basingstoke: Macmillan.

Tapsell, P. and Woods, C. (2010) 'Social entrepreneurship and innovation: self-organisation in an indigenous context', *Entrepreneurship and Regional Development*, 22(6): 535–56.

Teasdale, S. (2010) *What's in a Name? The Construction of Social Enterprise.* Birmingham: Third Sector Research Centre.

Teasdale, S. (2012) 'What's in a name? Making sense of social enterprise discourses', *Public Policy and Administration*, 27(2): 99–119.

Thompson, J. and Doherty, B. (2006) 'The diverse world of social enterprise. A collection of social enterprise stories', *International Journal of Social Economics*, 33(5/6): 361–75.

Thompson, J. B. and Held, D. (1982) 'Editors introduction', in J. B. Thompson and D. Held (eds), *Habermas. Critical Debates.* London: The Macmillan Press Ltd., pp. 1–20.

Tilly, C. (2004) *Social Movements 1768–2004.* Boulder, CO: Paradigm Publishers.

Tisdell, C. (2002) 'Globalisation, development and poverty in the Pacific Islands. The situation of the least developed nations', *International Journal of Social Economics*, 29(12): 902–22.

Touraine, A. (2004) 'On the frontier of social movements', *Current Sociology*, 52(4): 717–25.

Trivedi, C. and Stokols, D. (2011) 'Social enterprises and corporate enterprises: fundamental differences and defining features', *Journal of Entrepreneurship*, 20(1): 1–32.

Watkins, J. M. and Mohr, B. J. (2001) *Appreciative Inquiry: Change at the Speed of Imagination.* San Francisco: Jossey Bass/Pfeiffer.

Young, D. R. (2001) 'Organisational identity in nonprofit organisations: Strategic and structural implications', *Nonprofit Management and Leadership*, 12(2): 139–57.

Young, D. R. (2006) 'Social enterprise in community and economic development in the USA: theory, corporate form and purpose', *International Journal of Entrepreneurship and Innovation Management*, 6(3): 214–55.

PART V

The future for evaluation of social enterprise

13

SUMMARIZING AND PROJECTING INTO THE FUTURE

Simon Denny and Fred Seddon

The previous chapters in this book have provided a wide range of examples of definition, evaluation and critical reflection of social enterprise (SE), all of which have been securely based upon current and prior research. The purpose of this chapter is to summarize the content of these highly informative chapters and to speculate on the foci of future SE research.

It has been argued in this book that if we do not have a precise, clear and generally agreed definition of what SE is then evaluation of SE will remain a problematic process. Many similar definitions of SE are available (Birch and Whittam 2008; Department of Trade and Industry (DTI) 2002; Dees 1998; Thompson and Doherty 2006; Nicholls 2008) and in Chapter 2, Thompson and Scott provide us with a set of characteristics that they propose as critical criteria for identifying a SE. These critical criteria for identifying a SE are: it has a social purpose, its assets and wealth are used to create community benefit, it pursues this with (at least in part) trading activities (if it delivers services to clients which are paid for by a third party, as distinct from direct sales to a customer, this is still regarded as trading), its profits and surpluses are reinvested in the business and community rather than distributed to shareholders (Thompson and Doherty 2006). These criteria can help *identify* a SE but, as Thompson and Scott argue in Chapter 2, there is much more to *defining* a SE. Doherty, in Chapter 3, identifies two main attributes that distinguish SEs from other organizations: SEs trade in goods or services in a market and they have social aims as their primary purpose. Doherty explains the importance of the SE's strength of social vision and mission, which is often based upon utopian notions of fairness, justice and social change that legitimize the enterprise.

Many definitions of SE focus on revenue generation through trading but, as Bell and Hall indicate in Chapter 5, revenue can also be generated from grants and donations, even though these revenue sources are decreasing (SEC 2009). Flexibility of revenue sources is also highlighted by Hazenberg, in Chapter 8. Hazenberg draws from the 'Emergence de L'Economie Sociale' (EMES) five social dimensions in defining a SE. Hazenberg reports that EMES proposes that a SE should have: an 'explicit aim to benefit the community', be an 'initiative launched by private citizens', have a 'decision-making process not based upon ownership', have a 'participatory nature for all stakeholders' and operate a 'limited profit-distribution model' (Borgaza and Defourny 2001). Hazenberg also cites Campi *et al.* (2006) to propose a multi-stakeholder model that allows SEs to source income from a variety of sources (e.g. private, public and third sectors) but warns of the potential for 'mission drift' that can accompany such flexibility of income generation. In Chapter 4, Mason comments on the academic community's engagement in seeking to define SE as a concept and a practice, and proposes that this engagement contributes to tensions while attempting to clarify a universal agreement on the meaning of SE. Mason cites Peattie and Morley (2008) to propose that although definition-seeking is a necessary part of developing a coherent body of SE knowledge, the academic nature of these debates can cause confusion among other stakeholders.

The authors writing in this book provide us with a demonstration of the overall problems of the definition of SE. By attempting to be all-inclusive, some definitions of SE are too general yet more specific definitions run the risk of excluding organizations that would intuitively be regarded as SEs. No doubt, future academic research will continue to address the intricate problems of the definition of SE. However, instead of this academic pursuit to determine a single definition of SE contributing to increased tension for SE stakeholders, future research could contribute to an acceptance of a multi-definition concept of SE. Such a multi-definition concept of SE would allow for ambiguities in definition and provide all stakeholders with the opportunity to draw down a definition that most closely aligns with their organization. This flexibility of definition, provided by a small number of very precise definitions positioned under an overall 'umbrella' definition of SE, may reduce stakeholder tension and could have beneficial consequences for SE evaluation.

Many SE stakeholders require some form of social impact measurement, whether for purely altruistic reasons or investment justification. In Part III of this book, the contributing authors provide an extensive account of some of the 'tools' available for measuring the social impact of SE. In Chapter 6, Borgaza and Depedri present a net-cost benefit system that was employed to calculate the savings made by the Trento region of Italy through the provision of government financial support for work integration social cooperatives (WISCs). Savings in the region of 6,000 Euro per disadvantaged worker per year are reported by Borzaga and Depedri and this figure translates to a 4 million Euro saving for the public sector over a period of three years (see Table 6.1 for more detailed figures). Clearly, for governments seeking to find cost savings, especially at a time of economic crisis, this type of net-cost benefit evaluation is a powerful 'tool' to demonstrate the financial benefits of supporting efficient WISCs. In addition to the financial benefits these WISCs provide, they can also have a very positive effect on the lives of the disadvantaged individuals employed at the WISCs. It is these 'outcome' effects on individual's lives, accrued as a result of their engagement in employment enhancement programmes, that form the basis of the evaluation presented by Barraket in Chapter 7. In her chapter, Barraket focuses in part on the effects on the wellbeing of immigrants and refugees to Australia as an 'outcome' measure for evaluating the success of the 'generated employment opportunities programmes' provided by Australian SEs as an alternative to mainstream labour market programmes. In Barraket's study, the increases in wellbeing of the immigrants and refugees were demonstrated by self-reported perceptions of improved self-esteem and self-efficacy and positive inter-generational and intercultural effects. Other measures of the success of the generated employment opportunities, which were also reported by the immigrants and refugees, were: high employment retention rates, earned income, new skills, language acquisition, new personal relationships, a sense of common purpose and new social and professional networks. These participant-reported benefits of the programme were supported by the observations of programme staff and partner organizations.

When SEs are seeking investment, they often find that investors are more easily persuaded to invest in SE activities if elusive social impact concepts such as self-esteem and self-efficacy 'outcomes' can be demonstrated to be measured in objective statistical procedures. Hazenberg, in Chapter 8, presents a prior research validated general self-efficacy scale (GSE) as part of a mixed quantitative and qualitative comparative evaluation of 'outcome' benefits. In his study, Hazenberg compares and contrasts the 'outcome' benefits resulting for young people not in employment, education or training (NEETs) after engagement in two employment enhancement programmes (EEPs), one programme delivered by a work integration social enterprise (WISE) and the other by a for-profit company (for more details of the comparative study see Chapter 8). The survey, conducted as part of an intervention study, measured participant GSE before and after engagement in the EEPs. Results of the survey demonstrated a statistically significant rise in the level of GSE of the NEET participants in both programmes (see Table 8.1 for details). The statistically significant evidence of 'outcome' benefits such as GSE, especially when triangulated with qualitative evidence in the same study, can provide a convincing argument that EEPs do improve the psychological profile of programme participants.

Not all evaluation focuses on the benefits for the individual, some look more towards the benefits for society as measured by 'impact'. Hall and Arvidson, in Chapter 9, indicate the need for evaluation measures and highlight the UK government's policy on evaluation for the third sector as it partners with government to deliver public services. Within this context, Hall and Arvidson compare and contrast three evaluation frameworks that measure social 'impact': Social Return on Investment (SROI), 'Outcomes Star' (OS) and randomized control trials. SROI uses money as a unit of analysis and is based upon the principles of accountancy and cost-benefit analysis in an attempt to quantify social value creation. Results are expressed as a ratio of monetized value (see Chapter 9 for a more detailed account). In a similar way to the 'net-cost benefit' system described by Borzaga and Depedri in Chapter 6, SROI communicates potential cost savings to existing and potential funders and to the general taxpayer. 'Outcomes Star' (OS) offers a flexible measure of outcomes that can be tailored to the specific circumstances of the SE and its evaluation requirements. OS has three main principles: to empower service users, foster collaboration between users and providers and to integrate the evaluation process into the everyday working practices of the service. The ease of use and flexibility of OS makes it a very useful evaluation tool for developing programmes but the subjective nature of the tool raises concerns about its effectiveness and ability to convince potential investors. Hall and Arvidson present a good account, and a highly illustrative example, of randomized controlled trials (RCT) in Chapter 9 but explain that RCTs are not widely used to evaluate SE. RCTs are problematic in evaluating SEs because they require relatively high evaluator skill levels to collect and analyze evidence; they are also expensive. In addition, creating control groups can raise difficult ethical issues if groups are to be denied potentially beneficial 'treatments' to satisfy methodological constraints.

Throughout Part III of this book the contributing authors present a range of potential evaluation 'tools' available to measure the 'outcome' and 'impact' of SE. As with the proposal for a multi-definition concept of SE, compiled under a definition 'umbrella', there is also a need for a wide variety of evaluation tools that can be applied to evaluating a SE depending upon the definition of the SE concerned. This proposed diversity of evaluation 'tools' as part of a 'toolkit' of evaluation, when coupled with the proposed diversity of SE definition, presents the possibility of matching the appropriate evaluation tool to the specific SE. This combination of specific definition and appropriate evaluation tool could then be perceived as a more valid and reliable approach to SE evaluation. Future research could play a part in developing specific evaluation 'tools' to both strengthen and broaden the availability of rigorous and reliable SE evaluation. For example, an interesting 'tool' is proposed by contributing authors Bell and Haugh. Their 'tool' examined the role of altruism in SE employee motivation. In the study presented by Bell and Haugh in Chapter 5, altruism is measured by employees' acceptance of lower salaries when their social impact aspirations align with the SE's social mission. This is an example of an evaluation 'tool' designed for the specific circumstances of the SE under investigation and validated through research.

The contributing authors in Part IV of this book provide a critical reflection on SE that encompasses social, political, financial, ethical and moral viewpoints. Nicholls, in Chapter 10, describes the rise of 'social finance' and the growth in the number of 'owners of capital' seeking to invest in SE. According to Nicholls, these 'owners of capital' are often motivated by a desire to generate social value rather than solely maximising financial return. Nicholls proposes a spectrum of investors based on the balance between social impact and financial performance, with grants and philanthropy offering purely social returns at one end of the spectrum, to market or near-market financial returns at the other (see Chapter 10 for details). Nicholls also acknowledges the need for a universally accepted metric for social outcomes to ensure social returns can be measured and accepted as relevant outcomes for investors interested in having a social return on their investment. Nicholls proposes three scenarios for the future of 'social finance' by proposing it will: become absorbed by the mainstream of financial markets, remain on the margins of the mainstream (as it currently is) or become institutionalized and promote an ethical economy built upon fairness and interpersonal regard. Social finance is an area that offers future research opportunities, many of which are described in the closing pages of Chapter 10.

Bode, in Chapter 11, takes a broader governance of SE viewpoint to argue that the new 'social enterprise model' has brought pressure upon 'traditional non-profits' forcing them into what he describes as 'managerialism' based upon 'muddling through'. Non-profit organizations that traditionally provided what Bode describes as 'human care' (social services) previously operated with a focus upon the needs of the individuals they cared for by forming financial partnerships with government agencies. As the 'social enterprise model' gains transnational momentum, especially during times of austerity, these non-profit organizations are forced to become entrepreneurial and seek successful 'double bottom-lines'. In the 'social enterprise model', there has to be a balance between focusing on the care of the individual and providing an autonomous financial future for the SE. Bode indicates that some 'human care' cannot be delivered by organizations having to balance a 'double bottom-line'. He argues that there is still a need for partnerships between managerialist welfare bureaucracies and care providers based upon an understanding that the care services they provide may never generate surplus income. The problem being that, as the 'social enterprise model' becomes a normative vision, entrenched in the wider environment, traditional care providers have to compete for declining funding opportunities. Grant, in Chapter 12, continues this critique of SE by examining the balance between 'social' and 'enterprise' from a purely theoretical perspective. Grant warns that the market-based activity undertaken by SEs adds to the commodification of their activities, which can disturb the delicate balance between 'social' and 'enterprise'. Also, by adopting the language of the market place, Grant argues that service providers may be perceived as more business or 'enterprise' orientated than focused on 'social' care, prompting a polarization of perception by stakeholders and creating discord rather than social harmony. Grant urges continued critical reflection through research and theory-building to ensure SE maintains an appropriate balance between 'social' and 'enterprise', taking into account the cultural context in which the SE engages.

An overview of the previous chapters in this book reveals much consensus between the contributing authors. In relation to issues of definition, the authors acknowledge the need for definition but recognize that an over-emphasis on precision in definition may not result in the flexibility required to enable all SEs to fall within the criteria adopted. Future research can help to build SE knowledge and contribute to a range of definitions that reflect the nature of the diversity of current and future SEs. There is also broad agreement between contributing authors on the need for a number of social impact evaluation tools that are grounded in research, which can provide consensus and much needed 'proof' of validity and reliability. These evaluation tools should take into account the need to measure 'soft' and 'hard' outcomes in terms of 'output', 'outcome' and 'impact' (McLoughlin *et al.* 2009).

As with issues of definition, a broad range of evaluation tools is required to suit the focus of individual SEs. The overall picture emerging from previous chapters in relation to critiques of SE seems to be that the contributing authors perceive SE as a benign and potentially highly beneficial contributor to society. There is some consensus that there are potential problems in promoting SE as a panacea for global social, financial, political and ethical problems. Some contributing authors draw attention to the problems of balancing 'double bottom-lines' and the potential for 'mission drift', others indicate that some social support services must be provided by government subsidy even though they may never produce financial surpluses. In regards to 'social finance' there may be an emerging opportunity for consortia of ethical investors to provide positive ethical investment alternatives that can exist alongside current financial markets. This potential development in the social finance sector could be regarded as an opportunity to make ethical investment and working practices the norm rather than the exception.

Finally, in our opinion future research projects should focus on:

*   exploratory research designed to reveal and document the multiplicity of SE organizational and delivery models that can contribute to a 'continuum-style' definition of SE
*   developing flexible, user-friendly, empirically-tested evaluations tools for measuring the 'output', 'outcome' and 'impact' of SE
*   monitoring and evaluating the evolution of 'social finance' in order to promote ethical financial solutions to social problems.

References

Birch, K. and Whittam, G. (2008) 'The third sector and the regional development of social capital', *Regional Studies*, 42(3): 437–50.

Borzaga, C. and Defourny, J. (eds) (2001) *The Emergence of Social Enterprise*. London: Routledge.

Campi, S., Defourny, J. and Grégoire, O. (2006) 'Work-integration social enterprises: are they multiple goal and multi-stakeholder organisations?', in Nyssens, M. (ed.), *Social Enterprise*. Oxon: Routledge, pp. 29–49.

Dees, J. G. (1998) 'The meaning of social entrepreneurship', Working paper, Stanford University, Graduate Schools of Business, Stanford, California.

Department of Trade and Industry (2002) *Social Enterprise: A Strategy for Success*. London: DTI.

McLoughlin, J., Kaminski, J., Sodagar, B., Khan, S., Harris, R., Arnaudo, G. and McBrearty, S. (2009) 'A strategic approach to social impact measurement of social enterprises: The SIMPLE methodology', *Social Enterprise Journal*, 2(2): 154–78.

Nicholls, A. (2008) *Social Entrepreneurship: New Models of Sustainable Social Change*. Oxford: Oxford University Press.

Peattie, K. and Morley, A. (2008) 'Eight paradoxes of the social enterprise research agenda', *Social Enterprise Journal*, 4(2): 91–107.

SEC (2009) *State of Social Enterprise Survey 2009*. London: Social Enterprise Coalition.

Thompson, J. L. and Doherty, B. (2006) 'The diverse world of social enterprise – a collection of social enterprise stories', *International Journal of Social Economics*, 33(5/6): 361–75.

INDEX

Page numbers in italic refer to boxes and tables.